WORLDVIEWS OF ASPIRING POWERS

Peter,
A kindred spirit!
Henry

WORLDVIEWS OF ASPIRING POWERS

*Domestic Foreign Policy Debates
in China, India, Iran,
Japan, and Russia*

EDITED BY

HENRY R. NAU

AND

DEEPA M. OLLAPALLY

OXFORD
UNIVERSITY PRESS

OXFORD
UNIVERSITY PRESS

Oxford University Press is a department of the University of Oxford.
It furthers the University's objective of excellence in research,
scholarship, and education by publishing worldwide

Oxford   New York

Auckland   Cape Town   Dar es Salaam   Hong Kong   Karachi
Kuala Lumpur   Madrid   Melbourne   Mexico City   Nairobi
New Delhi   Shanghai   Taipei   Toronto

With offices in

Argentina   Austria   Brazil   Chile   Czech Republic   France   Greece
Guatemala   Hungary   Italy   Japan   Poland   Portugal   Singapore
South Korea   Switzerland   Thailand   Turkey   Ukraine   Vietnam

Oxford is a registered trademark of Oxford University Press
in the UK and certain other countries

Published in the United States of America by
Oxford University Press
198 Madison Avenue, New York, NY 10016

© Oxford University Press 2012

Library of Congress Cataloging-in-Publication Data
Worldviews of aspiring powers : domestic foreign policy debates in
China, India, Iran, Japan and Russia /
edited by Henry R. Nau and Deepa Ollapally.
p.   cm.
Includes bibliographical references and index.
ISBN 978-0-19-993747-9 (hardback)—ISBN 978-0-19-993749-3 (pbk.)
1. Middle powers—History—21st century.
2. International relations—Philosophy—History—21st century.
3. International relations—History—21st century.
I. Nau, Henry R., 1941–   II. Ollapally, Deepa Mary.
JZ1310.W68 2012
327—dc23
2012008751

1 3 5 7 9 8 6 4 2

Printed in the United States of America
on acid-free paper

To our children—Kavitha and Siddharth Anandalingam,
and Kimberly Nau—who will live in the world
of these aspiring and rising powers.

CONTENTS

CONTRIBUTORS

Farideh Farhi is an Independent Scholar and Affiliate Graduate Faculty at the University of Hawai'i at Manoa. Her publications include *States and Urban-Based Revolutions in Iran and Nicaragua* (University of Illinois Press) and numerous articles and book chapters on comparative analyses of revolutions and Iranian politics. She has been a recipient of grants from the United States Institute of Peace and the Rockefeller Foundation and was most recently a Public Policy Scholar at the Woodrow Wilson International Center for Scholars. Ms. Farhi has also worked as a consultant for the World Bank and the International Crisis Group.

Andrew C. Kuchins is a senior fellow and the director of the Center for Strategic and International Studies' (CSIS) Russia and Eurasia Program. He is an internationally known expert on Russian foreign and domestic policies who publishes widely and is frequently called on by business, government, media, and academic leaders for comment and consulting on Russian and Eurasian affairs. His recent publications include *The Key to Success in Afghanistan: A Modern Silk Road Strategy,* coauthored with S. Fred Starr (Central Asia–Caucasus Institute, May 2010), *Russia after the Global Economic Crisis*, coedited with Anders Aslund and Sergei Guriev (Peterson Institute, June 2010), "The Speeding Troika" (*Russia Beyond the Headlines*, September 2010), and "Keep on Truckin'" (*Foreign Policy*, October 2010).

Saideh Lotfian is Professor of Political Science, Faculty of Law and Political Science, University of Tehran, Tehran, Iran.

Narushige Michishita is Associate Professor at the National Graduate Institute for Policy Studies (GRIPS) in Tokyo, and the director of the Security and International Studies Program at the Institute. A specialist in strategic and Japan/Korea studies, he is author of *North Korea's Military-Diplomatic Campaigns, 1966–2008* (Routledge, 2009).

Nikola Mirilovic is Assistant Professor of Political Science at the University of Central Florida. Prior to joining UCF, he was Professorial Lecturer and a Postdoctoral Research Associate at the Sigur Center for Asian Studies, the George Washington University. Dr. Mirilovic's article "Explaining the Politics of Immigration: Dictatorship, Development, and Defense" was published in the April 2010 issue of *Comparative Politics*. He specializes in international political economy and in comparative politics.

Henry R. Nau is Professor of Political Science and International Affairs at the Elliott School of International Affairs, The George Washington University. He is the author of numerous books and articles, among them, *Perspectives on International Relations* (CQ Press, 2011), *At Home Abroad* (Cornell, 2002), *The Myth of America's Decline* (Oxford, 1990), "The Jigsaw Puzzle and Chess Board," *Commentary* (May 2012), and "Ideas have consequences," *International Politics* (July 2011). He served twice in government: from 1975–77 as a special assistant to the undersecretary for economic affairs in the U.S. Department of State, and again from 1981–83 as senior staff member responsible for international economic affairs on President Reagan's National Security Council. Nau also served two years as a lieutenant in the 82nd Airborne Division at Fort Bragg, North Carolina.

Deepa M. Ollapally, a leading expert on the international relations of South Asia, is Associate Director of the Sigur Center for Asian Studies and Associate Research Professor of International Affairs at the Elliott School of International Affairs, The George Washington University. Previously, she directed the South Asia program at the US Institute of Peace and was Associate Professor of Political Science at Swarthmore College. Her most recent book is *The Politics of Extremism in South Asia* (Cambridge University Press, 2008). Ollapally is a frequent media commentator. She holds a Ph.D. in Political Science from Columbia University.

Rajesh Rajagopalan is professor, Centre for International Politics, Organization and Disarmament (CIPOD), School of International Studies, Jawaharlal Nehru University, New Delhi. His publications include *Fighting Like a Guerrilla: The Indian Army and Counterinsurgency* (Routledge, 2008) and *Second Strike: Arguments about Nuclear War in South Asia* (Penguin/Viking, 2005).

Richard J. Samuels is Ford International Professor of Political Science and director of the Center for International Studies at MIT. He has been head of the MIT Political Science Department, vice-chair of the Committee on

Japan of the National Research Council, chair of the Japan-US Friendship Commission, and has been elected to the American Academy of Arts & Sciences. His most recent book, *Securing Japan: Tokyo's Grand Strategy and the Future of East Asia,* was a finalist for the Lionel Gelber Prize for the best book in international affairs.

David Shambaugh is Professor of Political Science and International Affairs and director of the China Policy Program at the George Washington University's Elliott School of International Affairs, and is recognized internationally as an authority on contemporary Chinese affairs and the international politics and security of the Asia-Pacific region. He is a widely published author or editor of numerous books, including *China's Communist Party: Atrophy & Adaptation; American and European Relations with China; The International Relations of Asia; Tangled Titans: The United States and China;* and *China Goes Global: The Partial Power.* He serves on several editorial boards and is a member of the International Institute of Strategic Studies, National Committee on U.S. China Relations, and the Council on Foreign Relations.

Ren Xiao is Professor of International Politics at the Institute of International Studies (IIS) and the director of the Center for Chinese Foreign Policy Studies at Fudan University, Shanghai, China. His recent publications include *New Frontiers of Chinese Foreign Policy* (coeditor with Allen Carlson) (Lanham, MD: Lexington Books, 2011). He worked at the Chinese Embassy in Tokyo from 2010–2011.

Igor Zevelev is the Moscow office director of the John D. and Catherine T. MacArthur Foundation. He holds a Doctor of Sciences degree in political science from the Institute of World Economy and International Relations (IMEMO) in Moscow, where he served as deputy director and head of department at the Center for Developing Countries. He has held visiting professorships at Macalester College, the University of California at Berkeley, San Jose State University, and the University of Washington, and taught for five years at the George C. Marshall European Center for Security Studies in Garmisch, Germany. He has also served as Washington Bureau Chief for the RIA Novosti Russian News and Information Agency. Dr. Zevelev has published five books and numerous articles.

ACKNOWLEDGMENTS

This book project has given new meaning to the word collaboration. Three years, three continents, and a dozen authors later, it's good to be able to thank the many people who have contributed to this collective endeavor.

It began with a big idea by one of us that would never have gotten off the ground without key institutions and scholars getting behind it. At the brainstorming session that Deepa called at the Sigur Center for Asian Studies in 2007 to test the waters, it became clear right away that the prospect of looking more closely at the foreign policy thinking in rising and aspiring powers of Asia and Eurasia excited people. And it was during that session that Henry's idea of applying a schools of thought approach to access domestic debates in these countries caught on and made the project seem actually workable. Among those who took part in our early discussions, we owe special thanks to our valued colleague and former dean, Harry Harding, an Asia specialist par excellence, who inspired his colleagues to work together.

Since then, we are happy to say that the two of us have worked seamlessly as a team (despite differing political perspectives, we might add). We're also pleased to report that whatever skepticism some colleagues initially had about doing a complex domestically oriented comparative study of China, India, Iran, Japan, and Russia melted away as the project progressed.

From the beginning, we designed the country studies to be done jointly by US-based and in-country authors. But our project also traveled to the region: we took most of the dozen of us to Beijing, New Delhi, and Moscow between January and November 2010 for regional seminars where we presented preliminary country papers to prominent academics, journalists, policy analysts, and policy makers for reaction (and a reality check).

We could not have pulled off our regional seminars without crucial help from partner institutions within China, India, and Russia, and we want to express our sincere thanks—respectively to China Foreign Affairs University in Beijing; Observer Research Foundation, Institute for Peace & Conflict Studies and the Institute for Defence Studies & Analyses in Delhi; Moscow State Institute of International Relations (MGIMO) and the

Carnegie Moscow Center. The leadership and staff at each of these prestigious and very busy institutions went out of their way to help us with meticulous logistics and to recruit commentators representing a spectrum of foreign policy opinions.

Back at home, we were fortunate to have an extremely supportive group at the Elliott School of International Affairs. At the top of the list is Dean Mike Brown, an early (and continuous) strong supporter who provided critical seed money for our pilot conference in September 2007 (with important intercession by former Associate Dean Kristin Lord, now at the Center for a New American Security). Doug Shaw, associate dean, jumped through many administrative hoops on our behalf so the two of us did not have to.

At the Sigur Center for Asian Studies, we could not have asked for a more conducive environment, starting with former director Shawn McHale, whose able leadership, especially his bureaucratic-circumventing vision and capability, we came to rely on repeatedly! His successor, Ed McCord, also gave us unquestioning support. Their selfless leadership has been a driving force of this project's success and that of other projects as well. The Rising Powers Initiative staff at the Sigur Center is a dream team with Matt Grieger's unerring judgment, innovative mind, and ability to anticipate requirements; Winnie Nham's unparalleled design and writing skills; and Amy Hsieh's superb academic talents.

Of course, none of this would have been possible without outside sponsorship. To the Carnegie Corporation of New York, and most particularly to Patricia Moore Nicholas, we express our deepest appreciation. Pat's keen insights and feedback were always helpful and truly welcome.

We also thank David McBride, Caelyn Cobb, Rick Stinson, and Shyam Ghosh of Oxford University Press for their expert handling of our manuscript and getting it out in record time.

As coeditors, we wish we could take all the credit, but in the end, the book was written thanks to the exceptionally collegial, intellectually driven, and fun-loving group of authors we've had the pleasure of working with.

Henry R. Nau and Deepa M. Ollapally

WORLDVIEWS OF ASPIRING POWERS

1

Introduction

Domestic Voices of Aspiring Powers

Henry R. Nau

The world is changing: China and other countries are rising; America may be falling. Everyone is asking: what are the likely implications? One way to answer this question is to look at how rising powers view the world and how they would like to change it. Even more interesting is to look at differing views within rising powers rather than assume that they have only one view, which is externally or structurally determined.

This study examines different domestic worldviews of foreign policy within five aspiring powers—China, India, Iran, Japan, and Russia. Power is shifting materially toward these countries. For three decades after World War II, Japan grew faster than other developed countries. And for the past three decades, the developing or emerging countries, such as China and India, have grown faster than developed countries. Relative growth is not the only indicator of rising power, so we included Russia and Iran. And, for reasons of resources and time, we could not include other rising powers such as Brazil, Turkey, and South Africa (although we explore implications for them in our concluding chapter). Moreover, because Japan is already a "risen" power, Iran a "prospective" power, and Russia, China, and India, as this volume describes, often "conflicted" powers, unsure what the rise in power means, we refer to our five countries as "aspiring" as well as "rising" powers.

Whether the power shift toward aspiring powers is significant depends on how these powers plan to use their enhanced power. They express and debate views about their role in the world, and these worldviews interpret what they want to do with their power. In this study, we call these world-views "foreign policy schools of thought." Schools of thought are concep-tual frameworks for thinking about the world. They differ in terms of the scope, goals, and means of foreign policy—whether a country aspires to be a global or local actor, seeks ideological or material goals, and prefers hard or soft power to achieve these goals.

Defined in these terms, different worldviews exist in all countries. They constitute a broad ideational variable affecting foreign policy outcomes. They are not always the most important factors. In specific cases, other factors may be more important such as a shift in the external distribution of power (external shock), domestic political ideology (whether a country is democratic or nondemocratic), bureaucratic politics (domestic institu-tions), interest groups (business and party competition), elite politics (class and ethnic differences), and public opinion (culture).[1] But debates about worldviews often suffuse these other factors. Competition among interest groups and bureaucracies play out between advocates of nationalist and globalist strategies, between agencies responsible for military and domestic affairs, and between leaders espousing moral/religious and secular views. We are not arguing that worldviews are always the primary causes of for-eign policy outcomes; sometimes they are consequences. But whether cause or effect, debates about worldviews cluster or hover around the decision-making process and become another way of tracking foreign policy developments within and between countries. Domestic debates are especially important when international structures are relatively stable. In the absence of wars or serious economic crises, domestic factors tend to dominate.

In this introductory chapter we explore the role of worldviews in the study of foreign policy, create a framework to compare foreign policy worldviews or schools of thought across aspiring powers, and assess some of the shifts in domestic debates within aspiring powers and their impact on US and other great power relations. Examples are drawn from the in-dividual country chapters, which reveal for the first time the complexity and richness of domestic debates about worldviews, even in authoritarian states such as China, Russia, and Iran.

POWER SHIFTS AND WORLD ORDER

According to the US Central Intelligence Agency (CIA), "the international system—as constructed following the Second World War—will be almost unrecognizable by 2025 owing to the rise of emerging powers, a globalizing economy, an historic transfer of relative wealth and economic power from West to East, and the growing influence of nonstate actors. By 2025, the international system will be a global multipolar one with gaps in national power continuing to narrow between developed and developing countries."[2]

The CIA's projections are probably overwrought. There is nothing new about a changing world. America's fall has been expected for a long time. Paul Kennedy predicted it almost twenty-five years ago.[3] Henry Kissinger agreed, arguing in 1994 that the world was heading toward multipolarity and the United States was ill-prepared for such a world.[4] I was a skeptic then and remain one today.[5] The terrorist attacks on September 11, 2001, did not change American supremacy as much as reinforce it. Almost singlehandedly America initiated and won two immediate military victories in Afghanistan and Iraq (overall outcomes, of course, remain in doubt) and, behind French–British leadership in NATO, conducted a third successful military intervention most recently in Libya. In addition, the United States contributed substantially to post-conflict reconstruction operations in Iraq and Afghanistan for some ten years or more after military interventions. So, even with unprecedented debt and the slowest recovery in history, America is hardly down and out. Conversely, the rise of China may be overdone. This too has been predicted for more than a decade. But no great power has emerged on the world scene following a trajectory of uninterrupted growth. By 2025 China is more likely to experience setbacks than great power status or supremacy. Both Prussia and the United States stumbled many times before uniting troubled nations and attaining world power at the end of the nineteenth century.

Moreover, the rise and decline of great powers may change the world, but some world structures accommodate power shifts better than others and make the rise and decline of great powers less contentious. Most projections, like the CIA's, focus on the impact of rising powers on the existing power structure.[6] Few consider the impact of the existing power structure on rising powers.[7] Yet the United States has superintended a world order since 1945 that has been extraordinarily peaceful. That world has accommodated rising powers one after the other—Germany and the European Union (EU) in Europe, Japan in northeast Asia, and now potentially China and India in all of Asia. Indeed that world also accommodated peacefully a major falling power, the Soviet Union. If America's dominance has served its own interests, it has also served the interests of others. As Colonel Liu Mingfu, an instructor at the National Defense University in China, points out, "America has had two strategic successes: the success of smoothly achieving its rise and the success of efficiently containing challenges to its hegemony from other powers."[8] Today's aspiring powers may have a high bar to hurdle if they hope to improve on the peaceful and prosperous world that the United States has led since World War II.

If or as American power accommodates more and more rising powers, and in that sense *relatively* declines, the voices of today's aspiring powers become more important. These voices will shape how future international structures may change and evolve.

EXTERNAL STRUCTURE AND DOMESTIC DEBATES

This volume is acutely aware that both domestic and international events determine foreign policy.[9] Domestic debates about foreign policy are likely to be more consequential when international events are stable or become less threatening. US foreign policy shifted in 2008 from an ambitious freedom agenda under George W. Bush to a more realist or security-oriented policy under Obama.[10] Aside from an emerging international financial crisis, this shift was largely a consequence of contentious domestic debates in the United States about Iraq. By contrast, when the Soviet Union collapsed from 1989 to 1991, the external power structure changed substantially, but it did so in a less threatening direction. In this case too, domestic developments came to the fore and probably accounted best for America's and other countries' (e.g., Russia's) foreign policies in the 1990s. On the other hand, when terrorist hijackers attacked the United States on September 11, 2001, an external shock accounted for the American foreign policy response. As the source of an attack on the American mainland, Afghanistan became a war of "necessity" not choice. Still, domestic debates became important again soon thereafter. President Obama called Iraq a war of "choice," concluding that domestic influences overrode structural ones.

Overall, since 1991, the structure of the international system has been relatively stable. In this kind of environment, domestic debates about foreign policy take on added significance. Today, as our concluding chapter suggests, domestic debates in many aspiring powers cluster around the nationalist and realist rather than globalist end of the spectrum. Does that suggest that structural or geopolitical factors determine domestic debates? Not really, because then the puzzle would be why China and India, while maintaining core nationalist views, have moved so decisively over the past two decades toward global institutional objectives—joining the world trading and financial systems in an aggressive manner.

Countries, even authoritarian ones, don't just have a single foreign policy.[11] They debate foreign policy priorities, and these domestic worldviews may acquire a repetitive or timeless aspect. Some points of view or schools of thought emerge over and over again, even if different schools prevail at different times.[12] Certain schools may associate with certain institutes and journals or with certain periods of a country's history. For example, the Jacksonian school of thought in the United States, which celebrates American independence and abstention from foreign entanglements, associates with the Monroe Doctrine in the nineteenth century and is prominent today in the publications of the Cato Institute in Washington, D.C.

If we could identify and understand these institutional sources and historical traditions of foreign policy schools of thought in other countries, we could better anticipate changes in the foreign policies of those countries and be less surprised when a new point of view emerges. For example, anyone following American foreign policy over the past ten years would have benefited from being aware of the neoconservative thinking on foreign policy that developed in the 1990s at think tanks such as the American Enterprise Institute.[13] This thinking anticipated some aspects of foreign policy under the George W. Bush administration, such as the invasion of Iraq. Or, similarly in the 2000s, foreign observers would have benefited from following the liberal internationalist critique of Bush's foreign policy emerging from the Brookings Institution and Carnegie Endowment for International Peace. This school of thought anticipated some critical aspects of foreign policy under the Barack Obama administration, such as the heavy emphasis on diplomacy and multilateral institutions.[14]

DO DOMESTIC DEBATES MATTER?

The study focuses, then, on domestic debates interpreting international events when international events themselves are relatively stable and cannot account for changes in foreign policies. Why focus on domestic debates? Don't other aspects of domestic policy matter more than debates or ideas? What is debated or said may not be related to what is actually done. Intellectual debates about foreign policy may be irrelevant, unrelated to official decisions made behind closed doors through unofficial channels. Or these debates may be epiphenomenal, reflecting rationalizations of policy rather than motivations or explanations of it. Bureaucrats, presidents, legislators, political parties, civil society actors such as military–industrial interests, political ideologies, and public opinion may all be more important.[15]

Our argument is not that these other factors are unimportant in making foreign policy choices, but that they all work to a considerable extent through the medium of intellectual ideas and debate. Bureaucrats base their policy actions on expertise, and expertise is developed through the application and testing of ideas against practical realities. In some countries, scholars become bureaucrats, while all bureaucrats may be slaves to some defunct scholar or economist, as John Maynard Keynes once told us. Even if decisions are made for purely material reasons, such as protecting budgets and bureaucratic turf, bureaucracies perform specific functions or roles, and those roles reflect intellectual orientations. Most foreign ministries, for example, stress diplomatic or institutional solutions to foreign policy problems, while most defense departments stress military approaches and most economic ministries commercial applications. Similarly, legislators, political parties, and private sector actors influence foreign policy not in the abstract but to advance the ideas and interests of specific constituents. Hyphenated Americans and multinational corporations have a view of the world in which they pursue benefits and profits and press these views on their representatives. While domestic political ideologies, such as liberal and conservative, may influence foreign policy views, foreign policy worldviews also act independently of domestic ideologies.[16] Finally, public opinion is shaped by media discourse and the packaging and sale of ideas through hearings, campaigns, and advertising. The new media world is rich with intellectual discourse and disagreements.[17]

Domestic debates may not matter more in all cases, but they matter enough in most cases that outcomes over the medium term do not usually deviate very far from the shifts and movements of domestic debates. In this study, we are not trying to explain specific day-to-day decisions. Nor are we trying to explain the social or institutional origins of various schools of thought. We are trying to track domestic debates *in terms of* these schools of thought, associate the schools with individuals or institutions to the extent we can, and identify shifts in the intellectual center of gravity of these domestic foreign policy debates, shifts from one point of view to another along a spectrum of views about how that country should relate to the world.[18]

These shifts occur and capture policy developments over the medium term. At any given moment, a specific decision may be better explained by bureaucratic expediency, secret maneuvering, lobbying, procedural and legal stratagems, or corruption. Even then, the individuals or groups making this decision may be influenced at least in part by their worldviews. But rather quickly that decision, if it is significant, feeds into a larger, more visible, medium-term intellectual discourse, because the decision generates consequences, requires explanation, triggers controversy, is challenged in courts, gets reported by the media, or becomes the basis for elite and public opinion disputes. Our argument is that within this medium time frame, say several months to a couple of years, domestic debates become a pretty good way to follow the intellectual thinking and majority consensus of a society regarding foreign policy, whether these debates are causes or effects of specific decisions. Over a medium term, shifts in domestic debates become good proxies for shifts in foreign policy.

Some examples from our case studies illustrate this point. In 2009 Japanese domestic politics experienced an unprecedented shift.[19] With little change in the external environment to explain it, Japan went from a one-party-dominated system to a two-party system. The Democratic Party of Japan (DPJ) took power and immediately advocated a different foreign policy approach. The DPJ favored less reliance on the United States, a nuclear-free zone in Asia, and more "Asianism" in trade relations. Meanwhile, the United States shifted in the same year from a democracy-oriented focus under President Bush, which spotlighted Japan as an ally, to a more great power, pragmatic-oriented foreign policy orientation under President Obama, which gave greater priority to relations with great powers such as China and Russia. Both countries moved away from one another, from globalist to more realist and regionalist positions. In some ways, these shifts preceded and predicted the foreign policy dispute that erupted subsequently between Japan and the United States over the implementation of the Okinawa base agreement negotiated in 2005–2006.

Another example comes from the China case study.[20] Between 2006 and 2010, China's foreign policy shifted visibly from a campaign to sell China's rise as a peaceful contribution to institution building in Asia to a tougher policy to assert China's territorial interests in the South and East China Seas and strengthen solidarity with rogue nuclear states in North Korea and Iran. Our interest here is not to explain that specific decision; in China's case it remains obscure. Rather, we seek to track the preceding and subsequent domestic interpretation or public relations trail of the decision. In this case, the center of gravity in China's debate moved from a globalist, economic-oriented, institution-building strategy to a more traditional military, security-oriented strategy. At the same time, the debate in the United States moved from a globalist ideologically oriented program under Bush to a more pragmatic, security-oriented policy under Obama. In the short run, greater realism in both China and the United States seemed to offer better prospects for cooperation on practical issues such as nonproliferation (North Korea and Iran), climate change, economic recovery, and terrorism. But China's shift from economic priorities to military assertiveness did not match up well with America's shift from ideology to diplomatic pragmatism. Recently, China has been unwilling to make concessions in economic areas while the United States has reacted to greater Chinese assertiveness by upgrading its alliance with Japan and South Korea.

A critical task for us therefore is to identify, track, and compare foreign policy views or schools of thought across diverse countries and judge whether the center of gravity in these debates has moved farther apart or closer together, particularly between the aspiring powers and the United States.

FOREIGN POLICY SCHOOLS OF THOUGHT

To explore and compare domestic foreign policy debates across diverse countries, we brought together both theoretical and country expertise. The literature on foreign policy schools of thought in the United States is well developed.[21] We use this literature to develop some analytical distinctions that help us identify and compare foreign policy schools in the domestic debates of other countries. But can these distinctions drawn from the American literature be applied to foreign countries? We thought so, although to safeguard against ethnocentrism, we employed foreign experts throughout the study. Each country chapter was done jointly by an American specialist *on* that country and a foreign specialist *from* that country. In addition, we held three regional seminars in the countries studied to delve into the domestic debates on their own terms—Delhi, India, in January 2010; Beijing, China, in May 2010; and Moscow, Russia, in November 2010. Details about our regional partners appear in the Acknowledgments of this volume.

Schools of thought are intellectual cultures that communicate by emotions and experience as well as abstractions. Normally the emotions and experiences of an intellectual culture are not accessible to outsiders. But abstractions are. In the schemata below, we identify abstractions that enable us to compare schools of thought across different cultural and emotional environments.

All countries and groups within countries debate foreign policy in terms of three broad parameters. Table 1.1 identifies these parameters and variations within them:

- **Scope of foreign policy**—whether foreign policy initiatives should be primarily isolationist, national, regional, or global in scope. How involved should the country be in world affairs? Does it prefer to view its foreign policy in a relatively limited, autonomous or independent fashion or does it believe it has a role to play at the global level through great power or multilateral initiatives and institutions?

- **Means of foreign policy**—whether foreign policy actions should give primary emphasis to military/economic, political/cultural/ideological, or diplomatic/institutional means to influence world events. Military and economic means are called "hard" power; political, diplomatic, cultural, ideological, and religious factors are often referred to as "soft" power.[22] Does the country react to the world largely through the prism of threats and the acquisition/use of military force, a competition for power and supremacy? Or does it deal with the world primarily through cultural, religious, or ideological programs? As part of its peaceful rise initiative in the mid-2000s, for example, China established some 350 Confucius Institutes (university-affiliated) and 430 Confucius Classrooms (at secondary schools) in 103 countries and regions to teach Mandarin Chinese and spread Chinese culture.[23] Or does a country emphasize the tools of cooperative diplomatic and institutional efforts to manage common resources, encourage disarmament, and solve problems peacefully? In other words, does a country implement its foreign policy primarily through traditional great power instruments, exceptionalist soft power tools or diplomatic and institutional initiatives?[24]
- **Goals of foreign policy**—whether foreign policy seeks to achieve largely geopolitical goals such as defense and the international balance of power; cultural and political goals such as nonviolence, human rights, and democracy; or institutional and diplomatic goals such as global governance of wealth, environment, and arms. Is the world envisioned as the outcome of foreign policy a Western, non-Western, post-Western, or post-modern world?

Note that the distinctions overlap and are matters of emphasis not exclusiveness. All schools of foreign policy thought contain elements of national, regional, and global scope. But they differ in terms of how they prioritize these elements. Groups that favor a national scope may expand their efforts when confronted by global threats. Nationalists are fierce defenders of sovereignty. But Nationalists incline toward dealing with faraway threats as

Table 1.1: *Parameters of Foreign Policy Debates*

SCOPE	National (Most Limited)	Regional	Global (Most Expansive)
MEANS	Military/Economic Tools (Hard Power)	Political/ Ideological Tools (Soft Power)	Interactive Tools (Diplomacy and Multilateral Institutions)
GOALS	Geopolitics (Defense, Balance of Power, Hegemony)	Spread of Culture, Religion, Ideology, or Civilization (Human Rights, Democracy, Non-Western world)	Consolidation of International Institutions (Global Governance of Commons, Environment, Nonproliferation, etc.)

expeditiously as possible and returning to a more limited foreign policy as quickly as possible. Similarly, military power and ideas are means as well as goals of foreign policy. But there is a difference between domestic groups that advocate the spread of a country's ideology, say democracy, and those that advocate the use of ideological or soft power to promote traditional military goals, such as cultural exchanges to strengthen alliances. The former sees ideology as a goal, the latter as a tool. Additionally, scope and means of foreign policy become entangled when groups differentiate themselves along the two axes simultaneously. Normal Nationalists in Japan, as we see in chapter 5, hug the United States, a global power, rather than China, a regional power (a scope issue), and emphasize the use of military force rather than economic integration (a means issue).

Furthermore, while the three-part breakdown may seem too simple to capture the complexities of individual country foreign policy debates, keep in mind that these three parameters, if allowed to vary in three different ways (such as national, regional, or global in the case of the scope of foreign policy), combine to produce at least twenty-seven different categories of foreign policy views. It's doubtful that any single country has twenty-seven different schools of thought debating its foreign policy. But, as we see in this volume, the range of views is often much more diverse than we assume.

This comparative framework offers three specific advantages. It helps us find schools of thought that we might otherwise leave out, make judgments as to which schools of thought may be more prevalent at a given time and which may be relatively weak or minor, and compare the resulting center of gravity of schools in individual countries and shifts among these centers across countries.

To illustrate the first advantage, we might assume that all schools of thought in the United States are global in scope since America is a unipolar power in the world. But this would overlook a very important voice in the American debate, the Nationalist school that favors a more limited or humble American foreign policy. George W. Bush asserted this view in 2000 when he appealed as a presidential candidate for a more "humble" America.[25] Similarly, a country such as Japan may define itself as a peace-loving, trading state, which sharply restricts the military means and goals of foreign policy. But, as chapter 5 on Japan shows, other groups within Japan may oppose this definition of Japan and advocate foreign policies that position Japan as a more normal or traditional, including military, state. Our framework makes us look for groups that do not share the dominant or official view as well as groups that may not be visible in official policy debates but are nevertheless present and often powerful. The military, hard-line school of thought in both China and India may be obscure but we know it is present.

Second, the framework allows us to ascertain at any point in time how contested that country's foreign policy may be (how many groups are involved) and where the center of gravity of the foreign policy debate lies. In some countries, such as Russia, there may be a clear consensus, at least for now; in others, such as India, there may be a fragmenting consensus. By looking for alternative schools of thought, even when there is an apparent consensus, we can better anticipate shifts in that country's foreign policy. The debate in some countries may be more restricted, in others more fluid. If the center of gravity shifts quite often, we might anticipate that schools of thought in that country are more personalized rather than institutionalized. It may not be possible to associate worldviews with stable, ongoing institutional sources. That may be the case in Iran.[26] Similarly, if the political environment is restricted, as in authoritarian states, schools of thought outside the official policy environment may not be allowed to develop and organize independently. Nevertheless, they voice their views through informal channels. That may be the case in China and to a lesser extent Russia. Even in India, which is a democratic state, public opinion beyond official circles still may not matter much except as a veto factor.[27]

Third, the framework allows us to make useful cross-country comparisons. Are economic-based schools of thought more prominent in some countries, while military- or ideological-based groups are more important in others? For example, economic approaches to the means and goals of foreign policy appear stronger in China and India than in Russia or Iran. In China and India, we need to know more about the groups that advocate military and nationalist approaches to foreign policy, while in Russia and Iran, we need to ask why modernizing groups that might advocate economic globalization are so weak. Similarly, ideological-based schools may be stronger in Iran and the United States than in Japan. These are useful comparisons to have in mind when considering the prospects of foreign policy cooperation and conflict among countries.

COMPARING COUNTRIES

Countries are in large measure unique. Country specialists emphasize this fact and often resist comparisons. Our categories therefore do not please all specialists including some of our own authors. Nevertheless, comparison is impossible unless we abstract beyond individual countries. In this study, we are focused on shifts in domestic foreign policy debates from one point of view on the spectrum to another, first within individual countries and then across countries. We do not argue that our distinctions capture the same realities in each country. Nationalists in Russia are not the same as Nationalists in China. The spectrum of foreign policy views in each country is to some extent idiosyncratic.

Thus, we are less interested in whether we have the right labels for each group in different countries than we are in identifying shifts within each country from say the globalist end of the spectrum to the nationalist end, or the reverse.[28] A shift along the spectrum in any country in the same or opposite direction, say toward nationalism in one and globalism in another, is significant for our purposes. We believe such shifts, especially if they go in opposite directions, have consequences for foreign policy relations among countries and may be as significant as external events for explaining foreign policy crises or opportunities. For example, if both countries shift toward the nationalist end of the spectrum (not becoming nationalist but moving along the spectrum in that direction), we might expect less opportunity for foreign policy cooperation between them. That happened between Japan and the United States in 2009. Both countries became less globalist. If one country became more globalist while the other more nationalist, we might expect the two countries to drift apart but not necessarily engage in more conflict. That happened between Russia and China after 2000. Russia became more nationalist, while China entered the World Trade Organization (WTO). Their relationships did not get worse, but they became less relevant to one another. On the other hand, India's foreign policy debate shifted from a nationalist to a more globalist focus. That made its relations with Russia less relevant, but its relations with China (and the United States) more relevant. As we note later, India and China are globalizing and may encounter and potentially conflict more with one another on the world scene. On the other hand, if as some commentators argue, the United States, Russia, and Japan are scaling back global commitments, they may conflict less with India and China.

Let's observe how the framework sorts out schools of thought in the countries we studied. The variety of schools identified here may seem overwhelming, especially before reading the country studies. But reality is not always simple, and the reader may find it useful to refer to this section as he or she examines the individual country cases. In our conclusions, we consolidate some of the schools into larger groupings.

Table 1.2 starts with ALL domestic groups that favor a national rather than regional or global scope for that country's foreign policy. In terms of scope, all groups are Nationalists advocating independence/autonomy, self-defense, perhaps protectionism, and no more involvement in foreign policy than absolutely necessary. We then ask what goals of foreign policy they relatively emphasize and what means of foreign policy they relatively prefer to implement those goals.

Nationalist groups that emphasize geopolitical goals and prefer military means include the Hyper-Nationalists in India, Hard Power Realists in China, Autonomists in Japan, and Nationalists in Russia. As observed in the India chapter, the Hyper-Nationalists in India "insist on a much more autarchic and autonomous path for India…, seek far greater military capability for India…, [and] are distinguished by their opposition to any measure, especially international arms control measures and domestic military policies which might even remotely or potentially limit such capabilities."[29] Note the national scope, military means, and geopolitical or defense-oriented goals (opposition to diplomatic/multilateral agreements on arms control) of this particular school of thought. Similarly, the Autonomists in Japan seek geopolitical goals, "security with sovereignty and dignity," and "an independent, full spectrum Japanese military that could use force" [military means].[30]

Now look further in Table 1.2 at schools that emphasize geopolitical goals but prefer political–ideological means. We have Offensive Realists in Iran and Nativists in China. According to the China chapter, Nativists in China seek autonomy (limited scope), apply Marxist ideological tools (ideological means), and oppose a capitalist world order (geopolitical goals). Offensive Realists in Iran exploit fundamentalist Islam (religious means) to achieve great power status in the tradition of ancient Persia (geopolitical goals).[31]

For geopolitical Nationalists that prefer economic means, we find Neo-Nationalists in India, and Mercantile Realists in Japan. The Neo-Nationalists in India oppose globalization because it endangers sovereignty and increases inequity [geopolitical goals]. They prefer "strict reciprocity in economic relations, particularly with South Asian neighbors, and alignment with other developing countries over developed countries in economic negotiations" [economic means]. In Japan Mercantile Realists

Table 1.2: *Nationalist Schools of Thought*

Geopolitical Goals
   • Military means: Hyper-Nationalists in India, Hard Power Realists in China, Autonomists in Japan, Nationalists in Russia
   • Political/Ideological means: Offensive Realists in Iran and Nativists in China
   • Economic means: Neo-Nationalists in India, and Mercantile Realists in Japan

Cultural/Religious/Ideological Goals
   • Military means: Normal Nationalists in Japan, Standard Nationalists in India, Ethnic Nationalists in Russia, and Soft Power Realists in China
   • Political/Ideological means: Leftists in India

Institutional Goals
   • Political/Ideological means: Soft Power Nationalists in India

"believe that Japan must remain a small power with self-imposed limits to its right of belligerency [limited scope] and that Japan's contributions to world affairs should remain non-military" [economic means]. At the same time, these Realists "hug" the United States to exploit global markets and enjoy a free ride on American security [geopolitical goals]. Power is sought through economic not military means, while the objective remains Japanese economic and military security, not global institution building (i.e., national not global scope).

So far we have considered only geopolitical goals. What if we ask if there are Nationalist groups that pursue primarily cultural/ideological goals? These groups espouse political/cultural values defended by various means. Those favoring military means now include the Normal Nationalists in Japan, Standard Nationalists in India, Ethnic Nationalists in Russia, and Soft Power Realists in China. As the Indian chapter explains, "the key difference here [between the Standard Nationalist and Hyper-Nationalist schools] is that the [Standard] Nationalist emphasizes the political objectives of military power rather than seeing military power as an end in itself." For Standard Nationalists, political values are the ends, military power just the means. For Hyper-Nationalists, military power is both the ends and means. Normal Nationalists in Japan, identified with the Koizumi wing of the Liberal Democratic Party (LDP), and Soft Power Realists in China also pursue sovereign cultural goals with traditional military means. Ethnic Nationalists in Russia advocate reuniting the Russian nation through a combination of military power and ethnic pride. The Leftists in India also seek cultural goals but they now prefer primarily cultural over military means. And, finally, as the table shows, the Soft Power Nationalist school in India favors political/ideological means but now seeks institutional goals. As the Indian paper suggests, this group "tends to emphasize autonomy [national in scope]...a rhetorical anti-Americanism...and anti-western rhetoric [focus on ideological means]...[and] a variety of third world causes...preferences for selective multilateralism, strict reciprocity in economic relations [institutional goals]."

Note here how the analytical framework helps us to understand differences even when we sometimes use the same labels. The Standard Nationalist or "Nehru"-vian Perspective in India, for example, differs somewhat from the Nationalist groups in other countries because it incorporates more universalist objectives such as nonviolence, not just traditional national, cultural goals. It is also more ambitious in scope and less military in means and ends. Nevertheless, it is still largely a traditional Nationalist school more limited in scope and more focused on military means than the Liberal Globalists in India, whom we discuss below.

Table 1.3 groups together schools that advocate a regionalist scope for their country's foreign policy. Groups preferring institutional goals and diplomatic means include the Asianists in Japan who want to bandwagon with China. They emphasize economic means and collective goals such as economic condominium, discounting military threats. In China, regionalist schools include the Asia First school, which advocates development and institutional goals and means, and the Global South school, which seeks development ends through ideological means (solidarity with the South). In Russia, the Great Power Eurasianist school takes a regionalist approach but now emphasizes more traditional military means and perhaps civilization goals seeking to offset Western influence. And, in Iran, the Regional Power Balancers constitute the dominant school. Some favor military means to achieve religious goals while others emphasize military means to achieve traditional geopolitical goals. An offensive variant prefers religious/ideological means and a defensive variant hopes to work through global institutions and integration to modernize Iran.

Table 1.4 shows the globalist schools of thought broken down by the goals and means preferred. Again, as the chapters suggest, practically all

Table 1.3: *Regionalist Schools of Thought*

Institutional Goals
 • Trade/Diplomatic means: Asia First and Global South Schools in China, and
  Asianist or Bandwagon School in Japan

Cultural/Religious/Ideological Goals
 • Military means: Eurasia/Orthodox School in Russia, Regional Power Balancers in
  Iran

Geopolitical Goals
 • Military means: Regional Power Balancers in Iran
 • Political/Ideological means: Offensive (Anti-West) Variant
 • Institutional/Diplomatic means: Defensive (Modernization/Detente) Variant

countries have a school of thought that is global in scope and ideological in goals, an exceptionalist school interested in projecting that country's identity abroad.[32] This exceptionalist school includes Islamic Idealists in Iran, a civilizational or Orthodox school in Russia, and a Moralist school in India. The Islamic Idealists in Iran favor ideological means while the Global Rejectionists prefer military means.

Other globalist schools downplay ideological ends and advocate institutional goals. They include the Liberal Globalists in India, the Dual Hedgers in Japan, the Pro-Western Liberals in Russia, the Globalists in China, and a small group of Global Accommodationists in Iran. These schools emphasize disarmament, diplomacy, globalization, and, to varying degrees, international institutions. For example, Pro-Western Liberals in Russia and Globalists in India and China seek integration with the West by trade and institutional means. The Dual Hedgers in Japan seek an integrationist Goldilocks solution for Japanese foreign policy: a Pacific or global scope, a balance between military and economic means (hedging with the United States on military matters and China on economics), and the hope that neither China nor the United States pursues ideological aims that might compromise Japan's military and economic hedges and destroy the "goldilocks" solution of a peaceful integrated world system (institutional goals). In short, this strategy depends upon an open integrated international system that permits Japan to express its unique ambivalence between China (East) and the United States (West).

Table 1.4: *Globalist Schools of Thought*

Geopolitical Goals
  • Military means: Great Power Balancers in Russia, Great Power Realists in India, Major Powers school in China, Balancers in Japan, Pre-Revolutionary Pahlavi State in Iran

Institutional Goals
  • Integration/Diplomatic means: Globalists in China, Dual Hedgers in Japan, Liberal Globalists in India, Pro-Western Liberals in Russia, and Global Accommodationists in Iran

Civilization/Cultural Goals
  • Political/Ideological means: Islamic (Revolutionary) Idealists in Iran, Orthodox school in Russia, Moralist school in India
  • Military means: Global Rejectionists in Iran

Still others schools emphasize a globalist scope but geopolitical/military rather than ideological or institutional ends. This category includes the Balancers in Japan, who, as the Japan chapter points out, favor "reinterpreting the constitution to allow Japan to defend its U.S. ally" and "prefer the global status quo in which Washington remains the dominant player in the system." Great Power Balancers in Russia, Great Power Realists in India, the Major Powers school in China, and the prerevolutionary Pahlavi regime in Iran also fall into this category. They seek a great power role on the world stage both to shape security regimes and to share responsibilities for global rules and stability. Economics serves that end, but it does not replace great power politics, as liberal globalist schools expect. In this context, China's strategy which subordinates economic advance to political and military competition may be the model. For Great Power Realists in Russia, China, and India (as well as Japan), the most important international partner is the United States because it sits at the "high table" of global power politics. In Russia, the New START treaty, in India the recent US–Indian Nuclear Agreement, and in China the prospect of a Group of Two (G-2) symbolize this status.

Therefore, theoretical distinctions, although ideal types, accommodate a great deal of empirical complexity, and indeed they are absolutely necessary if we are going to compare countries, which is the objective of this project. All countries may to some extent regard themselves as unique, but insisting on that proposition too much precludes any meaningful comparison with other countries.

POLICY IMPLICATIONS FOR THE UNITED STATES AND OTHER POWERS

There are at least three important foreign policy implications for aspiring powers and the United States, which derive from this approach emphasizing domestic foreign policy debates.

First, as we have noted, the center of gravity of foreign policy debates shifts. We witnessed such shifts in the United States in 2008 and in Japan in 2009 and may see such shifts again in 2013. In democratic countries, these shifts often coincide with the rotation of opposing political parties in and out of government. Republicans and Democrats in the United States are known to have different foreign policy preferences, and opposing parties in Japan may now be displaying similar patterns.[33] These changes still leave a lot unchanged. One can be as impressed with the continuity of American foreign policy between Bush and Obama as well as with the changes. The same can be said of Japanese foreign policy under the Democratic Party of Japan (DPJ). Nevertheless, the shifts, even if marginal within an underlying continuity, can produce big changes and controversies. And these changes may seem bigger from abroad than they are at home. Obama's policies are certainly perceived abroad as being very different from those of George W. Bush.

Second, it is important to track these internal foreign policy debates especially in countries that are not democratic. In these countries, the differences exist but are more obscure and emerge sometimes with little warning. The dramatic and unexpected shifts in China's foreign policies are obvious examples—in the early 1970s toward rapprochement with the United States, again in the late 1970s toward export-oriented growth policies, once more in the early 1990s toward integration with the West and WTO despite the domestic threat of democracy posed by the events in Tiananmen Square, and most recently in 2009–2010 toward greater national assertiveness. Russia and Iran experienced similar shifts in the early 1990s and late 1970s, respectively. While authoritarian countries will always be more opaque, our approach anticipates possible changes by looking for alternative opinions (schools). For example, in Russia and Iran today, where are the groups advocating modernization and membership in the WTO? If significant change occurs in these countries, it will come from these groups. The domestic debates approach deliberately searches for such groups.

A third important implication of following domestic foreign policy debates in terms of schools of thought is to anticipate better cross-country shifts in these debates and not to lock in on only one interpretation of such shifts. Scholars are often inclined to favor one school of thought over another. Realist scholars interpret domestic shifts in terms of geopolitics, while liberal scholars interpret them in terms of reactions to US policy. Because Realist schools dominate today in Russia, China, and India, realist scholars conclude that geopolitics is determining outcomes. Or, if China slides toward nationalism, liberal scholars conclude that the United States must have pushed it in that direction. The schools of thought approach compensates for this bias. The schools include all major approaches to international relations. Nationalist and Realist schools rely more on the logic of realism to interpret events, Globalist schools more on the logic of liberalism, and or Idealist exceptionalist schools more on the logic of constructivism. The schools of thought approach makes us aware of these different logics. We look at international shifts through different lenses, including those that we do not necessarily prefer.

SHIFTING DEBATES ACROSS COUNTRIES

The most important benefit of tracking domestic debates in aspiring powers is that it alerts us to shifts in the centers of gravity in debates between two or more countries and the directions in which these shifts occur.

While the distribution of foreign policy views in each country is unique, a broad spectrum encompassing the three parameters of our framework applies to all countries. Figure 1.1 illustrates this spectrum. On scope, as schools of thought move from left to right on this chart, they move from isolationist or nationalist positions to more global orientations. On means, they shift from an emphasis on military and economic or hard power to ideological and diplomatic instruments or soft power. And on ends, they move from military/geopolitical goals to cultural and exceptionalist goals and on to institutional and integrationist ones. Consolidation of institutions, or integrationist goals, generally implies collective decision making on global security issues (UNSC) and institutional integration in the world economy (WTO). That's clear enough. But institutional goals may be heavily flavored by cultural or civilization content. Do institutions advocate Western or non-Western, maybe post-Western, goals? Some Great Power Balancers in Russia today favor the idea of "democratic sovereignty" to distinguish their worldview from the contemporary Western concept of the "democratic peace."[34] They emphasize civilization concepts rather than common institutions. Groups in China and Iran too have different ideas about the normative orientation of an integrated world. Once again, the framework of this study helps us to make distinctions between cultural/ civilizational and institutional goals.

As a hypothetical example, let's say that the center of gravity of domestic foreign policy debates in the United States shifted such that US foreign policy became less global in scope, more dependent on economic than ideological instruments, and more focused on consolidating international institutions than balance of power goals. Indeed, shifts under Obama may be such an example. Even without considering policies or reactions in China, a more limited and economic/institution-oriented foreign policy in the United States might cause the United States to be less threatened by an expansion of China's military role in Asia, more inclined to preserve economic interdependence with China in which China finances American consumption of its exports, and more focused on multilateral solutions to solve security conflicts around the world. Indeed, for such reasons, some might argue, Obama was late in responding to China's more nationalist or assertive policies staking out territorial claims in the East and South China Seas and subtly supporting rather than condemning North Korean provocations in 2009–2010. But now, what if China's center of gravity also shifted and China became increasingly oriented toward globalist scope, economic instruments, and integrationist goals? China would press its economic and institutional solutions at the global level, while the United States would be less active. Now relations would depend on whether China favors integrationist goals with a different civilization content, one that is less Western and more Asian. A

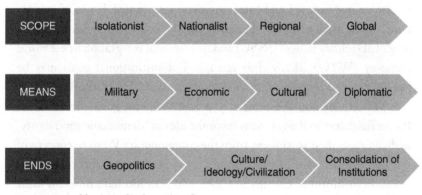

Figure 1.1: Tracking Shifts within Countries

"Beijing Consensus" might call for more statist rather than open market economic rules and set limits on financing of American consumption, different from the "Washington Consensus" that preceded it. Clearly the implications for the United States could be serious and might cause it to retreat further from the international stage or to reconsider its less globalist orientation and contest the Beijing Consensus.

The country case studies reveal several interesting shifts of this sort. Let us look at each one and its implications for the United States.

From 1996 to 2002, Russia domestic foreign policy debate shifted significantly from the integrationist or pro-Western liberal end of the spectrum to the nationalist/military-focused end. US foreign policy during the same period shifted from a democracy/integrationist center of gravity under Bill Clinton to a more nationalist/military-focused foreign policy under George W. Bush. There were no overriding international events that might explain these shifts, although Russia's dissatisfaction with the expansion of NATO in 1997 and the Kosovo crisis in 1999 constituted important external factors contributing to Russia's shift. More or less, the nationalist shift in both countries was driven by domestic factors and resulted in a cooling off of United States–Russian relations, as one might expect from a relative withdrawal of both countries from more expansive foreign policies. United States–Russian relations stabilized modestly in 2002 with the conclusion of SORT (the Strategic Offensive Reduction Treaty) and the re-creation of the NATO Russia Council.

Following the Iraq invasion, the Bush administration shifted again toward the ideological integrationist end of the foreign policy spectrum, emphasizing the spread of democracy particularly in the Middle East. Predictably, this shift, accompanied by a continuing nationalist orientation in Russia, made United States–Russian relations less relevant if not more contentious. Obama's strategy to "reset" United States–Russian relations (upgrade them to a more great power realist status) brought a new "realism" to American foreign policy and coincided with a shift in Russia under Medvedev toward a more realist school of thought, the Great Power Balancers school. United States–Russian relations warmed as they cooperated on Afghanistan, nuclear arms negotiations, and sanctions against Iran.

The future of the reset policy thus may depend on the center of gravity of the domestic debate in both countries remaining near the realist position on the foreign policy spectrum. A shift in the United States toward the nationalist end of the spectrum, which is a greater possibility if the Republican Party wins national elections in 2012, would undermine recent cooperation. Similarly, a shift toward the globalist end of the spectrum in Russia might cause other problems in United States–Russian relations. As the Russian chapter in this volume points out, some Russian liberals and economic elites (e.g., Club of November 4) favor joining NATO (to become PATO, Pan-Atlantic Treaty Organization) and the WTO. But, if they prevailed and the United States became more nationalist, the United States may not be in a position to follow through and get Congressional approval for Russian inclusion. The internationalist wing of American foreign policy is noticeably weaker today in face of the economic difficulties and protectionist sentiment among many constituents on both sides of the political aisle. Russia's decision to join the WTO may find little resonance in the United States, unlike the bipartisan support over the past thirty years for China's entry into global markets.

The China chapter in this volume describes a similar shift in China from a globalist, selective multilateralist center of gravity toward the nationalist end of the spectrum (labeled Realist school in the China case). In the short term, this shift is in line with the recent realist shift of Obama's foreign policy. The United States pounds less on human rights issues in China, and the United States and China collaborate more as great powers on a series of common problems—climate change, nonproliferation, and energy. If this cooperation stalls, however, as it has done on climate change and nonproliferation (given China's continuing support of an increasingly belligerent North Korea), the relationship is subject to potential shock. The United States may not be able to sustain a realist posture if nationalist sentiments build up in the United States to reject Chinese imports, which threaten American jobs. Already, the two countries may be locked in a competitive struggle to devalue exchange rates. China buys dollars to keep its exchange rate from rising and to continue its export-led growth, and the US central bank sells dollars (puts dollars into the economy by buying long-term Treasury bonds) to revive the economy and drive the dollar down and US exports up.

Improvement in United States–China relations therefore may depend on, more than anything else, a shift in both countries toward the globalist and economic engagement end of the foreign policy spectrum. The China paper warns the United States not to overreact to China's latest realist/nationalist surge. But this warning makes sense only if the driving force of China's policy is external actions on the part of the United States. Yet the United States has done little over the past several years that can be said to have provoked the more assertive Chinese behavior. Indeed, the United States was relatively neglectful of Asia, leading Obama to pivot back to Asia in late 2011. China is reacting to internal debates. As we suggest in this volume, domestic debates are often more important than reactive, process-driven external events.

A major shift in foreign policy debates occurred in India after 1991. The center of gravity moved from the nationalist (independence), moralistic (Nehru's approach) end of the spectrum to the globalist integrationist end, exactly the opposite of more recent movements in China and the United States. Perhaps this shift was provoked initially by external events. The disappearance of the Soviet Union took away India's principal ally. Over-shadowed increasingly by a rapidly growing China, India decided to join the globalized world economy. This decision was elite-driven and led rather than reflected a domestic foreign policy consensus. The bulk of foreign policy sentiment in India, as the India chapter suggests, still remains nationalist and independence-oriented. In this case, the decision to go global came ahead of a shift in the domestic foreign policy debate. Never-theless, as we anticipate in this study, domestic debates follow if they do not lead. The sustainability of India's decision now depends on the center of gravity of Indian foreign policy sentiment being dragged toward the globalist economic end of the spectrum.

But India is joining the global economy late. Support for globalization, as we have already noted, is weakening in both the United States and China. The domestic shift in India, like that in Russia as it joins the WTO, may find little resonance or support in the United States and rising powers. India would be well advised to sustain its course of globalization, regard-less of the short-term health of the world economy. China did so in 1999, when, despite the Asian financial crisis and subsequent global recession, it joined the WTO and doubled down on its bet to exploit the open competitive international economy. China's internal debate carried the day over external pressures. The future of India's globalist course may also depend on a stronger internal consensus to override external influences. Thus, while policy decisions sometimes precede policy debates, even in democratic countries, debates eventually catch up if that policy is to be sustained. Domestic foreign policy debates exert an important influence in their own right.

Japan is another country that has a lot at stake in the globalist, institution-oriented international system that currently exists. Its domestic debate at the moment is deadlocked between the globalist, trading state advocates adhering to the Yoshida Doctrine and more regular (in Japan called Normal) Nationalists or regionalists torn between hugging the United States, China, or both. Historically, Japan has approached the world system as a taker rather than maker of international rules and institutions. But its rising relative power, an external factor, is causing that stance to shift, and the shift is both reflected and amplified in the domestic debate.

While there seem to be few genuine globalist in the Japanese debate who advocate a strong Japanese contribution to multilateral institutions, UN collective security, and a free market-oriented world economy, there are an increasing number of Realist groups that push Japan to take a more activist stance regionally to align economically with China, militarily with the United States, and diplomatically with both. The latter or Goldilocks solution, as the Japan chapter suggests, is probably unrealistic. It assumes a stable external security environment superintended by a friendly United States, which benefits less and less from economic engagement in Asia while Japan makes the most of Chinese economic development.

But the United States is still the principal absorber of Asian exports and industrialization. Japanese and other Asian companies now export to the United States from China, ensuring that Asia's dependence on America's market for final product exports has probably not changed that much even as Asia's regional trade involving components has shown a relative increase. Whether the United States can continue to absorb all these end products is a crucial question. As we have noted, the domestic consensus in the United States underpinning import of Asian industrialization is weakening. A shift to the nationalist end of the foreign policy spectrum in the United States would doom the Doha Round (if it is not doomed already) and probably begin to reverse the open market policies of the past three decades. A more modest shift to the realist middle of the spectrum has already enflamed United States–China currency relations, as we noted above. And the more competitive nationalist orientation of Chinese foreign policy and of the domestic foreign policy debate in China has focused renewed attention on the United States–Japan alliance. If anything, as our conclusions suggest, a further shift toward the nationalist and military end of the spectrum in China or the United States will push other countries in the region toward a more realist configuration of confrontation and containment and an unraveling of the integrationist regional and global agenda of the past couple of decades.

Iran, whose domestic debate and foreign policy center of gravity are the most xenophobic of the countries we studied, has the least at stake in the current global system but potentially the most to lose if it should decide to change its foreign policy orientation to embrace that system. Iran, in short, is not a member of the global system and seems to thrive in defying it. Its foreign policy debate is highly constrained and centers on an exceptionalist self-image as an Islamic fundamentalist state (ideological ends) with strong regional if not global ambitions (scope) to be a great power (military means). If there are remnants of more moderate schools (e.g., the Accommodationist wing of the Global Balancers school) that might see Iran's goals in terms of more regular nationalist or statist aims and more globalist economic integration, they are largely silent or, more accurately perhaps, "silenced" under present circumstances. But what is equally worrisome is that support outside Iran for an open global economy is also weakening.

The situation for Iran today is very different from the one faced by China and India when they made their decisions to join the global system. In the 1990s, free markets were on a roll. The Uruguay Round and North American Free Trade Agreement had recently been concluded and implemented. The US economy was expanding solidly, and NATO offered security to one new democracy after the other. Today the world economy is still growing but the United States is no longer the leading market. Brazil, Russia, India, China, and South Africa, the BRICS markets, lead the way. They, along with the EU, oppose many US policies, particularly expanding fiscal deficits and unprecedented easy money policy. The opportunities for Iran in such a situation are few. Should it decide to globalize, would the

EU, Russia, or China offer it markets? For oil and gas perhaps, but probably not for light manufactures and other industrialized, including information age, products, which the other aspiring powers covet for themselves. These external structural factors may explain why there are so few advocates for globalization in the Iranian domestic debate today.

WHITHER THE PRESENT GLOBAL SYSTEM?

An important question here is the continued acceptability of the Western and United States–led model of economic growth and democratic statehood that has characterized the global system for the last two decades and more. Russian Nationalist and Realist groups speak about "democratic sovereignty" as a way of rejecting the "democratic peace" implicit in the Western global system. Iranian domestic groups reject the capitalist institutions of the West as well as the social and cultural implications of Western-style modernization as they understand it. China champions a mercantilist government-to-government global economic model. Is the world ripe for some non-Western vision of global politics and economics? If so, aspiring powers in particular have a hard sell to make, to convince not only their own people but foreign countries as well that they have a model for world development that is at least as peaceful and prosperous as the global system led by the United States since 1945.

It's easy to criticize that US-led system, but it should be remembered that world real GDP grew from 1980 to 2010 by over 150 percent or 3.4 percent per year, despite two recessions and a global financial meltdown.[35] That system provided the basis for managing not only the rise of earlier powers, such as Japan, the Asian Tigers, and the EU, but the rise today of the emerging markets of China, India, Brazil, Turkey, and others. It also provided the basis for greater equality in the global order, assisting more than 400 million people in China and nearly 200 million people in India, not to mention 60 million in Brazil, to escape poverty and join the middle-class lifestyle. Greater equality is also evident in the seamless transition of world economic management from the Group of Seven (G-7) and Eight (G-8) economic summits to the Group of Twenty (G-20) economic summits. Whether the G-20 maintains the capitalist market approach of the

G-7 is another issue. A "Beijing Consensus," by contrast to the "Washington Consensus," would allow less room for private sector activities and more room for direct and often secretive government deals. More of the world economy would be politically constructed in a zero-sum fashion. The ability of private markets to expand benefits in a nonzero-sum setting would be sharply curtailed.

The things that go well never make the headlines, and much has gone well over the last thirty, if not sixty, years under America's watch. So, aspiring powers have a responsibility to understand their new obligations as future makers rather than takers of the system and be aware of what worked and did not work in the past, whatever their grievances against specific aspects of the recent system. In our regional seminars, we struggled hard to elicit from Russian, Indian, and Chinese counterparts alternative ideas about how they might manage world order differently. Their silence suggested that their criticisms of the existing world order are not yet sufficiently urgent that they are thinking out the elements of an alternative approach. Even the CIA, whose latest futures report is generally optimistic about the emerging powers, warns: "While sharing a more state-centric view, the national interests of the emerging powers are diverse enough, and their dependence on globalization compelling enough, that there appears little chance of an alternative bloc forming among them to directly confront the more established Western order." [36]

America is undoubtedly still a dominant power for some time to come; therefore, the key domestic debates in the future will be in America.[37] The United States surprised the declinists and much of the rest of the world by pulling out of the stagflation of the 1970s and indeed "leading the world economy into the 1990s."[38] With modest compromises and bipartisan cooperation between a conservative Republican Congress and centrist Democratic president, the fiscal deficits of the 1980s were eliminated by the end of the 1990s. There is a reasonable chance that the United States might recover once again, overcoming the displacement and shocks of recent financial crises and reducing the structural deficits of domestic entitlement programs. The decisive factor will be American willpower not American power.[39]

In the meantime, rising powers will have an increasingly large role to play. In Asia and the rest of the world, they will construct cumulatively over time a new regional or international order to reinforce or reform the one established by the preeminence of the United States. This new order or international structure will arise ultimately out of the fuzzy and confusing domestic debates currently taking place in the aspiring countries of Asia and elsewhere. Thus, the focus of this volume offers an early window on the types of policies and programs that may emerge in the future and create the rules and agenda of a new post-American world order.

As we argued at the outset of this chapter, international orders both shape and are in turn shaped by domestic debates in aspiring and other powers. The payoff of this project is thus both broad in scope and long term in time. For years, scholars and policy makers have tracked the development and dispersion of military and economic capabilities around the world. In the future, they will also have to track the shifting contours of domestic foreign policy debates. These debates determine both how aggressively a country accumulates military and economic capabilities and what that country decides to do with these capabilities. The chapters that follow represent a first cut at identifying and tracking these internal debates in rising powers. The approach is both novel and exciting. And we have only begun to scratch the surface of this task for the future.

Notes

1 · For an up-to-date discussion of all these material, institutional, and ideological variables influencing American foreign policy, see Steven W. Hook and Christopher M. Jones, *Routledge Handbook on American Foreign Policy* (New York: Routledge, 2012).

2 · "Global Trends 2025: A Transformed World," National Intelligence Council, Central Intelligence Agency, Washington, DC, November 2008.

3 · Paul Kennedy, *The Rise and Fall of Great Powers* (New York: Random House, 1987).

4 · Henry Kissinger, *Diplomacy* (New York: Simon & Schuster, 1994); see also Kenneth N. Waltz, "The Emerging Structure of International Politics," *International Security*, 18 (Fall 1993), 44–79.

5 · Henry R. Nau, *The Myth of America's Decline: Leading the World Economy into the 1990s* (New York: Oxford University Press, 1990). See also Henry R. Nau, "Why 'The Rise and Fall of Great Powers' Was Wrong," *Review of International Studies*, 27 (2001), 579–92.

6 · The CIA is not alone. For similar accounts of America's relative decline, see, among others, Fareed Zakaria, *The Post-American World* (New York: W. W. Norton, 2008); Thomas L. Friedman and Michael Mandelbaum, *That Used to Be US: How America Fell Behind in the World It Invented and How We Can Come Back* (New York: Farrar, Straus & Giroux, 2011); and Charles A. Kupchan, *No One's World: The West, the Rising Rest, and the Coming Global Turn* (New York: Oxford University Press, 2012).

7 · Two exceptions are G. John Ikenberry, *Liberal Leviathan: The Origins, Crises, and Transformation of the American World Order* (Princeton, NJ: Princeton University Press, 2011); and Niall Ferguson, *Civilization: The West and the Rest* (London: Penguin Books, 2011).

8 · Liu Mingfu, *China Dream: The Great Power Thinking and Strategic Positioning of China in the Post-American Age* (Beijing: Zhongguo youyi chuban gongsi, 2010), 158–60.

9 · Debates about world events are often between structural and domestic-driven alternatives. See, among others, Dale C. Copeland, *The Origins of Major War* (Ithaca, NY: Cornell University Press, 2000); Richard Rosecrance and Arthur A. Stein, eds., *The Domestic Bases of Grand Strategy* (Ithaca, NY: Cornell University Press, 1993).

10 · For details, see Henry R. Nau, "The Jigsaw Puzzle and the Chess Board: The Making and Unmaking of Foreign Policy in the Age of Obama," *Commentary* (May 2012), 13–20; and "Obama's Foreign Policy: The Swing Away from Bush: How Far?" *Policy Review*, 160 (April/May 2010), www.hoover.org/publications/policy-review/article/5287.

11 · See, for example, John Pomprey, "In China, Officials in Tug of War to Shape Foreign Policy," *Washington Post*, September 24, 2010, A1.

12 · This is a central point in Walter Russell Mead's groundbreaking study, *Special Providence: American Foreign Policy and How It Changed the World* (New York: Routledge, 2002). He compares the foreign policy schools of thought to magnets that line up the iron filings of historical events and disclose the repetitive clusters of thought and action defining various foreign policy traditions. Mark L. Haas also tracks differing foreign policy views among domestic political groups to show how these views affect foreign policy outcomes. See his innovative studies, *The Ideological Origins of Great Power Conflicts, 1789–1989* (Ithaca, NY: Cornell University Press, 2005); and *The Clash of Ideologies: Middle Eastern Politics and American Security* (New York: Oxford University Press, 2012).

13 · See, for example, the influential article published by William Kristol and Robert Kagan, "Toward a Neo-Reaganite Foreign Policy," *Foreign Affairs* (July/August 1996).

14 · See, for example, Ivo H. Daalder and James M. Lindsay, *America Unbound: The Bush Revolution in Foreign Policy* (New York: Wiley, 2005).

15 · See, among others, Bruce W. Jentleson, *American Foreign Policy: The Dynamics of Choice in the 21st Century* (New York: Norton, 2007); Ole R. Holsti, *Public Opinion and American Foreign Policy* (Ann Arbor: University of Michigan Press, 1996).

16 · One recent example is neoconservative advocates, who were liberal Democrats in terms of domestic ideology but defected from support of Democratic presidents because they held different foreign policy worldviews. A colleague, Matthew A. Baum, and I are exploring this issue. See "Foreign Policy Worldviews and US Standing in the World," manuscript, March 2012.

17 · By emphasizing interpretations and not just capabilities of foreign policy, this study is self-consciously constructivist. Foreign policy is to a considerable extent what groups make of it. See Alexander Wendt. "Anarchy Is What States Make of It: The Social Construction of Power Politics," *International Organization*, 46, 2 (Spring 1992), 391–425.

18 · We are working, in some sense, in the conceptual space between, on the one hand, worldviews, images, and perceptions of individual decision makers, which affect specific policies, and, on the other, epistemic communities of individuals sharing similar worldviews that affect outcomes across time and multiple decision points. See Robert Jervis, *Perceptions and Misperceptions in International Politics* (Princeton, NJ: Princeton University Press, 1976); Ernst B. Haas, *When Knowledge Is Power* (Berkeley: University of California Press, 1990);

and Emanuel Adler and Michael Barnett, eds., *Security Communities* (Cambridge: Cambridge University Press, 2000).

19 · See chapter 5, this volume, by Narushige Michishita and Richard J. Samuels.

20 · See chapter 2 by David Shambaugh and Ren Xiao.

21 · See, among others, Dexter Perkins, *The American Approach to Foreign Policy* (Cambridge, MA: Harvard, 1952); Selig Adler, *The Isolationist Impulse: Its Twentieth Century Reaction* (London: Abelard Schuman, 1957); Felix Gilbert, *To the Farewell Address* (Princeton, NJ: Princeton University Press, 1961). Recent updates of this discussion include Mead, *Special Providence*; Henry R. Nau, *At Home Abroad: Identity and Power in American Foreign Policy* (Ithaca, NY: Cornell University Press, 2002), especially chapter 2; Henry R. Nau, "Grand Strategies: United States," in David Coates, Kathy Smith, and Will Waldorf, eds., *The Oxford Companion to American Politics* (New York: Oxford University Press, 2012), Vol. 1, 450–59; and David C. Hendrickson, *Union, Nation, or Empire; The American Debate over International Relations 1789–1941* (Lawrence: University Press of Kansas, 2009).

22 · Joseph S. Nye Jr., *Soft Power: The Means to Success in World Politics* (New York: Public Affairs, 2004).

23 · Mike Peters and Zhang Chunyan, "Confucius Lives," *Wall Street Journal*, October 20, 2011, A10.

24 · Richard Rosecrance, *The Rise of the Trading State: Commerce and Conquest in the Modern World* (New York: Basic Books, 1986).

25 · Stanley Renshon, *The Bush Doctrine and the Future of American National Security Policy* (New Haven, CT: Yale University Press, 2008).

26 · See chapter 4, this volume, by Farideh Farhi and Saideh Lotfian.

27 · See chapter 3, this volume, by Deepa M. Ollapally and Rajesh Rajagopalan.

28 · For example, the China chapter identifies no school of thought that is labeled Nationalist. Yet the chapter notes that both the Nativist and Realist schools are "staunch nationalists." The Major Powers school in China is, then, a more traditional great power "realist" school. Labels matter less than the substance of the foreign policy views they identify. A shift toward the Realist school in China is therefore a shift toward the nationalist end of the spectrum and has the same effect as a shift toward the Nationalist school in another country such as Russia.

29 · See chapter 3, this volume, by Deepa M. Ollapally and Rajesh Rajagopalan.

30 · See chapter 5, this volume, by Narushige Michishita and Richard J. Samuels.

31 · Offensive Realists use Islam instrumentally. Islamic Idealists pursue Islam as a goal. These are important distinctions highlighted by our comparative framework. See chapter 4 on Iran.

32 · The concluding chapter refers to these exceptionalist schools as "Idealist."

33 · In the United States, for example, Republicans perceive America as weaker or less respected in the world than Democrats when a Democrat occupies the White House; and the reverse is true when a Republican occupies the White House. See American National Election Studies (ANES), www.electionstudies.org/.

34 · See chapter 6, this volume, by Andrew Kuchins and Igor Zevelev.

35 · See Henry R. Nau, "Lessons from the Great Expansion," *Wall Street Journal*, January 26, 2012, A15; and Gary Becker and Kevin Murphy, "Do Not Let the 'Cure' Destroy Capitalism," *Financial Times*, March 19, 2009, www.ft.com/cms/s/0/98f66b98-14be-11de-8cd1-0000779fd2ac.html.

36 · "Global Trends 2025," 82.

37 · On this point, see Robert Kagan, *The World America Made* (New York: Alfred A. Knopf, 2012).

38 · This is the subtitle of my 1990 book, *The Myth of America's Decline*.

39 · See Robert J. Lieber, *Power and Willpower in the American Future: Why the United States Is Not Destined to Decline* (New York: Cambridge University Press, 2012).

2

China

The Conflicted Rising Power

David Shambaugh and Ren Xiao

China is the world's most important rising power. Every day and everywhere, China figures prominently in global attention. Wherever one turns, China is in the news—gobbling up resources, soaking up investment, expanding its overseas profile, throwing its weight around its Asian neighborhood, being the sought-after suitor in global governance diplomacy, sailing its navy into new waters, broadening its global cultural presence, and managing a mega-economy that is the engine of global growth.

But how will China behave on the global stage in the future, as it continues to accrue wealth and power? This is *the* grand strategic question of our era. One recent book was confidently titled *When China Rules the World.*[1] Another one was titled *Eclipse: Living in the Shadow of China's Economic Dominance.*[2] Yet another is apocalyptically titled *Death by China.*[3] All of these perspectives are overstated, as China remains far from being the world's dominant power.[4] Nonetheless, in two decades China has moved from the periphery to the center of international politics.

While the future of China and its impact on the world will depend on a wide variety of domestic and international determinants,[5] one key variable of importance is *how the Chinese perceive their nation's international position and roles.* This is the subject of this chapter.

While Chinese have, over time, possessed an extraordinarily singular sense of purpose and will to acquire wealth and power (*fu-qiang*), we argue that as China regains its former global status it is increasingly a *conflicted* rising power possessing a series of *competing* international identities that try to satisfy a variety of international (and domestic) constituencies.[6] This may consequently help to explain why China's foreign policy exhibits diverse—sometimes conflicting, sometimes complementary—emphases and policies simultaneously. This multidimensional and omnidirectional policy orientation reflects the different levels, regions, and priorities of China's diplomatic engagement.

Differing domestic perceptions play a role in shaping China's foreign policy,[7] while the foreign policy-making milieu itself has become increasingly pluralized with a wide range of voices and actors interacting in an unprecedentedly complex policy-making process.[8] As China continues its rise in world affairs, and its impact becomes more consequential, it will concomitantly become more important for foreign analysts to dig deep inside of and understand China's international relations (IR) discourse, in order to ascertain China's possible policy directions and actions. Understanding these competing perceptions is crucial to anticipating Beijing's increasingly multidimensional behavior on the world stage in the years to come. Each orientation carries different policy implications for other nations.

This chapter examines the perceptions of China's IR experts primarily based in research institutes and universities, as well as some foreign policy officials, rather than the general public. While the Chinese Internet, blogosphere, and newspapers are rife with opinion concerning world affairs (which tends to be hyper-nationalistic), very little systematic evidence is available concerning public perceptions of international affairs. The only recent published public opinion survey the authors are aware of appeared in December 2009, by the China Academy of Social Sciences.[9] Generally speaking this survey finds that the Chinese public's attitude toward the United States is mixed to poor, positive toward Russia, mixed but essentially optimistic about Europe, and mixed to poor about Japan.

OPEN DISCOURSE IN A CONSTRAINED ENVIRONMENT

Despite ongoing official censorship, self-censorship, and state propaganda, few nations (especially rising powers) have had as extensive, animated, and diverse domestic discourse about its potential as a major power as has occurred in China over the past decade. Official, semiofficial, and unofficial circles in China all actively debate the roles, opportunities, dangers, risks, and responsibilities of being a major power. China's academic IR community is, in fact, very diverse—now including proponents of virtually all major schools of IR theory. "In China, we have realists, liberal institutionalists, constructivists, the English School, *dependencia* theorists, interdependence theorists, and others," observed one scholar.[10]

While robust and diverse, China's international identity discourse still takes place in a highly constrained political environment—which impacts the parameters, terminology, content, and conclusions of discourse. Moreover, Chinese academic political culture does not have a tradition of scholars directly criticizing each other, thus it is difficult to ascertain who specifically advocates what. As one leading scholar put it succinctly, "We don't criticize others by name in our articles, but we openly attack other's ideas."[11] Unlike the public-policy culture in the West, Chinese scholars also rarely publicly advocate specific policies for the government and they certainly do not explicitly criticize existing government policy. Such specific policy recommendations are usually offered in internal (*neibu*) channels. Positions are thus often difficult to decipher, and require the venerable tradition of "Pekingology" (the China-watching version of "Kremlinology").

While scholarly debate is increasingly broad-gauged and animated, government officials tend to maintain tight Leninist discipline. Officials only occasionally publish under their names.[12] When speaking with foreigners, they are remarkably scripted—one rarely gets the sense that they are expressing an individual opinion as distinct from official policy (the presence of other officials and notetakers in the room ensures this conformity, as any variance would be reported to more senior authorities). All official speeches are carefully vetted by government agencies or propaganda authorities before public release. Chinese writings rarely discuss or analyze China's contemporary foreign policy decision-making process, although some outline the institutions involved,[13] and some diplomatic histories have illuminated the policy process in past events. Some Chinese officials occasionally discuss the policy process within the Foreign Affairs Leading Small Group, the Central Foreign Affairs Office, Foreign Ministry, and the military. But foreigners do have the opportunity to regularly interact with "think tanks" (government-affiliated research institutes) and universities that contribute to the policy process. That such academic institutions do play a role now, albeit still on the periphery, is one of the major changes over the past thirty years.[14] Nonetheless, the proverbial "black box" of foreign policy decision-making remains quite opaque.

PARSING THE DISCOURSE

What are the parameters of this discourse? To be sure, there is still a segment of official opinion (frequently heard) that *denies* that China *is a major power*—arguing instead that China remains a developing (socialist) country. Another significant segment of opinion *denies* that China is a *global power*, arguing the PRC is a regional power at best. Another tenacious self-identity, still deeply rooted in the Chinese mind-set and frequently articulated in media and specialist publications, is that of historical victimization and humiliation at the hands of other major powers. This traditional *weltanschauung* has fueled modern Chinese nationalism and expresses itself as a nation that was a great power historically and deserves to return to that status. Long-standing aspirations for restored pride and dignity, wealth, and power, animate both and are deeply embedded in China's psychological DNA.

While these traditional identities continue to be articulated in official government speeches and documents, over the past decade the preponderance of domestic discourse recognizes that China *is a major power*—or at least well on the way to becoming one. As a result, the discourse in recent years has shifted to discussing *what kind of major power should China be?*

While such discussions take place primarily in the semiofficial policy and academic communities, they have also extended to society at large. Bookstores are filled with "how to" books on how to become a great power.[15] The best example of the public's involvement was stimulated by the 2006 airing of the twelve-part CCTV documentary series "Rising Powers" (*Daguo Jueqi*). This popular television documentary series was re-aired several times and watched by hundreds of millions of Chinese. It portrayed the conditions that gave rise to other modern great powers in history (Portugal, Spain, Holland, France, Great Britain, Germany, Russia, the USSR, Japan, and the United States), so that China's own rise could be contextualized and informed by these historical experiences.

The CCTV series followed a series of lectures on the subject given by scholars to the Chinese Communist Party Politburo during 2005–2006. The impetus of the Politburo briefings was the same: to learn the lessons of other rising (and falling) powers, so that China could anticipate repetitive problems experienced by other previous powers and effectively manage them. Of particular Chinese concern was how to avoid the historically repetitive "asymmetry trap" between the major established power and the primary rising power, in which the latter challenged the former's hegemonic position in the international system—thus causing tensions, competition, clashes, and wars.

DEBATED ISSUES

In recent years Chinese international relations studies have displayed considerable intellectual diversity.[16] Previous conceptual constraints—ideological and political—have been eased and Chinese scholars are exploring an unprecedented range of new topics (both theoretical and policy-related). To be sure, there still remain "no go zones"—such as critically analyzing China's own foreign policy, human rights, or humanitarian intervention—but Chinese scholars are otherwise embracing a much broader menu of research subjects. Within the domestic discourse, several key topics have been notable.

"Biding time, hiding brightness, not taking the lead, but doing some things." One of the longest running debates is linked to the late Deng Xiaoping, who allegedly argued in 1989 that China should "bide its time, hide its brightness, not seek leadership, but do some things" (*taoguang yanghui, bu dang tou, yousuo zuowei*). This observation was offered at the time in the context of the collapse of communist regimes in Eastern Europe, but subsequently attracted much attention in the West—where it was seen as a blueprint for stealth development of Chinese power. *Taoguang yanghui* is often translated (incorrectly) as "biding time and concealing capabilities" (although the phrase can equally be translated as "maintaining a modest

demeanor"). In this way, Deng has been interpreted as calling for China to maintain a low profile in world affairs.

In the same twenty-eight-character statement Deng also argued that China could still "do some things" (*yousuo zuowei*), which has been interpreted as offering to make selected contributions to global governance. This latter phrase has caused intense debate in recent years (twenty-three years after Deng's original statement!), as scholars and officials wrestle with exactly *how much* China should do on the world stage. Says one scholar, "At the strategic level, everyone agrees we should continue to follow Deng's *taoguang yanghui* concept, but tactically there are many different views. Some think China is too reactive, while others think China should be more proactive."[17] Some Chinese scholars have challenged this dictum of Deng's, arguing that it is out of date and not appropriate to China's newfound international status. They argue that China should "do *more* things" (*gengyou zuowei*), while a few say China should "do nothing" (*wusuo zuowei*) or little in world affairs.

Yan Xuetong of Tsinghua University, a well-known advocate of a more robust Chinese foreign policy, argues that "China should take charge as a great, responsible power instead of maintaining a low profile. Deng Xiaoping's 'keeping a low profile' policy of the early 1990s was right for China at the time, given the international environment and China's former status, but now China's international status has undergone a fundamental change. Continuing such low-profile-type policies will bring more harm than benefit to China."[18] Wang Jisi, another leading scholar and dean of the School of International Studies at Peking University, also seemed to argue in an article that China should be more active and speak out more on the international stage: "Internationally, our country's goal should change from saying what we don't want to what we do want."[19] Other scholars, such as Ye Zicheng of Peking University argued as early as the early 2000s that *taoguang yanghui* was too vague to serve as a master (or grand) strategy for China, it suggested a sinister intention to many abroad, and that China should improve its transparency rather than conceal its capabilities. Others countered by arguing that ambiguity was *precisely* a good strategy for China at this stage of development.

Yet the mainstream consensus holds that *taoguang yanghui, yousuo zuowei* remains an appropriate guiding principle for Chinese diplomacy, given its developmental status and limited power. If anything, there has been a shift over time from *taoguang yanghui* to the *yousuo zuowei* dimension and that Deng's dictum is more useful as a guiding principle (*zhidao yuanze*) than as a "grand strategy" (*da zhanlue*). At the 2010 annual meeting of China's Association of International Relations in Lanzhou, participants heatedly debated the continuing efficacy of the *taoguang yanghui* paradigm and concluded that it was still a good guide for China's diplomacy. As a result of this macro conclusion, participants came to nine other principal policy recommendations: do not confront the United States; do not challenge the international system in general; do not use ideology to guide foreign policy; do not be the chief of the "anti-Western camp"; do not conflict with the majority of countries, even when we are right; learn to make compromises and concessions, and learn the game of reciprocal interests; do not compromise China's core interests concerning unification of the country; provide public goods in needed areas of international affairs; and change China's international image by taking advantage of important global events.[20]

Peaceful Rise. The preoccupation with rising powers (noted above) generated the theory of China's "peaceful rise" (*heping jueqi*)—a theory most forcefully articulated by leading Chinese Communist Party (CCP) theoretician Zheng Bijian.[21] While Zheng and other scholars did much to popularize the concept, it eventually fell into disfavor with the Chinese government.[22] The term "rise" was thought by some to be too threatening a term; others favored "revival" (*fuxing*). Instead an official terminology of "peaceful development" (*heping fazhan*) was authorized for use, which was consistent with Deng Xiaoping's dictum of "peace *and* development." This *tifa* (formulation) is embodied in the 2011 official White Paper on "China's Peaceful Development."[23]

Structure of the International Order. Chinese IR scholars actively discuss and debate the structure and nature of the international structure (*guoji geju*), international system (*guoji tixi*), or international order (*guoji zhixu*).[24] Most Chinese IR scholars are in the Realist tradition and thus (like realists everywhere) pay much attention to the structure of the international system. They are somewhat like geometrists—constantly looking for pivots, nodes, triangles, etc. More than anything, they are wed to the concept of polarity (*ji*) in international relations. Both official policy and

Chinese scholars have long posited that the international order is inexorably moving toward multipolarity (*duojihua*) over time.[25] But they debate whether all regional powers in the world constitute a "pole" in the international system—for example, Japan, India, Iran, Brazil, and possibly Nigeria and South Africa—or just the United States, Russia, China? What about collectivities of states like, ASEAN, the EU, SCO, and BRICs—should they also be considered as poles?

Closely related in this discourse has been the discussion concerning the dominance of the United States and its post-Cold War unipolarity. Why has American "hegemony" and unipolarity not collapsed, they ask? If the United States is in decline, is it absolute or relative? What is the pace of America's decline? Can it be reversed? Can it be hastened? How severely wounded is the United States from the post-2008 global financial crisis? These questions animate such discussions. It should be noted that Chinese IR analysts have several times (e.g., late-1970s, mid-1980s, 2001–2005) pronounced and predicted America's decline in world affairs—only to be proven wrong by America's resilience and staying power. "We consistently underestimated the United States," admitted one leading scholar.[26] Another scholar reflected, "There is a strange euphoria about the US decline and China's rise. Some (Chinese) analysts have been smoking opium and believe Chinese power is much greater than it is."[27] Some key analysts, such as Yang Jiemian, president of the Shanghai Institute of International Studies, argue, "While in relative decline, in 20–30 years the United States will *still* be the world's only superpower."[28]

While differing views exist, a consensus emerged among most analysts in the late 1990s that still prevails: the global structure is *simultaneously unipolar and multipolar (yichao, duoqiang)*. Yet another group argued just the opposite during the first year of the Obama administration—that the potential for United States–China global cooperation (G-2) meant that a *liangchao duoqiang* (two superpowers, many powers) world order could emerge—although this minority viewpoint soon disappeared. A smaller segment of opinion argued that the international system is in *transition* from unipolarity to multipolarity.[29] The transition from the Bush to the Obama administrations seemed to convince many Chinese analysts that indeed the US decline had finally begun to emerge and the pace of multipolarization is picking up.[30] The global financial crisis since 2008 has convinced many Chinese that America's decline has truly and finally come. The simultaneous rise of the BRICS (Brazil, Russia, India, China, South Africa) and emergence of the G-20 further fueled this perception,[31] with some analysts arguing that these "intermediate forces" were becoming the dominant actors in world politics.[32]

Global Governance, Multilateralism, and the "Responsible Power" Theory. One of the most animated and active discourses in China today concerns the issue of China's contributions to international global governance, its role in intergovernmental organizations, multilateralism, and what it means to be a "responsible power" (*fuzeren de daguo*). The discussion was stimulated by US Deputy Secretary of State Robert Zoellick's 2005 call on China to become a "responsible stakeholder" (*fuzeren de liyi xiangguanzhe*) in the international system. Chinese analysts ask: what are the roles of intergovernmental and regional institutions in the new world order? How should China think about the concept of global governance, and how much should China contribute? They also debate the concept of "global responsibility,"[33] the role of major powers' responsibilities,[34] and specifically China's responsibilities.[35]

A broad range of opinion on these questions has emerged.[36] A substantial segment is very leery of global governance and believes that the whole concept is a Western/United States "trap" that tries to undermine China's sovereignty, lure it into a variety of foreign entanglements where China does not belong, and retard China's growth. As one senior official put it, "First you [the United States] tried to subvert our political system in the 1980s, then you tried to contain us in the 1990s, now you are trying to bleed us through international entanglements in the 2000s!"[37] Many also argue that China is not ready and does not possess the capabilities to become fully engaged in global governance. As one scholar observed: "China cannot even manage itself—how can it manage the world?"[38] Another group believes that China *should* do more in contributing to global governance, commensurate with its newfound position and power. Yet others believe China should do more, but do so selectively. Still others argue that China should do more in tandem with the United States (G-2). So, diversity of opinion prevails.

Closely connected to global governance is multilateralism, over which a related but somewhat separate discussion has emerged.[39] Chinese scholars use the term "multilateralism" (*duobianzhuyi*) but have a very different concept of it than is commonly used in the West. Observed one scholar: "For Chinese, multilateralism is a *tool* and a *tactic*, not an intergovernmental mechanism or institutional arrangement. China also worries that multilateralism is a tool for others to contain China. Since the 1990s, China has used multilateralism to solve bilateral issues—to this end, multilateral meetings are a useful platform (*wutai*) to negotiate bilaterally. But we are still uncomfortable with multilateralism, and prefer bilateralism and multipolarity."[40]

Analysts also debate the relationship between multipolarism and multilateralism—how does the former phenomenon among individual sovereign nation-states relate to the latter phenomenon of collectivities of sovereign states? There is evidence of two competing camps of theorists in China on this question (the former rooted in realism and the latter influenced by European liberal institutionalism and Asian constructivism) with the former recently gaining the upper hand in debates.

Concerning international institutions, Chinese scholars have debated the role of the United Nations and other global institutions, as well as a wide variety of regional blocs and organizations. Interestingly, the Chinese government and scholars have become some of the world's strongest advocates of the United Nations. Regionally, China has also pushed forward what it describes as a "new type" of regional organization, based on the model of the Shanghai Cooperation Organization (SCO): based on "comprehensive, cooperative security" rather than alliances, respect for sovereignty and territorial integrity, and confidence-building measures.

Harmonious World. Another key concept in recent years is that of the "harmonious world (*hexie shijie*), although a discourse per se has not emerged.[41] This is because the concept is so closely identified with President Hu Jintao that no one would dare to criticize it. As one scholar put it: "Of course there are those who don't like the idea (of harmonious world), but nobody can openly criticize it. So the way that some oppose the concept is *not* to talk about it!"[42] Nonetheless, the concept permeates articles on Chinese foreign policy in academic journals in recent years.

According to Chinese president Hu Jintao, a "harmonious world" should have four principal attributes: (1) effective multilateralism with a strong role for the United Nations; (2) development of a collective security mechanism; (3) prosperity for all through mutually beneficial cooperation;

(4) tolerance and enhancement of dialogue among diverse civilizations.[43] Like "Peaceful Rise" theory, "Harmonious World" theory posits that China's rise will not be a threat or disrupt the existing global order. The Chinese government has invested enormous resources and effort in trying to popularize this theory in recent years—but with little effect abroad.[44]

Soft Power. One of the newest and most active areas of discussion in China's international relations community concerns the concept of "soft power" (*ruan shili*) in public diplomacy. The China National Knowledge Index (CNKI) contains nearly 600 articles published on the subject during 2008. (See Figure 2.1.)

Chinese have seemingly become obsessed with soft power: What is it? Does China have it? If not, why not? How can China get it? And what should China do with it? Chinese scholars and officials working in the media and propaganda system work overtime on the subject. None other than Chinese president Hu Jintao drew attention to the importance of building China's global cultural soft power in his official report to the 17th Congress of the Chinese Communist Party in 2007. Since then, China has become increasingly sensitive to its image abroad and has been on what some describe as a "charm offensive" in its public diplo-

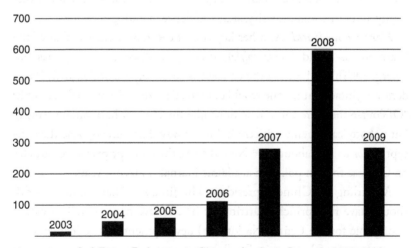

Figure 2.1: Soft Power References in Chinese Academic Journals, 2003–2009

macy. The Foreign Ministry has recently established an Office of Public Diplomacy and the State Council Information Office is accelerating its efforts in order to try and improve China's external image by reportedly pumping $8.7 billion into an external media and cultural blitz during 2009–2010.[45]

Hegemony. Finally, the concept of "hegemony" remains central to the major power discourse in China, although its usage has dropped off in recent years and it is not debated per se. But anti-hegemony (*fan ba*) remains the *sine qua non* of the Chinese worldview and foreign policy. While the term is not used as frequently as before in Chinese discourses, it remains an intellectual pillar of China's thinking about other powers—particularly the United States—as well as itself. Beijing steadfastly continues to remind the world that it will "never seek hegemony" once it emerges as a major international power. While eschewing hegemony, some scholars do discuss the possibility of taking a leadership role in world affairs. Observed one scholar: "China doesn't have the desire or history to be a hegemon. But we do want to be a leader!"[46]

Thus, the discourse inside China about what it means to be a major power has been both intensive and extensive, and has revolved around these key issues in recent years. The following section elucidates further the finer distinctions within the Chinese discourse and places these issues in the context of contending schools of thought.

THE SPECTRUM OF DISCOURSE ON CHINA'S INTERNATIONAL IDENTITY

While these concepts all compete within the marketplace of ideas in China's domestic discourse, different "schools" or "tendencies" of thought concerning China's international identity are evident.[47] While intellectually distinct, it would be incorrect to see these schools as mutually exclusive. While sometimes contradictory, they are also sometimes complementary. Our research reveals that individual IR scholars and officials in China are often *eclectic* thinkers—while strongly rooted in one school of thought, they often voice views associated with other schools of thought. Cognitive complexity prevails and schools of thought cross-cut institutions. While it would be nice to be able to label institutions as "Realist," "Globalist," etc. it is simply not so simple. The one exception to this generalization are writers associated with the Chinese military (People's Liberation Army), which pervasively exhibit a "hawkish" and "hard realist" perspective on many issues.

We argue that, as a consequence of competing international identities, China's foreign policy evinces several elements simultaneously. This is expressed in China's official policy of *daguo shi guanjian, zhoubian shi shouyao, fazhanzhong guojia shi jichu, duobian shi zhongyao wutai* (major powers are the key, surrounding areas are the first priority, developing countries are the foundation, and multilateral forums are the important stage). Thus, readers should be aware that while these are clearly different intellectual orientations—with concomitant policy prescriptions—they are not necessarily mutually exclusive.

Understanding the content and spectrum of discourse within the country is central to understanding what Chinese themselves are wrestling with as their nation has been thrust quickly into the international arena. While no doubt welcomed, China seems unprepared for its new international status—which has come much more quickly than anticipated. This rapid rise has challenged China's "traditional identities" of being a developing country, a socialist country, an Asian country, a country formerly subject to imperialism, and an insular country. These are all "comfortable" identities that the People's Republic of China has possessed and carefully cultivated for six decades through unrelenting education and propaganda. Taken together, they constitute the "DNA" of China's core national and international personality. It is thus, quite jarring, all of a sudden, to be confronted with a whole new set of questions about China's international status and roles.

In reading the discourse in China's IR community and talking with officials, seven different and distinct identities are evident. These are represented in Figure 2.2.

It is important for readers to recognize that this is a *spectrum* of opinion concerning China's alternative international roles, that is, *where the emphasis of Chinese foreign policy should lie*. It moves from the left end (which advocates an isolated perspective) to the right (advocating full engagement in liberal global governance). In between are a series of five separate orientations/emphases—moving from those advocating a "China First" Realist

Figure 2.2: Spectrum of China's International Identities

perspective, through three sets of "regional" advocates, to a group of "selective multilateralists." Again, we must emphasize that these orientations are not to be seen as mutually exclusive—they merely reflect those in the domestic discourse who advocate one or another *emphasis* or *priority* for Chinese foreign policy.

Also, this spectrum is useful when viewed in the context of other chapters/countries considered in this volume. Professor Nau's introductory chapter (as well as the India chapter in particular) identifies a tripartite grouping of three schools: Nationalist, Realist, and Globalist. The spectrum of views in China is *similar* but slightly different. Nau's "Nationalists" can be seen in the Nativist and Realist camps, while the three middle groups (Major Powers, Asia First, and Global South) can be considered as regionalists insofar as each of their proponents are primarily area experts, while the Selective Multilateralists are variations of Nau's "Globalist" category.

The Nativists

At one end of the spectrum are the "Nativists." This is a collectivity of extremely conservative, populist, often Marxist, Hyper-Nationalists. They distrust the outside world, seek national autonomy, and view international multilateral involvement as "traps" (laid by the West) to embroil China in costly overseas commitments. They are vociferous critics of the West. Some in this cohort bear a strong traditional Marxist orientation. This group is the twin of the "new left" (*xin zuopai*) in domestic policy debates, as they believe the "reform and opening" policy of the past thirty years has cost China its socialist integrity, corroded its culture with negative foreign influences, and has compromised China's sovereignty and autonomy in world affairs.

Earlier examples of this thinking emerged during the 1990s with the "China Can Say No" (*Zhongguo Keyi Shuo Bu*) discourse and the "10,000 word essays" (*wan yan shu*) penned by Marxist ideological guru Deng Liqun and his intellectual coterie. More recent manifestations have been the popular books *China Is Unhappy, Who in China Is Unhappy?* and *Why Is China Unhappy?*[48] The latter group of authors includes some who had contributed to *China Can Say No*.

The Nativists are a loose coalition spread across a number of institutions, and indeed a number of its leading advocates operate independently. To the extent that they have an institutional home, it is in research institutes under the Central Committee of the Communist Party that are involved in Communist Party history and ideology. A number of institutes in the Chinese Academy of Social Sciences (CASS) have also been a bastion of such Nativist–Marxist thought.

Since 1989 this group argued that the "reform and opening" policy has inevitably led to China's restoration of capitalism and destruction of socialism. For many in this school "peaceful evolution" (*heping yanbian*)—a policy whereby the West attempts to evolve China peacefully so as to undermine Chinese Communist Party rule—has become the main threat to China and they thus argue the main policy priority should be to counter peaceful evolution through ultra-vigilant domestic security policies, to minimize engagement with the United States (the main purveyor of peaceful evolution), and to close China's doors. For this group, every reform and opening measure was evaluated as to whether it was intrinsically of a socialist or capitalist nature, and whether it threatened the rule of the Chinese Communist Party–state. They argue that "globalization" is in fact a process of the globalization of capital, similar to Lenin's description of imperialism.[49]

The post-2008 global financial crisis further emboldened this line of thinking, as many argued that advanced "state monopoly capitalism" (*guojia longduan zibenzhuyi*) had finally brought the world economy to the brink of disaster, just as Lenin had predicted. Fang Ning, director of the CASS Institute of Political Science, argued that this phenomenon dated to the 2003 Iraq War—which marked the arrival of an era of "new imperialism."

For Fang and others, Deng Xiaoping's era of "peace and development" was over. Earlier in 1999, the outbreak of the Kosovo War already prompted Fang and others to conclude that the new imperialism had three major policies: economic takeover, political patronage, and military control.[50] Indeed, the foreign policy of the George W. Bush administration gave rise to a revival of Marxist—to be more accurate neo-Leninist—studies of international relations. A number of articles and books on "new imperialism" appeared.[51] While they regurgitated much earlier analysis from the 1980s, the new scholarship went much further in dissecting both the new developments in "state-monopoly capitalism" and the international order. With respect to the former, these analyses had premonitions concerning the sources of the global financial crisis of 2008–2010. With respect to the latter, they also challenged the long-prevailing Chinese prediction concerning the evolution to a multipolar world—arguing that (American) unipolarity was showing surprising tenaciousness.[52] These authors also accused China's US policy of being far too "soft" and that a Sino–United States "strategic partnership" is an illusion.

Thus, the Nativist School of thought contains extremely conservative, predominantly Marxist, hyper-nationalistic, and anti-American elements. These views were reinforced by similar voices in Chinese cyberspace. Throughout the Nativist discourse is a strong sense of aggrievement and entitlement. That is, Nativists regularly harp on the nationalist theme of the "century of shame and humiliation" and argue that China is entitled to global respect (particularly by those powers that previously humiliated China).

The Realists

The second cohort is the "Realists." Like the Nativists, they are staunch nationalists—but of a more pragmatic and less xenophobic variety. They may also be considered dogmatic "China Firsters," as they care little about the interests of other countries or constituencies in world affairs—unlike the subsequent schools that we consider. Realism has deep roots in China's intellectual worldview. Even during the more ideological periods of the People's Republic, Realist orientations of strengthening China were prevalent.

Chinese Realists take the nation-state as their core unit of analysis. They uphold the principle of state sovereignty above all else, and reject arguments that transnational issues penetrate across borders. Like realists elsewhere, they tend to see the international environment as anarchic, predatory, and dangerous. In such an environment, Realists argue for placing a premium on building up a strong state and nation that can navigate its way in the world, deter aggression, and resist outside pressures. As one Realist put it: "the world is a place where there are many wolves and tigers. Only when you are armed well and possess power, can you possibly have a civilization. After all, wolves and sheep cannot dance together."[53]

While they share some core assumptions in common, the Realists may be subdivided into "offensive" and "defensive" Realists, as well as "hard" and "soft" Realists. Each group believes that the nation-state has to build its strength, but what distinguishes them are the *purposes* to which such power is put. Hard Power Realists argue for the strengthening of comprehensive national power (*zonghe guoli*), but particularly the military and economic dimensions—while the Soft Power Realists emphasize diplomacy and cultural (soft) power. The Offensive Realists argue that China should *use* its newly built military strength, economic strength, and diplomatic influence to essentially coerce others toward ends China desires. They believe that power is worth little if it is not used. They argue, for example, that China should leverage its holding of US Treasury bonds to get Washington to stop selling arms to Taiwan, or penalize large US corporations for selling weapons to Taiwan. They argue that China should establish a much broader military (particularly naval) presence in the western Pacific in order to force the United States from operating close to China's coastline. Defensive Realists agree that China should possess strong military might, but instead argue that China should "keep its powder dry" and use it essentially to deter aggression and Taiwan independence.

Realists are also pessimists about China's external environment and particularly the United States. That is, they find the world a dangerous place and are particularly distrustful of the United States. Like many Realists in the United States, they see an intrinsic competitive—even adversarial—dynamic at work in US–China relations; as such, they counsel that China should prepare for long-term competition, and even conflict, with the United States.

Discussions with Realists also reveal a certain frustration. Many *want* China to *use* its newfound power, but feel constrained in doing so by the official policy of nonaggression and noninterference. One Realist reflected: "As China's posture abroad grows, our investments and interests abroad are growing. We need to think about how to protect our nationals, investments, and interests. One way is to behave as an imperialist country with gunboat policies—but given our past history this is not feasible."[54] Such inclinations to be more assertive have been reflected in China's relations with Asian nations and the United States in 2009–2010.

There is also a strong sense of triumphalism among the Realists in the wake of the post-2008 global financial crisis. They feel the Chinese development model of mixed state capitalism and socialism has been vindicated, while the Western laissez faire system has been vanquished. This has contributed to an upsurge in writings about the so-called China Model. (Figure 2.3.)

Yan Xuetong of Tsinghua University and Zhang Ruizhuang of Nankai University are widely recognized as China's archetypal Realists. Yan holds a number of hawkish views. For him, "peaceful rise" is a dangerous theory because it gives potential adversaries (including Taiwan) a message that China will not act forcefully to protect its

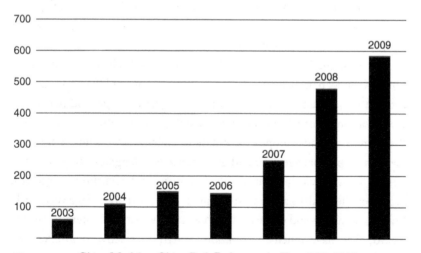

Figure 2.3: China Model or China Path References by Year 2003–2009

national sovereignty and interests. In the past Yan argued that China should resort to the use of force when necessary and without hesitation to counteract Taiwan's move toward legal independence and he predicted that such conflict was inevitable (although he later backed off from, and apologized for, this prediction).[55] Yan's 1997 book *China's Rise* was a manifesto for building *and using* China's comprehensive and hard power.[56] Today, Yan argues for a much more robust Chinese foreign policy and an abandonment of Deng Xiaoping's low-profile strategy. He also advocates building up China's military strength and establishing alliances in Asia to counter the United States.[57]

Zhang Ruizhuang similarly sees the official "peaceful development" view, taken together with the "multipolar world" and "US–China strategic partnership" theses, as badly flawed ideas that misjudge the international situation and base China's foreign policy on false premises. Zhang particularly argues for a much more assertive policy toward the United States. In 2010 he argued, "The United States has been damaging China's interests for a long time. China should be *dis*satisfied, not satisfied, with the state of US–China relations. It is not a relationship in good condition. If China does not oppose the United States, the US will abuse China's interests and China will become America's puppet."[58] Zhang also thinks multipolarism is an overly optimistic view of the post-Cold War order, underestimating the daunting challenges China faces, and loosens China's vigilance toward American hegemony. Yan Xuetong also recognizes the role of soft power in China's foreign policy,[59] and both Yan and Zhang argue for increased Chinese activism on global issues.

Above all, the Realist School takes a narrow and self-interested definition of China's national interests. They are suspicious of US or EU calls for cooperation as ruses for entrapment. They reject concepts and policies of globalization, transnational challenges, and global governance. They argue that American and European attempts to enlist greater Chinese involvement in global management and governance is a dangerous trap aimed at tying China down, burning up its resources, and retarding its growth. However, the Realists are not isolationists—they just argue for a very hardheaded definition and defense of China's narrow national interests. In this regard, they have much in common with the "selective multilateralist" school.

The Major Powers School

Another group, which we identify as the "Major Powers School," argues that instead of closing China's door (Nativists) or concentrating on national strengthening (Realists), China should concentrate its diplomacy on managing its relations with the world's major powers and blocs—the United States, Russia, and European Union—while paying relatively less attention to the developing world or multilateralism. Their watchword is *daguo shi shouyao* (major powers are of primary importance). Not surprisingly, scholars in this school are almost entirely regional specialists on the United States, Russia, and EU. As Figure 2.4 reveals, however, the vast majority of Chinese IR writings remain concerned with the United States.

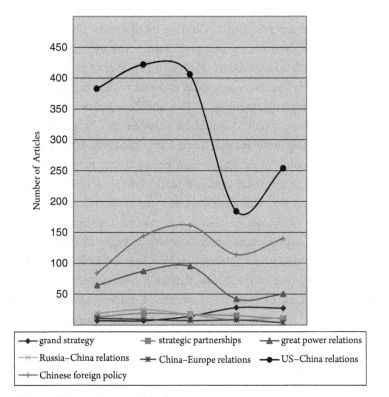

Figure 2.4

Source: China National Knowledge Index (CNKI) database.

As a group of analysts, the Major Powers School stresses the crucial importance of maintaining sound relations with other great powers, arguing that if China's ties with the major powers are not strong, then it will be detrimental to a range of Chinese interests and will complicate China's other regional relationships. One obvious reason for the major power orientation is China's modernization drive, that is, the Western powers are the major source of advanced technology as well as of capital and investment. Russia is a separate case, but is seen as a significant supplier of energy resources and military equipment.

Analysts in this school predominantly see the Sino–US relationship as the "key of the keys" (*zhongzhong zhi zhong*) for China, arguing that maintaining harmonious ties with Washington should be the Number 1 priority in Chinese diplomacy. This group was dominant during Jiang Zemin's tenure as president, and has remained important under Hu Jintao. Over the past decade, however, as Chinese power rises and frictions with Washington occur more frequently, Chinese intellectuals and the informed public increasingly advocate a tougher posture toward the United States. Like Zhang Ruizhuang (above), Professor Pan Wei of Peking University sees China's US diplomacy as a dead end and wishful thinking to seek a "Sino–US strategic partnership."[60] Pan and like-minded thinkers argue that China's foreign policy should be adjusted and be geared toward a closer relationship with Russia. Some other academic Russia specialists, Marxists, and some in official foreign policy circles further believe that Beijing and Moscow share intrinsic worldviews concerning sovereignty, the use of force, the United States, etc. As such, they argue that it is Moscow—not Washington—that is China's real "strategic partner." This cohort should not be exaggerated, however, as many in China recognize that Russia is a *declining power* that actually has very little to offer China.

A third subgroup of the Major Powers School advocated, until a few years ago, that China should emphasize the European Union in its diplomacy, as the EU was a key pillar in the emerging multipolar world and had much to offer China in terms of trade, investment, and technology transfer. Not surprisingly, many of these voices were Europeanists (based primarily in the CASS Institute of European Studies and China Institutes of Contemporary International Relations). But their voices began to dissipate in 2006–2007 as various frictions emerged in Sino–European relations, and they have almost completely disappeared since 2008 given the disorganization in Brussels, the impotence of EU foreign and security policy and the Eurozone crisis. Chinese analysts have become very disillusioned and dismissive of the EU, after having hoped for a long time that the EU would emerge as a "new emerging pole" (*xinxing ji*) in world affairs.

Despite the critics, a majority of senior leaders and policy makers still endorse a major power orientation, particularly focused on the United States. Their logic is that it would just be too costly for China to have strained ties with any of the three major powers noted earlier.

Asia First

Another group in the middle of the spectrum argues for concentrating China's diplomacy on its immediate periphery and Asian neighborhood. We call them the "Asia Firsters." They argue that, if China's neighborhood is not stable, it will be a major impediment to development and national security. Thus, they argue priority should be placed on building ties and a stable environment all around China's periphery. As one scholar put it, "Every power must protect its own backyard."[61]

In this context, Chinese scholars discuss a variety of regional trends, including the evolving regional institutional architecture, the role of the United States, the role of India, the North Korean issue, the role of ASEAN, nontraditional security issues, Sino–Japanese relations, Shanghai Cooperation Organization, and other regional issues. These discussions are more of a discourse among area specialists without significant cleavages and lines of debates.

The "Asia First" contingent first found expression in China's foreign policy in the late-1990s. During that time, following the 1997 Asian Financial Crisis and the "Peace and Development Debate" of the same year, China began to emphasize much more of its neighborhood diplomacy (*zhoubian waijiao*).[62] The result of this debate was that China decided to become much more proactive on its periphery to shape a peaceful environment. China embarked on a sustained period of proactive and cooperative regional diplomacy under the rubric of "establish good neighborliness, make neighbors prosperous, and make them feel secure" (*mulin, fulin, anlin*). This policy produced much fruit, as China managed dramatically to improve and stabilize relations all around its periphery. Formerly adversarial relationships (Vietnam, India) were turned into normalized, productive, and cooperative ones. While certain tensions remained in Beijing's ties with Japan during the Koizumi era, subsequently, bilateral ties stabilized. China's ties with ASEAN were particularly strengthened through concerted diplomacy, confidence-building measures such as the Declaration of Conduct on the South China Sea, China's acceding to the Treaty of Amity and Cooperation (TAC), and the inauguration of the China-ASEAN Free Trade Area (CAFTA).

One important subgroup of this cohort are those who push for "multilateral regionalism" and East Asian community building, as distinct from a more state-based strategy. These individuals are "constructivists with Chinese characteristics," drawing their intellectual inspiration from IR constructivism abroad. They emphasize normative behavior and push for institutionalizing cooperative and collective behavior. Professor Qin Yaqing of China Foreign Affairs University and Zhang Yunling of the Chinese Academy of Social Sciences have been at the forefront of this movement, and have each contributed significantly to building regional institutionalism in Asia and increasing China's involvement in such institutions.

Those that emphasize China's ties within Asia do not do so to the exclusion of relations with other regions or nations, but they do argue for prioritizing Asia—giving Asia a relatively greater emphasis over relations with the United States, Russia, Europe, or the developing world.[63]

The Global South

The next cohort is the "Global South" School, which argues that China's main international identity and responsibility lie with the developing world. They advocate for at least a more balanced foreign policy that takes account of China's longtime partners and client states in developing countries, and that Beijing should advocate their interests. This reasoning finds expression, for example, in China's strong support for the UN Millennium Development Goals, "no strings attached" aid programs and debt relief, and placing the climate change burden on developed countries. Not surprisingly, this school is a staunch advocate of the BRICS group, and they also strongly support the G-20—both as an effort to build global multipolarity and increase South–South solidarity—and to redefine and redistribute power from North to South in global institutions.

The Global South School's identity has much to do with China's long-standing self-identification as a developing country (*fazhanzhong guojia*), and the fraternal feeling China shares with other nations subjected to colonialism and imperialism. It dates back to the "Bandung era" of the mid-1950s.

There has always been a tension within China's international relations community between those whose work focuses on the Northern developed countries and those who work on the Southern developing countries. Within the latter group, since the 1990s Chinese analysts have increasingly taken note of the differentiation and fragmentation occurring in the developing world.

For example, according to Yu Xintian, the former president of the Shanghai Institute of International Studies, developing countries have broken into three economic categories. The first is newly industrializing economies, such as South Korea, Taiwan, Brazil, Mexico, Turkey, and South Africa; the second group is average developing countries, with per capita GDP varying from $800 to $7,000; and the third group is the least developed countries. Since they are considerably differentiated, Yu and others argue that the developing countries should not be seen as a whole, and more concrete policies need to be formulated to replace a more general approach.[64] However, the strategic goal of development that China has set to become a medium-level developed country by mid-twenty-first century means China's eventual departure from developing country status. Nevertheless, proponents of this school of thought argue that China should continue to see itself as a developing country indefinitely into the future, and China is still obliged to work with the developing countries for common development even when China has already risen to global power status.[65] From this perspective, continuing the self-identity as a developing country is required by the need for indispensable diplomatic support from the developing world on issues to fend off the West on issues like Tibet, human rights, Taiwan, and climate change.

Some in this school have noted that China is beginning to experience something of a backlash in Africa and Latin America over some of its economic and aid policies, and particularly rising criticism of its natural resource–and energy-driven foreign policy. While cooperation between China and those countries has been growing on the whole, new frictions are proliferating.

Not surprisingly, many analysts in this school advocate a fundamental restructuring of the global system in order to redistribute financial resources, institutional influence, and power from North to South.[66] They perceive the *existing* international institutional order to be unjust and weighted in favor of developed countries. In this regard, China is a *revisionist* and dissatisfied, not a status quo and satisfied, power.

Selective Multilateralism

Moving along the spectrum to the right, another group are the "selective multilateralists"—who believe that China should expand its global involvements gradually, but only on issues where China's national (security) interests are directly involved. There are several variations and splinter factions of this group: one argues China should only engage in UN-mandated activities, another argues that China should only become involved on its periphery and far away, while another believes it should not so constrain itself from getting involved in multinational (as distinct from multilateral) actions together with other major powers.

The Selective Multilateralists generally eschew increasing China's global involvements, but realize that China must be *seen* to be contributing to global governance. For them, contributing to global governance is a *tactic* not a *philosophy*. They are *not* Liberal Institutionalists, but more an internationalist version of Realists. The Selective Multilateralists are wary of foreign entanglements but they recognize that China must "do some things" (as Deng Xiaoping said) in the international arena so as not be perceived as self-interested "free riders" on the international community. They have advocated increasing China's participation in UN peacekeeping operations (today China has 2155 peacekeeping personnel deployed in eleven of the UN's current nineteen global operations), contributing to disaster relief (the 2004 Southeast Asian tsunami, the 2005 Pakistani earthquake, the 2007 Philippines typhoon, 2009 Haiti earthquake, 2010 Chile earthquake,

2011 Japanese earthquake and tsunami), fighting international piracy in the Gulf of Aden, being diplomatically involved in the North Korean and Iranian nuclear issues—but they eschew deeper involvement in sensitive and risky areas like Iraq and Afghanistan. And they essentially reject the entire transnational nontraditional security agenda. There remains a strong reluctance to engage in international security operations for "humanitarian" reasons.

Actually, the selective multilateralists are not in favor of multilateralism per se (in the sense of international institutions); they are perhaps more appropriately described as "selective multi*nationalists*." They are more comfortable working within small ad hoc groups of nations than institutions per se, reflecting China's general discomfort with global regimes. The Six Party Talks on North Korea and the Sextet on Iran are prime examples.

The Globalists

At the far end of the spectrum are those "Globalists" who believe that China must shoulder an ever-greater responsibility for addressing a wide range of global governance issues commensurate with China's size, power, and influence. They are the equivalent of Liberal Institutionalists in the West. They are also more philosophically disposed toward humanitarianism, embrace globalization analytically, and believe that transnational challenges require transnational partnerships. They are more supportive and trusting of multilateral institutions than the Selective Multilateralists, and they believe China should become much more fully engaged in global governance across the globe. This group is a very eclectic grouping comprised of individuals adhering both to "Constructivism" as well the "English School," but indeed others from other schools. This group is ideational and normative in its orientation. They are interested in soft not hard power, and put their faith in diplomacy and pan-regional partnerships.

The Globalists are of the view that it is incumbent upon China, given its global rise, to contribute much more to global governance and to act as a responsible power (*fuzeren de daguo*) in the international arena. The Globalists are "interdependence institutionalists" in essence, and their analytical starting point is globalization. They believe in multilateral institutionalism. For scholar Su Changhe of Shanghai Foreign Studies University, China's multilateral institutional diplomacy has joined its major power diplomacy and the two have become the most important components of China's foreign affairs.[67] Even leading officials sometimes evince a strong commitment to global governance. The official view, from Foreign Minister Yang Jiechi, is that:

> A more developed China will undertake more international responsibilities and will never pursue interests at the expense of others. We know full well that in this interdependent world, China's future is closely linked to that of the world. Our own interests and those of others are best served when we work together to expand common interests, share responsibilities, and seek win-win outcomes. This is why while focusing on its own development, China is undertaking more and more international responsibilities commensurate with its strength and status.[68]

As with their liberal institutionalist counterparts in the West, China's Globalists recognize that in the era of globalization sovereignty has its limits as various "nontraditional" challenges regularly cross sovereign borders and must be dealt with in a multilateral manner. Much of their analytical focus therefore is on nontraditional security—for example, human security, economic security, counterterrorism, public health, organized crime, smuggling, cyber hacking, piracy. The Globalists are strong advocates of the United Nations and China's activism in the Security Council. They are also strong proponents of China's participation in regional diplomatic groupings all over the world (especially in East Asia but also in Central Asia, Middle East, Africa, and Latin America) where China has been centrally involved in forming new dialogue groupings as well as becoming observers or full members of existing ones.

Articles in China's IR journals evince a growing interest in globalist and transnational issues and concepts associated with Liberal international relations discourse—globalization, global governance, international cooperation, interdependence, multilateralism, and international organizations. This is reflected in Figure 2.5. While there has been a surge of interest in more liberal IR topics, it continues to contend with traditional realist topics and a growing interest in social constructivism.[69] Interestingly, however, rising interest in these liberal concepts does *not* translate into Chinese government support for the liberal postwar order (although China has been a beneficiary of it). There continues to be deep-seated suspicion of the liberal order and particularly American calls for China to be a "responsible power."[70]

The Globalists are not the only ones who support China's growing global involvement. There seems to be a general consensus across the spectrum from the Realists to the Globalists over the necessity for China *to be involved* in international institutions—although there is disagreement among these groups over *how* and *where* China should participate. Only the Nativists reject international cooperation altogether. Some scholars believe that China should still essentially benefit from and "free ride" on international institutions (keeping a low profile as Deng Xiaoping suggested). This cohort asks: "what can international institutions do for China?" The "Globalists" instead ask: "what can China contribute to international institutions (and the world)?" In between, there are those who believe that international institutions and international commitments require selective involvement. One leading IR scholar divided views on China's involvement in global governance into three camps:[71]

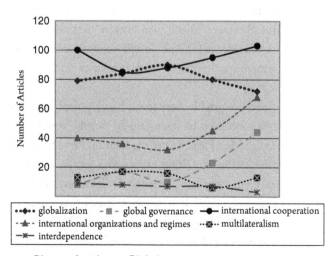

Figure 2.5 Chinese Articles on Globalism

- Those who oppose it and see it as a Western trap. They also argue that China is still a poor developing country and should build its national strength before becoming involved in international commitments.
- Those who argue that China is part of international society and should contribute proportionately.
- Those that argue that China should "do some things" (i.e., selective multilateralism).

Another scholar notes that, "Global governance is a Western concept. The West emphasizes 'governance,' while China emphasizes the 'global' dimension. We care more about equality of participation than about governance."[72] This is what China means by "international democracy." Not only do many see global governance as a trap for China, they also question the concept of "responsible power." "Responsible to whom? To whose standards? The United States? Never!" shouted one scholar.[73]

Constructivism has also contributed to the Globalist school. For example, both Zhang Yunling (CASS) and Qin Yaqing (CFAU) have actively been involved in institution-building for closer regional cooperation in East Asia. Su Changhe of Shangai Foreign Studies University and others concentrate their research on the inner workings of multilateral international institutions. Wang Yizhou of Peking University characterizes his own approach as "half globalist," which has a concern with the common destiny of the humankind (basing it even on human value and rights), and "half realist."[74] But Professor Wang also admits that the Globalists are swimming against the tide, as China's developmental needs remain pressing and there remains a hesitancy and insularity in Chinese global diplomacy.[75]

Globalists also show a predilection toward soft power. They argue that China has much to contribute to international norms from its traditional culture and philosophy. Men Honghua of the Central Party School, a leading scholar of soft power studies in China, argues that four key values of Confucius and Mencius are particularly pertinent: *he* (harmony); *de* (morality); *li* (ritual); and *ren* (benevolence).[76] It is on these bases that Globalists argue China is an "ethical country" (*deguo*) and thus "responsible power."

While debates about global governance have become very animated, by the end of 2009 and into 2010, however, it seemed that the Globalists were in eclipse both in the Foreign Ministry and academic circles—as China began to pursue a much more "Realist" and self-interested global policy.

THE SPECTRUM IN CONTEXT AND POLICY IMPLICATIONS

This is the spectrum of opinion in China today regarding China's international identity and global roles. The fact that China has such a broad spectrum of opinion says much about the identities that are competing with each other in China's IR discourse today. On this basis we argue that China possesses *multiple* international identities and is a conflicted country in its international persona. China wants to please everyone, but is only out for itself. Narrowly self-interested realism is dominant.

To summarize, we can contextualize and distinguish these schools of thought comparatively in terms of their respective ideational origins, policy goals, and policy tactics. This is reflected in Table 2.1. Figure 2.6 contextualizes the schools vis-à-vis the United States foreign policy. We can see from Figure 2.6 that different schools advocate more and less active Chinese diplomacy, with implications for the United States.

When the spectrum of opinion described in this chapter is considered in its totality, it is clear that China's international identity is not fixed. It remains contentious and under debate, and is fluid rather than static. As such, the United States and others can influence the ongoing debates (as well as policy outcomes) through both actions and words, both negatively and positively. Harsh words and tough actions are likely to have a reinforcing effect on China, producing more troubling behavior from Beijing as domestic voices push the government to stand tall and be tough against Washington.

Yet, more conciliatory statements and encouragement for China to act as a "responsible international stakeholder" and become more deeply involved in global governance will likely not produce the intended outcome either. This is because, today, the "center of gravity" on the spectrum does not lie in the middle or toward the Globalist end of the spectrum—rather it resides down toward the left-hand end, anchored on the Realists but

Table 2.1

SCHOOL	IDEATIONAL ORIGINS	POLICY GOALS	POLICY TACTICS
Nativists	Leftist/Maoist/ Marxist; Hyper-Nationalist and Xenophobic	Withdraw from World	Criticize the West; limit engagement with outside world
Realists	Qing "Self-Strengtheners"; Deng Xiaoping; Defensive Nationalism	Strengthen China; resist external pressure; internal balancing; "China First"	Economic and military modernization; eschew foreign entanglements; protect China; suspicious of multilateral institutions
Major Powers	Pragmatism; Sense of China as Great Power	Emphasize United States; work to build Russia and EU into independent "poles" in multipolar world	Reduce tensions with Washington; maintain strong ties with Moscow; try to divide Europe from United States
Asia First	Imperial Tribute System	Pacify and stabilize periphery; prioritize the region; create regional dependencies on China	Emphasize commerce and build webs of ties dependent on China; be unthreatening; work to exclude United States
Global South	Mao; Bandung era "intermediate zone"; nonaligned movement; antiimperialist	Fraternal solidarity; self-appointed leader of Third World; advance developing world causes; redress North–South inequities	Criticize Western dominance; advocate causes of the South; redistribute resources from North to South
Selective Multilateralism	Pragmatism; Realism	Drive for acceptance as "status quo" power; deflect Western criticism	Minimal involvement in global governance, but be *seen* to be contributing
Globalism	Liberal Institutionalism	Contribute proportionately to global governance; help to address global problems	Participate actively in multilateral organizations

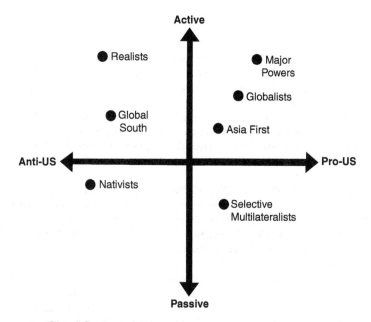

Figure 2.6: China's Diplomatic Proclivities

with strong pull from the Nativists and weaker influence from the Major Powers and Global South schools. The People's Liberation Army is a core element of the Realist School. Government officials in the Foreign Ministry and Central Committee Foreign Affairs Office are pragmatically centered between these two schools (Major Powers and Global South), but they must respond to Nativist and Realist voices in society, the military, and the Communist Party. What the world saw from China during 2009–2010 was an increasingly assertive but narrowly self-interested nation, seeking to maximize its own comprehensive power and throw its weight around. This behavior owes itself to the prevalence of these institutional actors and dominance of the Realist school.

China's intense discourse on the nation's international roles will continue to evolve. As it does so, it is likely to become more diverse but also possibly more polarized, as views may harden. Certainly, an incident could also shape the debate—if a Chinese embassy was seized, or workers were killed in large numbers, or a Chinese naval vessel attacked. But for the foreseeable future we anticipate a multiplicity of voices and policy advocates—which will sustain China's multidimensional and omnidirectional foreign policy.

Notes

A preliminary version of this chapter was published as David Shambaugh, "Coping with a Conflicted China," *Washington Quarterly*, 34, 1 (Winter 2011), 7–27, and an expanded version appears in David Shambaugh, *China Goes Global: The Partial Power* (Oxford: Oxford University Press, 2012).

The authors are most grateful to coeditors Henry Nau and Deepa Ollapally, as well as David M. Lampton and Gilbert Rozman, for their stimulating comments and constructive criticisms on earlier drafts of this chapter. We also benefited a great deal from the input from our Russian and Chinese colleagues at the Moscow and Beijing conferences associated with this project.

1 · Martin Jacques, *When China Rules the World* (London: Allen Lane, 2009).

2 · Arvin Subramanian, *Eclipse: Living in the Shadow of China's Economic Dominance* (Washington, DC: Peterson Institute for International Economics, 2011).

3 · Peter Navarro and Greg Autry, *Death by China: Confronting the Dragon—a Global Call to Action* (Upper Saddle River, NJ: Pearson Education, 2011).

4 · See Shambaugh, *China Goes Global*.

5 · For recent assessments of China's future, see David Shambaugh, ed., *Charting China's Future: Domestic and International Challenges* (London: Routledge, 2011).

6 · For earlier studies that also argued China possessed multiple identities, see Hongying Wang, "National Image Building and Chinese Foreign Policy," *China: An International Journal*, 1, 1 (2003), 46–72; Samuel Kim and Lowell Dittmer, eds., *China's Quest for National Identity* (Ithaca, NY: Cornell University Press, 1993); Yong Deng, *China's Struggle for Status* (Cambridge: Cambridge University Press, 2008).

7 · Despite the critical importance of the linkage between domestic perceptions and foreign policy, surprisingly few foreign scholars or analysts of Chinese foreign policy have focused on ideational variables and this linkage. Over the years, Bonnie Glaser, Banning Garrett, Alastair Iain Johnston, Evan Medeiros, Gilbert Rozman, Philip Saunders, and David Shambaugh have pioneered work on Chinese international perceptions. For a more recent assessment, see Daniel Lynch, "Chinese Thinking on the Future of International Relations: Realism as the *Ti*, Rationalism as the *Yong*?" *China Quarterly*, 197 (March 2009), 87–107.

8 · See the excellent recent study by Linda Jakobson and Dean Knox, *New Foreign Policy Actors in China* (Stockholm: SIPRI, 2010).

9 · Li Shenming and Zhou Hong, eds., *Zhongguo minzhong de guojiguan* [The Chinese Public's View of the World], Vol. 1 (Beijing: Shehui kexue wenzhai chubanshe, 2009). Professor Alastair Iain Johnston of Harvard University has also collected and published some data on Beijing residents' perceptions of international issues. See Johnston, "Chinese Middle Class Attitudes towards International Affairs: Nascent Liberalization," *China Quarterly*, 179 (September 2004), 603–28.

10 · Interview, Chinese Academy of Social Sciences (CASS), Institute of World Economics and Politics, January 28, 2010.

11 · Interview with leading IR scholar, April 30, 2010, Beijing.

12 · One example was an article published under the name of Chinese foreign policy czar State Councilor Dai Bingguo, "Persisting with Taking the Path of Peaceful Development," Ministry of Foreign Affairs of the People's Republic of China website, December 6, 2010, www.fmprc.gov.cn.

13 · See, for example, Wang Fuchun, ed., *Waishi Guanli Xue Gailun* [Introduction to Foreign Affairs Administration] (Beijing: Beijing daxue chubanshe, 2006); Zhang Lili, *Waijiao Juece* [Foreign Policy Decision Making] (Beijing: Shijie zhishi chubanshe, 2007); Wang Jun and Dan Xingwu, *Zhongguo Guoji Guanxi Yanjiu Sishinian* [Forty Years of China's International Relations Research] (Beijing: Zhongyang bianyi chubanshe, 2008), 33–55.

14 · See David Shambaugh, "China's International Relations Think Tanks: Evolving Structure and Process, *China Quarterly* (September 2002); Bonnie Glaser and Philip Saunders, "Chinese Civilian Foreign Policy Think Tanks: Evolving Roles and Increasing Influence," *China Quarterly* (September 2002).

15 · See, for example, Xue Yong, *Zenmeyang Zuo Da Guo?* [How to Be a Great Power] (Beijing: Zhongxin chubanshe, 2009); and Yu Defu, *Daguo Faze* [The Rules for Great Nations] (Beijing: Zhongguo Huaqiao chubanshe, 2009).

16 · See David Shambaugh, "International Relations (IR) Studies in China: History, Trends, and Prospects," *International Relations of the Asia-Pacific* (Fall 2011).

17 · Interview, People's University, January 29, 2010.

18 · Yan Xuetong, "China's Foreign Diplomacy Should Reflect Its World Number 2 Status," *Guoji Luntan Bao* [International Herald Leader], December 6, 2010, http://news.xinhuanet.com/herald/2010-12/06/c_13636783.htm.

19 · Wang Jisi, "Zhongguo de guoji dingwei wenti yu 'taoguang yanghui, yousuo zuowei' de zhanlue sixiang" [The Issue of China's International Position and "Hide Brightness, Modest Demeanor, Do Some Things" in Strategic Thought], *Guoji Wenti Yanjiu*, 2 (2011), 9.

20 · "Zhongguo Guoji Guanxi Xuehui 2010 nian nianhui zai Lanzhou zhaokai" [China's International Relations Society 2010 Annual Meeting in Lanzhou Review], *Waijiao Pinglun*, 4 (2010), 157.

21 · See Zheng Bijian, *China's Peaceful Rise: Speeches of Zheng Bijian, 1997–2005* (Washington, DC: Brookings Institution, 2006).

22 · See Bonnie Glaser and Evan Medeiros, "The Changing Ecology of Foreign Policy Making in China: The Ascension and Demise of the Theory of China's 'Peaceful Rise,'" *China Quarterly* (July 2007).

23 · Xinhua, "Full Text: China's Peaceful Development," www.gov.cn/english/official/2011-09/06/content_1941354_2.htm.

24 · See Yu Xingtian et al., *Guoji Tixi zhong de Zhongguo Jiaose* [China's Position in the International System] (Beijing: Zhongguo dabaike quanshu chubanshe, 2008); Yang Chengxu, *Guoji Da Geju* [The Global Grand Structure] (Beijing: Shijie zhishi chubanshe, 2006); Xia Liping, *Dangdai Guoji Tixi yu Daguo Zhanlue Guanxi* [The Contemporary International System and Major Power Strategic Relations] (Beijing: Shishi chubanshe, 2008);Yang Jiemian, ed., *Guoji Tixi Zhuanbian he Duobian Zuzhi Fazhan* [The Transforming International System and Development of Multilateral Organizations] (Beijing: Shishi chubanshe, 2007); Qin Yaqing, *Guoji Tixi yu Zhongguo Waijiao* [The International System and China's Diplomacy] (Beijing: Shijie zhishi chubanshe, 2009); Zhu Liqun, *Guoji Tixi yu Zhong Ou Guanxi* [The International System and China-Europe Relations] (Beijing: Shijie zhishi chubanshe, 2008).

25 · See Shang Shu, *Guoji Duoji Geju Zouxiang* [The Trajectory of Global Multipolarity] (Beijing: Shishi chubanshe, 2010).

26 · Interview, March 9, 2010, Beijing.

27 · Scholar's statement at conference at Zhongshan University, May 8, 2010.

28 · Interview, November 9, 2010, Shanghai.

29 · See, for example, Yu Zhengliang, "Global Power Structure Has Shifted and Transitional Multipolarity Has Emerged," *Global Review* (July–August 2010), 1–12.

30 · Ibid., pp. 2–3.

31 · See Wang Yusheng, "The BRICS: Rhythm of the Era," *Foreign Affairs*, 96 (Summer 2010), 32–37.

32 · See, for example, Xu Jian, "Rise of the Intermediate Forces and Structural Changes in the World Pattern," *China International Studies* (Spring 2008), 4–19.

33 · See Li Jie, "The Transition of the International System: From the Perspective of the Theory of Responsibility," *China International Studies* (Winter 2007), 138–58.

34 · Shanghai Academy of Social Sciences World Economics and Politics Research Academy, eds., *Fuzeren Daguo de Lujing Xuanze* [Responsible Major Powers' Choices of Routes] (Beijing: Shishi chubanshe, 2007).

35 · See Ma Zhengang, "China's Responsibility and the 'China Responsibility' Theory," *China International Studies* (Summer 2007), 5–12.

36 · For an excellent assessment of this literature (albeit somewhat dated), see Hongying Wang and James N. Rosenau, "China and Global Governance," *Asian Perspective*, 33, 3 (2009), 5–39.

37 · Interview, July 14, 2010, Beijing.

38 · Scholar's statement at conference, Zhongshan University, May 8, 2010.

39 · Shanghai Academy of Social Sciences World Economics and Politics Research Academy, eds., *Duobian Jizhi yu Zhongguo de Dingwei* [The Multilateral System and China's Position] (Beijing: Shishi chubanshe, 2007); Shanghai Academy of Social Sciences World Economics and Politics Research Academy, eds., *Duobian Hezuo yu Zhongguo Waijiao* [Multilateral Cooperation and China's Foreign Policy] (Beijing: Shishi chubanshe, 2010).

40 · Interview, May 3, 2010, Beijing.

41 · For one review of the concept and discourse, see Zhang Yuquan and Michael Chang, "'Harmonious World': China's New Strategy of Cultural Diplomacy," *Ya-Tai Pinglun* [*Asia-Pacific Review*], 1–2 (2009), 239–56.

42 · Interview with IR scholar, April 30, 2010, Beijing.

43 · Hu Jintao, "Build towards a Harmonious World of Lasting Peace and Common Prosperity," speech at the United Nations Summit, September 15, 2005, www.fmprc.gov.cn/ce/ceun/eng/zt/shnh60/t212915.htm.

44 · See, for example, the findings of a recent survey of Asian countries, in which large majorities in surveyed countries had never heard of the concept of "harmonious world." See Chicago Council of Global Affairs, *Soft Power in Asia: Results of a 2008 Multinational Survey of Public Opinion* (Chicago: Chicago Council of Global Affairs, 2009).

45 · For more on China's efforts to acquire and project soft power, see Shambaugh, *China Goes Global*, chapter 6.

46 · Interview, May 9, 2010, Guangzhou.

47 · It is better to think of these cohorts as "tendencies of analysis" than rigid schools of thought. The pioneering work on "tendency analysis" is H. Gordon Skilling and William Griffiths, *Interest Groups in Soviet Politics* (Princeton, NJ: Princeton University Press, 1973).

48 · Wang Xiaodong et al., *Zhongguo bu Gaoxing* (Jiangsu renmin chubanshe, 2009); He Xiongfei, *Zhongguo Weishenme bu Gaoxing?* (Beijing: Shijie zhishi chubanshe, 2009); Ye Dinghua et al., *Shei zai Zhongguo bu Gaoxing?* (Guangzhou: Huacheng chubanshe, 2009).

49 · Zhang Wenmu, "Shijie lishi zhong de qiangguo zhilu yu Zhongguo de Xuanze" [The Road of the Great Powers in World History and China's Choice], in Guo Shuyong, ed., *Zhanlue yu Tansuo* [Strategy and Exploration] (Beijing: Shijie zhishi chubanshe, 2008), 33,54.

50 · Fang Ning, "Xin diguozhuyi yu Zongguo de zhanlue xuanze" [The New Imperialism and China's Strategic Choice] in Guo Shuying, ed., *Zhanlue yanjianglu* [Lectures on Strategy] (Beijing: Peking University Press, 2006), 132–33.

51 · Illustrative is Wang Jinsong, *Diguozhuyi Lishi de Zhongjie: Dangdai Diguozhuyi de Xingcheng he Fazhan Qushi* [Imperialism Is the Final Stage of History: Contemporary Imperialism's Formation and Development Trends] (Beijing: Shehui kexue wenzhai chubanshe, 2008).

52 · Ibid.

53 · Zhang Wenmu, *The Road of the Great Powers*, 42–43.

54 · Interview with scholar at China Reform Forum, January 20, 2010.

55 · Yan Xuetong, "An Analysis of the Advantages and Disadvantages of Containing Legal Taiwan Independence by Force," *Strategy and Management*, 3 (2004), 1–5. He subsequently publicly apologized for these views.

56 · Yan Xuetong, *Zhongguo Jueqi* (Tianjin: Tianjin renmin chubanshe, 1997).

57 · Yan Xuetong, "China's Foreign Diplomacy Should Reflect Its World Number 2 Status."

58 · Statement at conference at Zhongshan University, May 7, 2010, Guangzhou.

59 · Interview, January 20, 2010, Beijing.

60 · See Pan Wei, "Yetan heping jueqi" [Again Discussing Peaceful Rise], www.360doc.com/content/07/0831/17/41440_708164.shtml. Also see Pan Wei's "Diqiushang conglai mei fasheng guo 'heping jueqi' zhezhongshi" (There Was Never Such a Thing as "Peaceful Rise" in the World's Past), www.360doc.com/content/09/1102/17/346405_828157.shtml.

61 · Interview, March 25, 2010, Beijing.

62 · See David Shambaugh, "China Engages Asia: Reshaping the Regional Order," *International Security*, 29, 3 (Winter 2004/2005).

63 · For an excellent survey of commentaries by China's Asianists, see Gilbert Rozman, *Chinese Strategic Thought toward Asia* (New York: Palgrave Macmillan, 2010).

64 · Yu Xintian, "Zhongguo ying zhuanbian dui fazhanzhong guojia de zhanlue" [China Should Change Its Strategy towards Developing Countries], *Strategy and Management*, 3 (2003), 40–45.

65 · *Huanqiu* [Globe], ed., *Baiwen Zhongguo Weilai: Zhongguo Jingying Duihua Quanqiu* [A Hundred Questions on China's Future: Dialogues with Chinese Elites] (Beijing: Xinhua Press, 2009), 12.

66 · See, for example, Men Honghua, "Daguo jueqi yu guoji zhixu" [The Rise of Great Powers and International Order], *Guoji Zhengzhi Yanjiu*, 2 (2004), 133–42; Zhang Wenwu, "Jianli guoji zhixu de xin linian" [New Concepts of Establishing International Order], *Xueshu Tansuo*, 6 (2005), 73–80.

67 · Su Changhe, "Faxian Zhongguo xin waijiao—duobian guoji zhidu yu Zhongguo waijiao xin siwei" [Rediscovering China's New Diplomacy—Multilateral International Institutions and China's New Thinking in Foreign Affairs], *Shijie Jingji yu Zhengzhi*, 4 (2005), 11–16.

68 · Yang Jiechi, "A Changing China in a Changing World," address to the Munich Security Conference, February 5, 2010.

69 · See Qin Yaqing, "Zhongguo guoji guanxi lilun yanjiu de jinbu yu wenti" [China's International Relations Theory Research: Progress and Problems], *Shijie Jingsjiyu Zhengzhi*, 11 (2008), 18.

70 · For a Chinese view, which stresses Chinese recognition of "international responsibility" and embrace of liberal IR, see Zhu Liqun, *China's Foreign Policy Debates*, Chaillot Papers No. 121 (Paris: European Institute of Security Studies, 2010).

71 · Interview with IR scholar, May 2, 2010, Beijing.

72 · Interview with scholar at CICIR, April 19, 2010.

73 · Ibid.

74 · For a full explanation, see Wang Yizhou, *Zhongguo Waijiao Xin Gaodi* [High Land over China's Foreign Affairs] (Beijing: Zhongguo shehui kexue chubanshe, 2008), 13–14; interview, January 30, 2010, Beijing.

75 · Interview, January 30, 2010, Beijing.

76 · Interview, May 2, 2010, Beijing.

3

India

Foreign Policy Perspectives of an Ambiguous Power

DEEPA M. OLLAPALLY AND RAJESH RAJAGOPALAN

As India rises, it faces a number of foreign policy choices. Some of these choices are influenced by the great power system in Asia, but because the Asian—and global—power system is evolving, India's choices are unsettled ones. Irrespective of what these conditions are, however, India's choices will ultimately be determined by how Indian decision makers and opinion shapers see these choices. Unlike other major powers, India does not have a well-articulated grand strategy or national doctrine to guide its foreign policy. India's rise has not been accompanied by White Papers, Prime Ministerial doctrines, or any other clear and open statements by the government about what its objectives are for India's global role. This is not surprising—official India rarely spells out its long-term vision with discrete steps to be taken to achieve its goals. Without considering whether this is due to a lack of purposeful thinking or whether it is a clever attempt to maintain flexibility, the outcome either way is a certain amount of ambiguity. Thus, it would be fair to term India "an ambiguous rising power."

At the same time, there has been an abundance of public, expert, and media discussion on this issue over the last five years. There are contending perspectives promoted by domestic groups that could potentially influence Indian foreign policy choices. This chapter outlines the main schools of thought in India, their historical roots, and their likely impact on critical regional and global issues—from dealing with India's neighborhood, to relations with major powers including the United States, and the use of force.

The strong foreign policy consensus that India enjoyed after independence in 1947 had become increasingly brittle by the late 1980s as India's economy stagnated and its most important strategic partner, the Soviet Union, faced a precipitous decline. The end of the Cold War has given rise to new foreign policy directions in India, but there has been no clear replacement of the consensus forged by the first prime minister, Jawaharlal Nehru. The absence of a dominant consensus as in the previous era does not mean that the current competing schools of foreign policy thinking are equally strong or influential. But it does mean that it is hard to see an identifiable consensus about the nature of India's rise to power—its foreign policy goals, means, or scope.

In this chapter, we outline different Indian conceptions of foreign policy, broadly defined to include grand strategy. We make this clarification because grand strategy is usually broader and encompasses the means–ends chain (while foreign policy can be seen as only one of the means).[1] As this book argues, foreign policy is determined as much by domestic political processes as by the international condition in which states find themselves. For example, India's post–Cold War quasi-bandwagoning with the United States is as much a consequence of the changed *structure* of global power after the Soviet collapse, as a *reaction* by Indian decision makers to that changed global balance. But how coordinated Indo–US policy will be is strongly conditioned by domestic attitudes in India about the nature of US power and preferences. Structural conditions thus strongly *influence* the strategic options that states face, but these structural conditions do not *determine* the choices that states make. This chapter, like this book, focuses more on how Indian opinion makers view India's choices and how they view the structural conditions that give rise to these choices.

This chapter is divided into four sections. In the first section, we examine which opinions matter in the making of Indian foreign and security policy. This is important in the Indian context because there appears to be a considerable distance between the public debate and policy making in India. The second section outlines the new debate about India's foreign policy, which is critical to the discussion that follows. The subsequent section outlines six major perspectives on Indian foreign policy that we suggest are key. The final section links these perspectives to particular foreign policy issues facing India and draws out what each perspective offers as policy prescriptions.

WHICH OPINIONS MATTER IN INDIAN STRATEGIC POLICY?

Although there is an active Indian strategic policy debate outside the confines of the central government in New Delhi, its consequences for policy making are unclear. Indeed, it is unclear if opinions outside of government have any significant impact on choices made by Indian decision makers. The Indian Foreign Service (IFS), the "bureaucratic guardians" of Indian foreign policy making, rarely seek or entertain outside opinions on matters of India's foreign policy.[2] Even the semiofficial National Security Advisory Board (NSAB), set up by the Atal Vajpayee government in 1998 to provide "nongovernmental" expertise to decision makers, has been largely filled with recently retired civil and military service officers thus undermining its "nonofficial" status. In addition, it is not clear if even this group is taken seriously within the government. Certainly, current and former NSAB members have complained of feeling that the group and its work were ignored by the government.[3]

To the extent that nongovernmental opinion matters, it appears to matter negatively as a constraint on or as a veto against particular choices rather than positively in promoting policy initiatives such as through policy lobbying. Such veto opinion was clearly very active and important during the Comprehensive Test Ban Treaty (CTBT) debate in 1995–1996. Once suffused with strong domestic opposition, key political decision makers appear to be reluctant to seek to change opinions or alter policy. Thus, opposition to the CTBT has become difficult for subsequent administrations to overcome, although both the Vajpayee administration (in 1999–2000) and the current Manmohan Singh government appear to have thought of altering existing policy.[4] The strength of such veto opinion varies in effectiveness: during the 2005–2008 debate over the United States–India nuclear deal, the Congress-led coalition government went ahead with the deal despite fierce and very public opposition from a variety of opinion makers. On the other hand, this appears to have been the result of Prime Minister Manmohan Singh's personal commitment to the deal because many even within his own Congress Party were lukewarm toward the deal, especially when Congress's allies threatened to withdraw support and pull the government down if it persisted with the deal.[5] Similarly, fear of such veto opinion is likely to limit Indian policy flexibility on issues such as the CTBT, Non-Proliferation Treaty (NPT), and Fissile Material Control Treaty (FMCT), as also on other strategic policies, especially key relations with Washington, Beijing, and Islamabad. For example, though FMCT negotiations have not yet started with any seriousness at the Conference on Disarmament (CD) in Geneva, Indian analysts have already outlined concerns and objections.[6]

Thus, the transmission belt between opinion makers on the outside and policy decisions on the inside is much more indirect than it is in many other states. Indeed, it is not even clear that such a transmission belt exists in the Indian context except in the form of veto. We suggest four reasons on both the demand and supply side why this is so: first, on the supply side, this appears to be the consequence of the insularity and the organizational culture of the Indian bureaucracy that rewards risk avoidance more than innovation. Second, again on the supply side, two decades of coalition governments have made both major political parties equally risk averse. Third, India's civil service is large and comprises career civil servants. It limits the links between government and the private sector, unlike the United States, where actors often move from the public to the private sector and vice versa. Fourth, on the demand side, India's international condition has consistently improved since the early 1990s as a consequence of its economic growth and power profile, and there have been few great challenges that required risky responses. Opportunities for additional gains may have been lost, but this is seen as less important. One consequence of this policymaking insularity is that there is considerable continuity in Indian strategic policy. Radical departures in policy are rare, and they have been the consequence of dramatic changes in structural conditions rather than domestic politics. Examples of such change include Indian response to the China war in 1962, to Nixon's China opening in 1971, and to the end of the Cold War.

Clearly, therefore, the influence of opinion makers outside the adminis-tration appears to be limited. What about opinion within the government? The key problem in delineating perspectives within the government is the opaqueness of the Indian state. There is also very little in-house institu-tional capacity to provide intellectual guidance and forward-looking strat-egies through White Papers and the like that can be made available to the strategic community. For example, the Ministry of External Affairs'(MEA) Policy Planning Division is well known to be a decrepit, virtually defunct, part of MEA.[7] In most important capitals, policy planning is an integral section of the foreign policy establishment. Occasionally, as in the case of the United States–India nuclear deal, differences within the government get public airing. But such instances are rare, and it is unclear if these are because of differences of personality, bureaucratic politics, or perspectives about India's role in the world. In the United States–India nuclear deal, for example, these appeared to have been more differences in personalities rather than of bureaucratic politics, while in some other cases, such as issues of the Chief of Defence Staff (CDS) or of some military strategies, they appear to be institutional disagreements such as interdepartmental and interservices rivalry.[8] Thus, because *most* policy disagreements within the government (at least those that are visible on the outside) are the result of personality rather than institutional/bureaucratic politics, they are dif-ficult to predict. Perhaps in India more than elsewhere, the role of key personalities in foreign policy cannot be underestimated.[9]

NEW DEBATES ON INDIAN FOREIGN POLICY TRADITION

In the Indian case, a self-conscious grand strategy or a comprehensive long-term assessment of goals and appropriate means, has historically been missing.[10] Still, Indian foreign policy seemed to evolve based on a fairly deep-seated shared understanding of India's broad international role until the end of the Cold War. Over the last two decades however (at least since the mid-1990s), there has been a debate among Indian analysts about whether Indian foreign policy has been "realist" or "idealist." This debate is not entirely about the past: many of those who argue that India's orientation has been realist are also proposing that India should adopt a more realistic and pragmatic strategy.[11] Indeed, their adumbration of the realist strands in India's traditional approach, especially such realist strands in Jawaharlal Nehru's foreign policy, usually appears as a prelude to their advocacy of a much more power-oriented stance for contemporary India. K. Subrahmanyam, considered the leading Indian realist strategist, characterized Nehru as "one of the most pragmatic and realist politicians."[12] The essence of the revisionist argument is that Indian foreign policy has been suffused with unnecessary moralism, which, according to these critics, is mistakenly traced back to Nehruvian ideals.[13] By showing that Nehru was much more realist than he is generally given credit for, these advocates seek to establish a case for greater realism in contemporary policy.[14] Indeed, some revisionists have even argued that Gandhi was a Realist.[15]

Their case itself is open to question: independent India's foreign policy practice has demonstrated an understanding of power, and used balance of power approach at key points especially in balancing China after 1962, in balancing the United States during the 1971 war, and when India shifted to quasi-bandwagon with the United States in the post–Cold War period. But from a power politics perspective, India demonstrated significant failures at different periods: its underbalancing of China in the 1950s and its uncertain pursuit of nuclear weapons are the best illustrators, but others include an excessive focus on the nonaligned movement (NAM) and nuclear disarmament. At some critical points, Indian decision makers have clearly demonstrated understanding and use of power politics but Indian diplomatic history records many instances when such power imperatives have been ignored to India's detriment. Moreover, one of the most distinguishing features of India's foreign policy has been its tendency toward being a "moralistic running commentary."[16] Thus, the picture is much more mixed than how it is painted in this new revisionist literature. But that is not the main point: what is important here is not the "reality" because clearly our interpretation of the periodic shifts between hard power and ethical imperatives is only one interpretation and not necessarily more valid than the revisionist ones above. What is relevant here is how traditional Indian foreign policy is interpreted in order to suggest lessons for contemporary policy. On the other hand, while agreeing that Nehruvian foreign policy has been misinterpreted, there are differences in this new revisionist literature about what should be the constituents of a "realist" foreign policy. In other words, reinterpretation of the Nehruvian and traditional model of Indian foreign policy serves different ends.

There is, of course, another side to this debate: some invoke Nehru to emphasize the need for greater ethical content in an Indian grand strategy, such as for nuclear disarmament, reduced militarization, or anticolonialism and third world solidarity.[17] This holds Nehru's approach as an ethical template for India's policy and as a critique for the current policy choices. It disagrees with much of the post–Cold War changes in Indian foreign policy, in particular India's quasi-bandwagoning with the United States, and its new relationship with US allies such as Israel, Japan, and Australia. But it is also noteworthy that democracy promotion, a key issue in American post–Cold War foreign policy—as well as that of a number of other Western powers—is not a major issue in India. Neither Nehruvians, nor those calling for change, suggest that India should join the West in democracy promotion mainly for reasons of pragmatism.[18]

That both sides of the debate draw from Nehru is not surprising—India's post-Independence foreign policy was overwhelmingly dominated by Nehru in conceptual development and practice. The hallmark of Nehru's thinking was its eclectic and expansive nature, understanding that power matters in international relations, but unwilling to let India become entangled in outside conflicts that would lead to Indian loss of blood and treasure, and perhaps even more important, erode India's autonomy and close off India's options. Such thinking should not be confused with actual practice: both Nehru and other Indian leaders were capable of seeking military assistance and even an alliance under extreme circumstances. For example, Nehru sought military assistance from President Kennedy to deal with the Chinese invasion in 1962 but this was a short-term, almost panic, reaction, and the policy was rescinded almost immediately after the crisis passed.[19] Thus, if we can identify one meta-narrative in post-independent India, it is this perspective. Despite remaining aloof from conventional power politics, Nehru and India managed to play an outsized role in international relations during the first twenty or so years after independence. Then and to some extent, even now, India tended to place an inordinate amount of importance on attaining international status. In turn, India still seems to place a good deal of stock on its "power by example" as a way of gaining global status.[20]

STRUCTURAL AND DOMESTIC DETERMINANTS

Both structural and domestic variables matter in the making of foreign policy. It would probably be unwise to emphasize one over the other. Indeed, in addition to traditional approaches that focused on domestic-level variables, even the most self-consciously structuralist approach, neo-realism, has been giving way for well over a decade to other approaches that give greater weight to domestic-level variables. Such neoclassical real-ist approaches do not reject structural insights but argue that such structural insights need to be complemented by other domestic-level variables for more comprehensive foreign policy explanations.[21] Nevertheless, the key question is whether domestic or structural conditions play a more prominent role.

Clearly, for a number of reasons, domestic variables need to be taken seriously in the Indian case. First, structural influences are not particularly strong in the Indian case because India faces a relatively benign international condition. Although the larger Asian power structure does intrude into South Asia, that does not challenge Indian dominance in the region. Second, domestic variables are likely to matter more in democracies because matters of policy are likely to be not only partisan but also openly discussed. Third, additionally, the fractured nature of India's polity ensures that such internal debates will be vociferous, as the United States–India nuclear deal demonstrated. Because neither of India's national parties—the Congress and the Bharatiya Janata Party (BJP)—are likely to achieve national dominance in the near future, these differences are likely to be played out much more vigorously. Finally, India's size and diversity will ensure that domestic variables will remain an important input into foreign policy making.

Even when international structure seems compelling as in the case of India's post-1991 foreign policy shift, it is only part of the picture. The Nehruvian paradigm of inward-looking economics and nonaligned foreign policy had been increasingly challenged by domestic critics since the early 1980s. By the end of the Cold War, domestic opinion that saw the limits of the earlier approach, especially in economics, was already ascendant.

Outlining the various Indian perspectives on Indian foreign policy is somewhat difficult because they fall within a fairly narrow range.[22] Moreover, as Figure 3.1 suggests, these are intersecting views, with plenty of commonality across these perspectives. Thus, they do not represent straight-line spectrum from the left to the right. The differences are not as great as might seem at first sight. It is difficult to find, within the variety of views about foreign policy, any perspective that suggests that India should actively use military power to promote itself to either a greater status in Asia or in the global community.[23] This clearly recognizes that India does not need to do much to dominate South Asia, where it is already dominant, and that it does not have sufficient capability to dominate Asia irrespective of the effort expended. In essence, India faces a military power gap: adding more military power resources is unlikely to make much difference to its existing dominance within South Asia, but India does not have the wealth needed to make a bid for Asian military dominance, even if we were to define Asia in such a way as to exclude US military presence. For example, Indian defense budget has remained between 12 and 15 percent of total budget and slightly over 2 percent of the GDP for much of the last two decades.[24]

Thus, there is broad agreement about the need to modernize and enhance India's military capabilities, although this is about gradual and moderate enhancement rather than about any dramatic or revolutionary increase in Indian military capabilities. Indeed, most of these arguments are being driven by the need to keep up with Chinese or Pakistani military capabilities. For example, news about China's infrastructure development

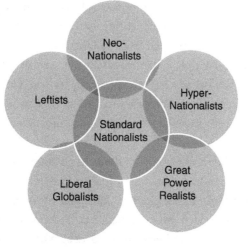

Figure 3.1: Major Schools of Foreign Policy Thought

along the India–Tibet border has resulted in concern about the poor state of the infrastructure on the Indian side of the border, resulting in greater budgetary allocation and public and parliamentary attention to the issue.[25] But there is also reasonably broad consensus on the need for enhancing Indian military power resources against China (and to a lesser extent, Pakistan) within and outside the government, thus reducing the weight and uniqueness of these arguments. But what is absent in these perspectives is as noteworthy: there are no suggestions, even among the advocates of hard power, that India should seek to use military power to recapture territory lost to either Pakistan (in Jammu and Kashmir) or China (in the 1962 war), despite the fact there are parliamentary resolutions that claim these territories, which possibly results in less suspicion about India's military build-up than about China's in the wider Asian context. India has, of course, used military force proactively before, in Goa (1961) as well as in the Bangladesh War (1971).

It should be noted that there is some frustration in two key areas close to home that could nudge India toward greater military activism in the future: terrorist attacks on Indian soil, and competition in the Indian Ocean from China. It is not surprising that the navy's top brass was the first to come out with a "doctrine" that evoked Clausewitz though couched in typical restraint. A 2004 analysis by the navy declares: "If India is to exude the quiet confidence of a nation that seeks to be neither deferential nor belligerent, but is aware of its own role in the larger global scheme, it will need to recognize what constitute strategic currency in a Clausewitzian sense."[26] Likewise, the perceived inability to respond to terrorism from groups associated with Pakistan, especially in the wake of the 2008 Mumbai attacks, has given rise to a new army strategy termed "Cold Start," utilizing small, rapid deployment forces trained to strike and retreat. As word of such a strategy got leaked however, the government was quick to deny its adoption.[27]

Thus, even the most extreme of the hard power perspective is limited to suggesting that India improve its capacity to defend its territory from a Chinese or Pakistani attack rather than proactively use military force to settle disputes—indeed, we were unable to find any recommendation that India proactively use military force to deal with any external security problem. Apart from a power gap, India's posture reflects long-standing self-restraint on the use of force as well as offensive military buildup, epito-mized by the twenty-five year hiatus between the two nuclear tests. Thus, though there are very distinct perspectives on India's foreign policy, they fall within a fairly narrow range.

We distinguish four separate schools among these perspectives. We characterize these as the Nationalists, the Great Power Realists, the Lib-eral Globalists, and the Leftists.[28] We further refine the Nationalist school into three subgroups: Standard Nationalists, Neo-Nationalists, and Hyper-Nationalists. As our framework in this study recognizes, these ag-gregations might not do justice to all the different opinions available and that some viewpoints might not fully fit these labels, just as there might be spillovers between the views in these different strands. (See Table 3.1.) But they do represent a spectrum along which we can assess period shifts. It is somewhat difficult to assign relative weight to these perspectives. Our in-terpretation is that Hyper-Nationalists and Leftists are less influential than the other perspectives. We also believe that a pragmatists strain, which is mostly made up of Great Power Realists and Liberal Globalists, have gained strength over the last two decades though they are by no means dominant.[29]

Nationalists

Standard Nationalists

The roots of the Standard Nationalist perspective are found as far back as Indian independence.[30] This is also most closely identified with the domi-nant Congress Party, and it tends to emphasize autonomy in decision making and a rhetorical anti-Americanism as its main elements. But it also represents a middle path in a variety of ways: despite the anti-American and anti-Western rhetoric, it remains mostly centrist in actual policy; it also takes a centrist position by rhetorically abjuring power politics, even though there has been little reluctance to use power politics/balance of power logic in critical situations such as in Goa, East Pakistan, or Sri Lanka (1987). The Standard Nationalist position also includes sympathy for a variety of "third world" causes including Palestine and, more recently,

Table 3.1: *Indian Foreign Policy Perspectives*

MAJOR SCHOOLS OF THOUGHT	GOALS & ATTITUDES	ROOTS
NATIONALISTS		
Standard Nationalists (1947–)	Aim for developed country status Pursue balanced growth	Nehruvianism
Neo-Nationalists (Post-1991)	No to idea of Great Power Domestic consolidation first South–South solidarity	Soft Nehruvianism Gandhian Indian civilization Socialist theory
Hyper-Nationalists (Post-1998)	Achieve global power India first Tight internal security	Kautilya Selective realist theory Hindu nationalism
GREAT POWER REALISTS (Post-1998)	Become global player	Kautilya Realist theory
LIBERAL GLOBALISTS (Post-1991)	Aim for global economic power	Economic theory
LEFTISTS (Post-2004)	Third World coalition against United States hegemony	Marxist theory

Iran.[31] This centrist position has been remarkably resilient, and this element of Nehruvianism has yet to be replaced.

This perspective may be considered to be the "establishment perspective plus." As such, their views are inconsistent, sometimes advocating power imperatives in policy and at other times moral imperatives. Thus, the Standard Nationalist emphasizes military power but it also pays heed to India's traditional ethical and moral concerns in foreign and strategic policy. For example, Standard Nationalists want India to be represented in the UN Security Council, even as they rail against the Security Council as a reflection of power politics. As with the Hyper-Nationalists, the Standard Nationalist perspective advocates greater military strength and greater military expenditure. The key difference here with Hyper-Nationalists is that the Standard Nationalists emphasize the political objectives of military power rather than seeing military power as an end it itself. This is most clearly evident in the case of nuclear weapons: while all shades of Nationalists support the nuclear weapons program, the Standard Nationalists see nuclear weapons as essentially political tools that give greater negotiating leverage and support a strategy based on a minimum deterrent force.[32] But this does not mean that they are not mindful of the need for a credible, second-strike nuclear force, including nuclear submarines.[33]

During the Cold War, the Standard Nationalists were at the forefront of India's intellectual opposition to the nuclear nonproliferation regime and its associated institutions, the export-control institutions in particular. They continue to be suspicious of many of the nonproliferation regime institutions and maintain fierce opposition to the NPT because of its discriminatory nature.[34] They traditionally viewed power politics in Nehruvian terms as immoral and occasionally continue to see power politics as passé, although, contradictorily, they also advocate it at other times.

The Standard Nationalist perspective also supports greater defense spending and capabilities, including developing indigenous military technology both because of the need for strategic autonomy and because of the fear that it would be insecure to depend on foreign sources for military hardware. As one former ambassador put it, "India will win respect internationally only when projects like the LCA, the Main Battle Tank, and the Advanced Technology Vehicle are successfully implemented. The development of an indigenous nuclear submarine should be treated as a national challenge and goal."[35]

One of the key areas of disagreement between the Standard Nationalists and Hyper-Nationalists is in terms of nuclear policy. For the former, nuclear weapons are political tools and they tend to be deterrence optimists, arguing that only small numbers of nuclear weapons are needed to assure deterrence. Thus, they have supported the idea of a minimum nuclear deterrent for India and associated ideas such as No First Use. In addition, they are skeptical about the need for more nuclear tests. Although they were supportive of the 1998 nuclear tests, they did not necessarily campaign for the tests, arguing for a decade that India did not necessarily have to test. The Standard Nationalist perspective also tends to be supportive of global nuclear disarmament initiatives, which the Hyper-Nationalists are dismissive of. Such support for nuclear disarmament is justified on the realist rather than moral grounds that nuclear disarmament will actually increase

India's military leverage by bringing India's superior conventional strength to bear on international politics.

Contradictions also abound in the Standard Nationalist views about international politics and the balance of power. They have traditionally been advocates of Nehruvian notions of South–South solidarity, but are also supportive of the changed Indian foreign policy that pays less heed to these concerns in favor of closer relations with the United States and other Western powers. One way to distinguish Standard Nationalists from Neo-Nationalists, who also draw heavily from Nehru, is that the former may be seen having been more closely allied with the external face of Nehruvianism—strategic autonomy and sovereignty in particular, while the latter emphasizes domestic concerns in Indian foreign policy. The main goal of Standard Nationalists is for India to achieve developed country status in a balanced manner in terms of India's economy and defense. Standard Nationalists are attracted by the notion of India as a great power, but are reluctant to expend the resources required for it.

The contradictions that result from such perspectives is reflected in a number of issues such as, for example, India's relations with other powers. Standard Nationalists appear to want India to have good friends in the international community who will stand by India, but without India necessarily having any obligations in return. As one former ambassador put it, "Our concern should be limited to our position in this fast changing world. Our first worry should be whether we have any real friends—friends of the kind that Indira Gandhi managed to get onside during the Bangladesh crisis."[36] The United States–India nuclear deal served to divide opinions *within* the Standard Nationalists. Some whom we would characterize as Standard Nationalists expressed apprehensions about the deal, even if they broadly supported the deal, while others were more forthcoming in their support.[37]

Thus the Standard Nationalist school tends to espouse ideological goals and a robust military, but increasingly will pragmatically trade them off against high costs or domestic needs. Proponents view military means as a way of augmenting the country's political status, and while some of their ideological goals have a global scope, the strategic sphere of action is largely limited to the broader Asian region, including India's "West Asia."

Neo-Nationalists

The Neo-Nationalist perspective is also "Nehruvian," but it clearly privileges domestic economic needs over external ambitions. This group coalesced in the aftermath of India's economic liberalization in 1991, in response to concerns that globalization would result in loss of economic and political sovereignty and increase domestic disparities. Neo-Nationalists are mostly comprised by the left of center sections of the Congress Party that over time has fragmented, as well as left parties, civil society groups, and some regional parties that represent dispossessed communities and frequently band together with the Leftists. To Neo-Nationalists, domestic consolidation is the most important national objective. The best representation of such positions are politicians (and former bureaucrats) such as Mani Shankar Aiyar of the Congress Party and N. K. Singh of the regional Janata Dal (United) Party who have asserted the need for economic growth to be translated into actual human development rather than leading to increased economic disparity in the country.[38]

A key strand of thought identified with the Neo-Nationalist position is that of "India as a Developing Country." The historic willingness of successive Indian governments to tolerate lower growth rates was to both protect Indian domestic business sectors and meet requirements of equity as outlined by Nehru. Although this is the aspect of national thinking in India that many observers view as having been overtaken by the new liberal economic outlook, such an assumption seems overly hasty. There is a strong lingering belief in the need to protect weaker sections of the population as well as certain business sectors, such as retail. While the Neo-Nationalists are the strongest advocates of this, the Standard Nationalists and even the Liberal Globalists are supportive of some form of equity considerations, the latter at least in rhetoric.

This acknowledgment of the need to pay some attention to equity sits rather uncomfortably next to the growing acceptance by all the schools of thought except the Neo-Nationalists and the Leftists of the "trickle down" economic model as a means of lifting the lower social strata. The change in terminology from "equity" to "inclusive growth" points to a shift in discourse and mind-set that now recognizes the importance of the growth model— something that was shunned prior to 1991. Given the almost unavoidable tension between "growth" and "equity" (at least politically), Singh's United Progressive Alliance (UPA) government is trying to have it both ways: embracing globalization and protecting domestic popular interests.

The Liberal Globalist economic managers of the country are increasingly at pains to note how economic growth is contributing to balanced development. The argument is that there are more and more opportunities at the bottom of the pyramid. It has been pointed out, for example, that between 2004 and 2007, banks more than doubled the amount given as farm loans to small landholders. In addition, India now runs the largest program of microcredit in the world.[39] Poverty estimates also show significant reductions of population below the poverty line over the last two decades: from 36.0 percent in 1993–1994 to 27.5 percent in 2004–2005, the latest figures that have been calculated in the Planning Commission's 2011 report. More than anything else, these accomplishments are attributed to the new growth.[40]

During its first term in 2004, Manmohan Singh's government lost little time in announcing special programs to benefit the poorest, most notably the Guaranteed Rural Employment Scheme. This was not only because of the political lesson learned from the Atal Vajpayee government's loss, but more broadly due to the ruling coalition drawing support from the left parties. Despite poverty reduction, one in five Indians lives in extreme poverty, a fact that the government cannot ignore. The point is that the belief in growth with equity has hardly evaporated. This is not due to political calculations alone; there seems to be residual ideological sentiment from the earlier period for the Standard Nationalists at the helm of the state.

As such, India's strategies for international engagement may be circumscribed by the Neo-Nationalist group as well as political considerations for the Standard Nationalists: a preference for selective multilateralism, strict reciprocity in economic relations, particularly with South Asian neighbors, and alignment with other developing countries over developed countries in economic negotiations. However, the same UPA government comprised largely of Standard Nationalists has shown a willingness to buck significant domestic fears about opening up Indian markets to potential competitors—the push for Free Trade Agreements is one telling example.[41]

Among the Nationalist groups, Neo-Nationalists hold positions closest to the "traditional" Indian Nehruvian foreign policy goals of global disarmament and nonalignment. The roots of such thinking may be traced beyond Nehru to Gandhian notions of nonviolence and seeing India's greatness deriving from its nonaggressive and accommodating civilizational antecedents. Although this traditional viewpoint has been transcended, it does correspond at times to the rhetorical position that the Indian government continues to take on some issues. The recent move of the Indian government to revive the Rajiv Gandhi action plan for nuclear disarmament, which did not garner much interest even when it was presented in the late 1980s by Rajiv Gandhi, is one indication of the continued rhetorical appeal of the Neo-Nationalist sentiment within the Congress Party.[42] Indeed, it is not clear that it ever represented actual policy as much as an idealized rhetoric around the policy. Thus, Prime Minister Nehru, despite being a strong advocate of nuclear disarmament, built the foundations of an independent Indian nuclear deterrent. Nevertheless, this idealized Nationalist position continues to find adherents among Indian foreign policy opinion makers, mostly among leftist sections of the Congress Party. It is also a view held by some well-regarded independent scholars and commentators.[43] In particular there continues to be an instinctive third-worldism and anti-Westernism in certain sections of the Indian foreign policy opinion community. However, it is unlikely that this position will correspond to Indian policy or will determine Indian policy any time soon.

Hyper-Nationalists

The Hyper-Nationalist perspective in Indian foreign policy is also a post–Cold War phenomenon. While there may have been similar opinions on the fringes of political discourse in the past, associated mostly with the minuscule Indian right-wing opinion, they were never allowed to enter the mainstream. In the post–Cold War period, these views became prominent after it splintered from another major perspective, the Standard Nationalists, because the latter supported changes in Indian foreign policy orientation after the Cold War, while the Hyper-Nationalists continued to insist on a much more autarchic and autonomous path for India. Hyper-Nationalists seek far greater military capability for India.[44] As the 2009 election manifesto of the BJP stated, "The Indian Army, Air Force and Navy need to be strengthened in view of rapidly changing regional and global realities."[45] The

Hyper-Nationalists are distinguished by their opposition to any measure, especially international arms control measures and domestic military policies, which might even remotely or potentially limit such capabilities.[46]

Indian Hyper-Nationalists tend to be suspicious of international interactions, seeing traps that might serve to constrain the development and exercise of Indian power. Thus, they strenuously campaigned against the United States–India nuclear deal, arguing that it was an American attempt to trick India into the NPT and that it would constrain the Indian nuclear weapons program.[47] They were of course not alone in expressing such views but others such as the political Left and Right and members of Indian scientific establishment had other reasons for opposing the deal.[48] What distinguished the Hyper-Nationalists was that their argument about the potential emasculation of the Indian nuclear weapons program was not a proxy argument as it was for some others like the left parties who were in reality against closer ties to the United States, or members of the BJP who wanted to oppose its rival, the Congress.[49]

What advocates of the Hyper-Nationalist argument find particularly galling is what they regard as India's propensity to limit its own military capabilities. India can only rely on its own power to make its way in the world. This requires military power and in their judgment, India devotes insufficient attention to enhancing its military potential in many ways, including by not spending enough.[50] Again, such views are also held by others, including some Standard Nationalists and Liberal Globalists. Indeed, even government ministers routinely state that Indian military spending, which is proportionately only about half that of China and Pakistan, needs to be increased. What sets Hyper-Nationalists apart is that they advocate much greater military spending and greater need for military power than others. They usually cite other countries, including China, as an example because China has not allowed economic development requirements to stand in the way of its military spending. Such opinions do find some resonance among Indian military officers, especially retired officers, although this is usually justified in terms of the need to either match the spending of India's adversaries or to deter war.[51] However, one caveat needs to be mentioned. Although we have argued there is no "war party" within the spectrum of foreign policy opinions in India, there have occasionally been calls for India to respond to Pakistan-sponsored terrorism with force, including with cross-border military strikes.[52]

Hyper-Nationalists are strong critics of the moderation in Indian nuclear policy. They oppose both the No First Use (NFU) principle as well as the minimum deterrent force posture, both of which, they think, are exhibitions of India's traditional moralism and reluctance to exploit its full military potential.[53] Although there is no agreement among them about the right size of the nuclear arsenal, they are of the opinion that it should be in the hundreds rather than in the dozens, and that at the very least it should match the size and capabilities of the Chinese nuclear arsenal and include thermonuclear weapons.[54] They oppose India's voluntary nuclear test moratorium and strongly oppose any move to sign any international treaty that might limit India's nuclear arsenal before it reaches its full potential.[55] They would have India develop its nuclear forces, especially long-range delivery capabilities, much faster than has been the case, although they are not alone in the criticism of India's rather relaxed progress on these capabilities.

They are also opposed to any treaty or agreement that does not grant India the same rights and privileges as the most powerful actors in the global system. Thus, they also oppose international arms control measures such as the CTBT and the NPT and are likely to oppose the FMCT if serious negotiations for such a treaty were to begin.[56] Hyper-Nationalism tends to boil down to just being in favor of much greater military power for India. This is a critical distinguishing trait from Great Power Realists in the Indian arena, who have a more nuanced understanding of realism. Hyper-Nationalists tend to justify their views with selective use of realist theory and a narrow evocation of the Indian equivalent of Machiavelli—Kautilya (who actually preceded Machiavelli by 1800 years).[57] The Hyper-Nationalist viewpoint at times comes close to conflating India's greatness with legacies of ancient Hindu kingdoms, and the need to reclaim that "glorious" past.

It is unclear what Hyper-Nationalist views mean in terms of India's power projection. Although they support stronger military forces and more assertive military policy, it is unclear what these general sentiments translate into in terms of specific policies. One area where India might be able to project power would be in the seas because of India's easy access and the availability of chokepoints to constrain other powers. Indeed, there are some alarmist warnings from the Hyper-Nationalists about China's "string of pearls" strategy in the Indian Ocean to encircle India in its own backyard. But there have not been very active calls for India to adopt a very assertive position in the Indian Ocean, yet.

Who are the Hyper-Nationalists? Although there might be a larger community of support for such views even within the government, these opinions are as yet confined to a set of independent analysts and former civil and military service officers. Their influence on policy making is unclear, but shades of such views appear much more widespread, even within the government. In the rather murky blogosphere of the Hindu right wing, figures from the Hyper-Nationalist school tend to be portrayed as the true defenders of Indian nationalism and pride.[58] While factions in the BJP may sympathize with this school of thought privately, during their one term in power (1998–2004), they kept such preferences in check when it came to policy making. Where Hyper-Nationalist views lack purchase is among the key political (and even bureaucratic) decision makers, who tend to be far more cautious.

Great Power Realists

The Great Power Realist school in India began emerging after the end of the Cold War, but became more prominent after the nuclear tests in 1998. In the earlier period, Indian strategic discourse studiously avoided the language of Realism, although Indian foreign policy showed some level of competency in practicing realism as noted earlier. This perspective is gaining increasing traction as India's rapid rate of economic growth propels it into the major power category. Despite India's low per capita income (China's per capita is two and half times that of India, for example), the aggregate Indian economy amounts to an important global presence. India is projected to become the third largest economy (in purchasing power parity terms) by 2030, following only the United States and China and displacing Japan to fourth place. For Great Power Realists, it is not a question of *whether* India will achieve major power status, but *when*.

As noted, Great Power Realists have a broader understanding of power and the use of diplomacy drawing from realist theory than the Hyper-Nationalists.[59] In this sense, they are closest to the Standard-Nationalists, although they have more global scope to the Standard-Nationalists's national and regional scope. They believe in the comprehensive development of India's economic and military power, although they are likely to emphasize the utility of military capabilities.[60] Thus, they dismiss foreign policy concerns based on moral grounds alone.[61] For Great Power Realists, the focus of Indian foreign policy should be managing relations with the major powers in the international system. The goal of Great Power Realists for India is to join their ranks as another major power, although some, such as C. Raja Mohan, also point out that India cannot do that unless it resolves its differences with Pakistan.[62] Like the Hyper-Nationalists, this school sees the biggest obstacle to India reaching major power status as India's own lack of purposefulness in strategy and its continuing reluctance to exercise power.[63] They bemoan this state of affairs because the international community's receptiveness to Indian rise provides the country a unique opportunity. This stands in stark contrast to Hyper-Nationalists who view the international system with great suspicion.

Great Power Realists argue for greater involvement and integration into the international system. Autarky will leave India isolated, not make it stronger. They would argue that even the long-held concept of strategic *autonomy* needs to yield to the concept of *responsibility*.[64] This is the biggest break from past Indian strategic thinking, and those transformed include some of India's best-known and most influential analysts like K. Subrahmanyam. These same sovereignty hawks of earlier period have changed their attitudes to a remarkable extent, and are now willing, for example, to trade off sovereignty to gain power in multilateral institutions. Indeed, strategists like Subrahmanyam have argued that India's nonalignment was really a strategy.[65] For Great Power Realists, India can protect its position better by becoming more engaged abroad and no longer relying solely on the autonomy argument to keep the country safe from outside influence.[66]

Great Power Realists believe that at this historic juncture, India's best bet is to partner with the United States, especially because both India and the United States share common interests in containing China.[67] As Realists, they understand that there are no permanent friends or enemies, and they, too, like every other foreign policy school in India (for different reasons), are averse to forming exclusive alliances with other powers.[68] They recognize the United States as the single most important state in the system and the only one willing and able to provide support that is aligned with India's interests—America's military action against terrorism in Afghanistan is seen as one of the most important contributions to Indian security. Whether it is to gain acceptance as a nuclear weapons power or secure a seat in the Security Council of the United Nations (two key objectives of this school), Great Power Realists see no option but to cooperate closely with the United States.

Great Power Realists' stand on the need for diversified power capabilities puts them at the forefront of those who hold a strong view about economics not just for the sake of economic power, but in the service of global power projection. This group would call for the development of more refined economic statecraft, basically leveraging India's economic strength for political goals. In this view, China is seen as the archetype, and Indian decision makers are called upon to adopt a steep learning curve from Chinese behavior. Such a view is found mostly among strategic thinkers rather than industry leaders or economic planners. If such a view exists within the government or economic class, it is hard to decipher. In terms of state behavior, it is difficult to see cases in which such a posture was effectively utilized—for example, was India able to leverage any foreign-policy advantages by the large-scale purchase of fifty aircraft from Boeing over Airbus for its state-owned airlines in 2005? Will India be able to gain any quid pro quo with the ongoing international bid to buy multi-combat fighter jets valued at $10 billion—the biggest aircraft sale globally in decades? The detractors of this approach such as the Neo-Nationalists and the Liberal Globalists would argue that India is no China, and that such a strategy would unnecessarily antagonize important international players without a credible economic "threat."

In terms of strategies, those who see economic power inevitably leading to global power would recommend fast track multilateralism; taking decisions that would land India at the international "high table" (e.g., voting against Iran at the International Atomic Energy Agency despite the importance of Iran to India's energy needs); showing a willingness to sacrifice domestic interests for international policy in terms of making trade-offs; and cultivating less developed countries through economic aid.

The idea of using foreign aid to gain traction and influence in other less developed countries seems to be catching on and is being promoted by foreign policy analysts and government policy makers encompassing Standard Nationalists, Great Power Realists, and even some Liberal Globalists. Neo-Nationalists argue that India's focus should be on internal development and that the notion of becoming a donor country is misguided and unaffordable. In 2003, India launched the Indian Development Initiative, a mechanism to intensify developmental collaboration with countries of the global South. At the same time, the current finance minister, Jaswant Singh, announced that India was suspending acceptance of bilateral development aid from twenty-two donor countries.[69] India's own aid programs, estimated around $300 million annually, are focused regionally on South Asia and Africa. There is clearly a strategic aspect to the aid: India's aid engagement is large in Nigeria, which happens to be India's largest African trading partner; it is also an important energy partner. Sudan receives substantial assistance, and is the most significant target country for Indian foreign investment in Africa. In 2005, the Indian government pledged $10 million in subsidies and $10 million in loans at the same time that the ONGC Videsh (India's national oil and gas agency) entered firmly into the Sudanese market.

Closer to home, Indian aid to Afghanistan is turning out to be an unexpected model of success. India has also found new ways to transfer aid via the South Asian Association for Regional Cooperation (SAARC) to circumvent the sensitivities of neighbors to direct bilateral assistance. The modalities of a new SAARC aid mechanism (mostly funded by India) are still being worked out; meanwhile, India is allowing bilateral aid flows under the SAARC umbrella, thus protecting the recipient's public image. This reveals a newfound willingness by India to accommodate sensitivities of neighboring countries in the interest of promoting longer term goals in the region.[70]

Great Power Realists are a growing minority in India, finding common cause with Hyper-Nationalists against the Indian tendency to take a relaxed view of security, but aligning with Standard Nationalists on the need for balanced growth in economics and military, and all three agreeing on the need for security sector reforms. India's postcolonial foreign policy and security institutions have not kept pace with India's changing status, and these groups call for changes in intelligence and defense, foreign office and the armed forces. Although India's armed forces are depoliticized, there are a number of key retired military brass who fall into the Great Power Realist category.[71]

The Indian navy is emerging as a particularly important tool for pursuing great power aspirations: it can provide an effective power projection platform, without being perceived as offensive as land-based weapons or airpower. Under BJP rule, the navy apparently toyed with the idea of revising the Nehru-era defensive doctrine that focused on coastal protection.[72] Jaswant Singh, defense minister at that time, was said to be an enthusiastic backer. The navy's new maritime doctrine outlining the need for a credible minimum nuclear deterrence and pursuit of littoral warfare to ensure the navy's dominance in the Indian Ocean was unveiled by then Chief of Naval Staff, Madhvendra Singh, one month before the Congress-led government came to power in 2004. The navy could point to its increasing rescue and disaster relief missions and antipiracy operations in the Indian Ocean since 2008 as an impetus for change, but the political leadership is unlikely to move in a significantly new direction in the near future. Given India's clear political control over the military, the navy will have little recourse but to wait.[73]

Liberal Globalists

The Liberal Globalist is the third main category of power perspectives and as with all but the Standard-Nationalist, it represents a post–Cold War evolution. It is a breakaway category from the Standard Nationalist perspective and the differences between them remain somewhat slim. Liberal Globalists are increasing in numbers but are also butting heads with Neo-Nationalists who have a greater political presence across India's political parties, nationally and regionally. Liberal Globalists stand in greatest opposition to the Hyper-Nationalists whose autarkic orientations the Globalists believe will kill the golden goose of Indian economic globalization.

The key difference between the Liberal Globalists and the other perspectives is that Liberal Globalists pay far less attention to military power than the others, and to ideology or moralism in foreign policy. Liberal Globalists see diplomacy and trade as playing a much greater role in international politics, particularly between India and its various neighbors. Commercial ties and diplomacy are seen as helping to ameliorate conflict between India and its neighbors, particularly Pakistan and China. Unlike the Chinese perspective on liberal international order, which emphasizes both trade and international institution building as a way to reduce potential conflicts, the Indian variant does not involve institution building probably because India's natural disadvantages as an international institutional builder, given its turbulent domestic politics.

For the Liberal Globalists, India's newfound international prominence is the result of its economic growth rather than military prowess, although they do not dismiss military power entirely. Rather, much more so than the other two perspectives, Liberal Globalists see military force as primarily needed for defensive purposes rather than seeing military power as a means for India to expand its global profile. For this group, India's primary means to expand its influence is through innovative and bold diplomatic engagement and trade. Advocates tend to share the Standard Nationalist view that military force, especially nuclear force, are largely political instruments and thus support notions of minimum deterrence and NFU. None of this means that Liberal Globalists do not support Indian military power; indeed they do. The difference between them and the Standard Nationalists is in terms of the degree rather than the kind of emphasis.

A major difference between this group's perspective and the Standard Nationalist and Neo-Nationalist perspective is in terms of what might be called the traditional moral foundations of foreign policy. Liberal Globalists rarely use moral arguments for policy, preferring interest-based arguments. Somewhat similar to the Hyper-Nationalists, they are dismissive of such arguments, but unlike Hyper-Nationalists, they are much more supportive of the changed orientation in post–Cold War Indian policy, especially the closer relations with Washington, seeing in that reorientation a much-needed shift toward pragmatism. But like the other perspectives, at least for tactical reasons, they are unlikely to support greater Indian involvement in the nuclear nonproliferation regime.

In this framework, economics is the leading edge of India's global rise. India's biggest asset to support the county's major power aspiration is clearly seen as economics—specifically by becoming a developed country. This would describe the current view of India's national decision makers, led by the prime minister. India's global influence is viewed as flowing primarily from its economic success. Unlike strategic discourse in India, there is little effort to hide the pride, confidence, or ambition to become an economic superpower. But there is nothing in India like the Chinese government's approach to economic primacy: in 1999, the Chinese government adopted an explicit "go global" policy, with the goal of getting thirty to fifty Chinese firms on *Fortune*'s Global 500 list. The Chinese government then proceeded to steer funds to these selected companies through state-owned banks.[74]

The idea of India as a global economic power can easily find roots in Nehru's thinking, which was fundamentally one that saw economics making India world-class, and enabling India to protect its autonomy. Nehru's orientation was arguably first and foremost global—his preoccupation with international affairs and India's global role is legendary. According to Nehru, "Ultimately, foreign policy is the outcome of economic policy, and until India properly evolved her economic policy, her foreign policy will be rather vague, rather inchoate and will be groping."[75] Thus the idea that current-day economics is post-Nehruvian is true in the specifics, but, it can be argued, not in the spirit. As Om Prakash Bhatt, the State Bank of India chairman who turned the stodgy bank around, describes his goal for the bank's globalization, "I want us to be where we can serve India Inc., whether it's through acquiring resources, technology, products, or skills. We don't need to build a footprint in the world just to be global; I want us to be able to serve our primary clientele—India and Indians. So wherever I go, I keep this in mind. How does it strengthen our ability to serve India?"[76] What seems to have brought around economic policy makers and major industrial actors steeped in the inward-looking approach is the realization that India could be a net gainer through globalization.

Thus, Indian perception is changing. Because the Indian economy is becoming highly reliant on foreign markets for its survival and growth, foreign policies toward Indian exports matter more. India's growth in its exports of goods, services, and people create a big stake for India in sustaining open markets globally. Multilateralism is being seen as an important means for India's economic management, especially in dealing with major powers. The rise of the G-20 means that India is recognized as a global player. Although India does not have veto power like China, it is being seen as belonging to the world's steering committee. As one expert puts it, "India has been invited to the party...[so] it cannot be a party-spoiler."[77]

Indeed, the confidence that is exuded by Indian entrepreneurs is striking when compared with the apprehension of the 1980s and 1990s as to how Indian companies—public and private—would weather global competition. A case in point is the remaking of the State Bank of India in the midst of intense rivalry with Indian private and foreign banks subsequent to liberalization in the early 1990s. Known for its legacy of being state-owned with no competitive spirit, SBI under new management and the liberalized environment, managed to turn itself around. Between 2006 and 2009, SBI went from being fourteenth in terms of market cap, to the country's fifth, and joined the Fortune Global 500. Indeed, in 2007, SBI was rated the best bank in terms of customer service, brand loyalty, and branch strength in India. Showing its global ambition, the Bank aims to have at least 25 percent of its balance in international business in the future, compared to 10 percent today.[78]

India's economic success has also led to the notion of an "Indian Brand"— a positive image and positive externality that buys more international recognition and influence than can be measured by the number of international transactions. The lavish 2006 "India Everywhere" campaign at the World Economic Forum at Davos masterminded by the Confederation of Indian Industries (CII), government ministries, and the Indian Brand Equity Foundation (a government-CII partnership), marked a turning point. For the Liberal Globalists, this is a huge spillover benefit that needs to be capitalized on. Like the Great Power Realists, a major assumption of the Liberal Globalists is that for India to keep on the path to developed country status, India's interests are best served by cultivating primary relationship with the United States, preferably without prejudice to other countries. In case of having to make trade-offs such as over the proposed Iran–Pakistan–India gas pipeline, the tendency would be to accommodate United States preferences, although there is some tension on this.

Leftists

The Leftist perspective is identified primarily with India's two major communist parties, the Communist Party of India (CPI) and the Communist Party of India-Marxist (CPM), as well as with Left-leaning newspapers such as *The Hindu*. The Left opinion has traditionally not been very important in Indian foreign policy calculus. Indeed, previous attempts at categorizing Indian foreign policy perspectives have not considered the Leftists.[79] However, the Left did become prominent because they led the effort against the United States–India nuclear deal, and have been very vocal in opposing new trends in Indian foreign policy including India's closer relations with Israel. Part of their importance came because they performed remarkably well in the 2004 national elections and partnered with the Congress-led United Progress Alliance (UPA), which formed the government. But their clout has declined after their failed gamble to pull the UPA government down in 2008; in the national parliamentary elections in 2009, their parliamentary strength dropped to about half of what it was in the previous parliament. The Leftists, understandably, take a strongly ideological position on foreign policy, opposing closer ties with the United States almost as a matter of principle. They have generally opposed greater role for multinational corporations in the Indian economy and efforts to liberalize Indian economy and its integration with the global economy,[80] oppose India's nuclear program,[81] but have argued in support of "Iran's principled position" on the nuclear issue.[82] Although their influence on policy was fairly brief, they nonetheless represent one extreme in Indian foreign policy perspective.

OVERVIEW AND POLICY IMPLICATIONS

The following tables capture the implications for particular viewpoints for specific Indian policy. Table 3.2 lays out some of the key policy issues facing India in the contemporary period and what the policy preferences are from the different schools of thought. Table 3.3 focuses on the most salient issues in India's relations with the United States and likely responses.

An examination of these different perspectives suggests, as we indicated at the beginning, that the variations between them are not as great as might seem, although there are some significant differences, especially between the Hyper-Nationalists and the others. But there are also significant areas of commonality. If these perspectives reveal some ambiguity about what kind of great power India wants to be, it is partly because of the military gap that was mentioned earlier, and partly because of India's historical proclivities and domestic pluralism that has demanded accommodating competing and even contradictory tendencies.[83]

Below we first outline three policy areas where there are continuing differences between these different perspectives. Subsequently, we also outline briefly areas where there is broad agreement between these perspectives, hence, where current Indian policies should not be expected to change.

Areas of Clashing Perspectives

Relations with the United States

The key dispute between these perspectives relates to India's US policy. Indeed, it is difficult not to suspect that all the other differences in perspectives are subsumed under this key issue: in other words, each of these perspectives appears to define its position on other issues on the basis of where it *thinks* the United States stands on each issue. This is most clearly visible in issues like Iran, where Indian analysts have seen India's position as a "litmus test" of whether India is following an independent foreign policy, defined as independent of American interests.[84] But it applies also to other areas of policy. For example, Indian military exercises with the United States have been opposed by Leftists, leading the Indian government to deny any intention of creating a military bloc with the United States.[85]

The most serious opposition to closer United States–India relations comes, understandably, from the Leftists, but there is also significant opposition from both Neo-Nationalists and Hyper-Nationalists. Neo-Nationalists, like the Left, oppose closer ties with the United States on ideological grounds.[86] For Hyper-Nationalists, the United States is seen as

Table 3.2: *Major Policy Issues and Responses by Perspective*

	NATIONALISTS			GREAT POWER REALISTS	LIBERAL GLOBALISTS	LEFTISTS
	STANDARD NATIONALISTS	NEO-NATIONALISTS	HYPER-NATIONALISTS			
Military Power	Need more	Adequate	Much more	Need More	Adequate	Need Less
Use of Force	Oppose	Oppose	Support	May Support	Oppose	Oppose
Nuclear Weapons	Adequate	Adequate	Much Larger Arsenal	Larger Arsenal	Adequate	Oppose
US Nuclear Deal	Supported/Mixed	Opposed	Opposed	Supported	Supported	Opposed
Strategic Ties/ Alliances	Possible	Suspicious	Dangerous	Possible	Necessary	Oppose
Globalization	Costs & Benefits	High Costs	High Costs	Costs & Benefits	Benefits	Oppose
United States Relations	Support/Mixed	Suspicious	Suspicious	Support	Support	Oppose
China Relations	Suspicious	Seek Rapprochement	Suspicious	Suspicious	Seek rapprochement	Strong Support
Iran Relations	Mixed	Favorable	Favorable	Mixed	Mixed	Very Favorable
Pakistan Relations	Suspicious; reluctance to compromise	Rapprochement; sentimentalists; for compromise	Military response; no compromises	Resolve to facilitate global role for India	Peace through dialogue, trade; for compromise	Favor peace even with big compromise

Table 3.3: *Current Issues with Policy Impact on United States–India Relations*

	NATIONALISTS			GREAT POWER REALISTS	LIBERAL GLOBALISTS	LEFTISTS
	STANDARD NATIONALISTS	NEO-NATIONALISTS	HYPER-NATIONALISTS			
Nuclear Liability Bill	Mixed on compromise	No compromise	No compromise	May compromise	Compromise	Oppose
Afghanistan	Rely on United States but fears uncertainty	United States is unreliable; More Indian economic activism	More military and political activism	More political, military, and economic activism	Rely on United States	Oppose United States intervention
China	Tend to oppose	Rapprochement	Oppose	Tend to oppose	Rapprochement	Want closer ties
Iran	Dual stance	Keep ties	Keep ties	Dual stance	Dual stance	Want closer ties
Pakistan	Deep frustration with United States reliance on Pakistan military	Against United States support for Pakistan military over civilians	Deep suspicion of United States support for Pakistan	Some frustration with United States but may entertain role for conflict resolution	May favor role for United States for sake of economic stability in area	Against any United States role in South Asia

a constraint on Indian power, which seeks to direct Indian foreign policy toward US rather than Indian interests.[87] Support for closer, working relationship between the United States and India come mostly from Great Power Realists and Liberal Globalists. The former, more pragmatic in foreign policy orientation, see closer ties with the United States as necessary for India's rise.[88] The latter, more interested in economic liberalization and trade for growth and dismissive of the ideological concerns of both the left and the right, also see partnership with the United States as necessary for India's economic development.[89]

Figure 3.2 is another rendition of the different schools of thought on relations with the United States, as well as their propensity for political and economic means of foreign policy versus military instruments.

We see little likelihood that the dispute over partnering with the United States will end any time soon. But it should be noted that whatever the differences in the public debate, Indian governments since the end of the Cold War have consistently sought closer relations with the United States. Private assurances by senior BJP leaders to the US ambassador that their public

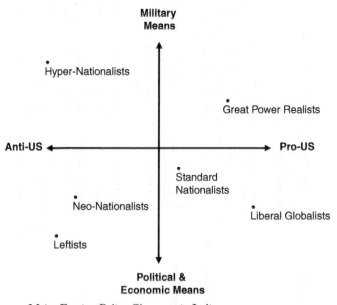

Figure 3.2: Major Foreign Policy Cleavages in India

rhetoric against United States–India nuclear deal was only political rhetoric suggest that this trend will continue.[90] At the same time, as Figure 3.2 shows, no group apart from the Great Power Realists seems inclined toward any serious military partnership with the United States. Thus, the notion of India being amenable to any form of military "burden sharing" internationally in a United States–led effort does not appear on the horizon.

Arms Control Policy

Another area of significant difference between these perspectives is on India's arms control policy. Although India's opposition to the NPT remains relatively firm (although some Indian analysts are now willing to consider joining the NPT if India can join as a NWS),[91] there have been disputes about Indian policy on other treaties such as the CTBT and the FMCT. India's nuclear control policy traditionally had two legs: it advocated abolishing nuclear weapons, a position that has continued even after India became overtly nuclear; and India refused to accept any arms control treaty that did not have equal obligations on all parties. India saw nuclear nonproliferation as simply an excuse for putting off nuclear abolition, a position that put a convenient moral shine on its opposition to countenance any compromise with the NPT. In any case, this led to opposition to all other half-measures such as the CTBT. But since 1998, both the BJP-led government and the subsequent Congress-led government have periodically floated trial balloons to gauge the public mood on signing the CTBT, without much success. Neo-Nationalists and Hyper-Nationalists have generally opposed any compromise, the former because of their commitment to India's traditional nuclear disarmament agenda[92] and the latter because they see most arms control treaties as constraining India.[93] However, Standard Nationalists, Great Power Realists, and Liberal Globalists are more likely to suggest that India should at least be more open-minded in considering arms control measures, mainly because they would prefer that India move toward the "managerial" side of global governance rather than stay on the "trade union" corner. As in other areas, the Leftists are the outliers, both opposing Indian nuclear program, but also opposing many international arms control initiatives such as the NPT and CTBT because they are not tied to a plan for comprehensive nuclear disarmament.[94] This debate is likely to become more intense if the CD begins negotiations over the FMCT, although there is little prospect of such development in the immediate future.

Iran and Third World Solidarity

Although India remains a member in good standing in the NAM, and while its NAM rhetoric has not entirely ended, this issue has been largely sidelined in Indian foreign policy. There is greater focus on specific coalitions that include other regional powers, many of them from the third world. Such coalitions include BRIC (Brazil, Russia, India, China), BASIC (Brazil, South Africa, India, China), and IBSA (India, Brazil, South Africa). Nevertheless, some traditional third world policy issues on which India has modified its position, such as on Palestine and Israel, remain controversial in India, with the Left as well as Neo-Nationalists strongly opposing such policy changes.[95] India's policy toward Iran has become the new issue of controversy, with the Left and the Neo-Nationalists in particular, keeping close tabs on any diversion from what is viewed as India's traditional policy of friendship with Iran.[96] The Standard Nationalists, as well as the Great Power Realists and Liberal Globalists, are less concerned about Iran, some seeing Iran as complicit in Pakistan's nuclear weapons and strategic programs.[97] Indian foreign policy has tried to split the difference, arguing that Iran has an obligation to live up to its treaty commitments, but not explicitly suggesting that Iran is pursuing a nuclear weapons program. This issue is likely to continue to confound Indian decision makers, and the shrillness of the Left in particular is likely to make the government cautious about routinely associating itself with US-backed initiatives on Iran.

Areas of Agreement

There are also many areas where the differences between these perspectives are not easily discernible. These are issues where we judge that current Indian policy is likely to continue. For example, on policies toward three of India's key neighbors—China, Pakistan, and Myanmar—the differences between these perspectives are not very great. To the extent that there are differences, these differences are at the extremes: both the Left (including also some sections of the Neo-Nationalists) and the Hyper-Nationalists are sufficiently far outside the mainstream that even though they have different perspectives, they are unlikely to matter. On China, for example, Left opinion makers would suggest closer relations and partnership with China rather than the United States,[98] while Hyper-Nationalists would suggest a much more confrontational posture with regard to China.[99] Nevertheless, the broad middle, which includes Standard Nationalists, some Neo-Nationalists, Great Power Realists, and Liberal Globalists, all broadly agree that India should expend effort on developing closer ties with China although all are also wary of China and its policies toward India. Similarly on Pakistan, between the sentimentalism of the Neo-Nationalists and the hard-line recommendations of the Hyper-Nationalists, the broad middle supports cautious policies that will seek a resolution with Pakistan, while also being on guard against any Pakistani adventurism. A third area of agreement is on Myanmar and democracy promotion. Western interests in democracy promotion have almost no takers in India and no support within any of the perspectives, all of whom see Western appeals as hypocritical given the long association that Western powers have had with many unsavory dictators around the world. On each of these issues, though, there is greater agreement than difference among the various perspectives, which suggests some stability in Indian policy.

CONCLUSION

India's traditional Nationalist consensus embodied by the Neo-Nationalist school has not only declined and splintered; it faces competition from new worldviews. The greatest challenge comes from Hyper-Nationalists and Great Power Realists, both a creation of the post-1998 environment following India's nuclear tests. The latter groups pose a challenge in terms of India's foreign policy goals, means, and scope, calling for a buildup and sharpening of the country's military means, shifting its goals to achieve major power status, and showing a willingness to be more proactive in the global arena. At the same time, these two challengers do not see eye to eye on the emphasis placed on military means, nor do they agree on whether to engage with other major powers or go it alone as India plays a greater international role. These are important distinctions that prevent them from coalescing, ceding the greatest political space to Standard Nationalists.

In India's diverse and active democracy, it is not surprising that dominant opinion hews to an ambiguous middle ground, providing a continuing basis for Standard Nationalists to retain power. The base for all other groups is too narrow, particularly for the tiny Hyper-Nationalists and the small, but growing Great Power Realists. Liberal Globalists are proving to have excellent traction, in large part due to the Standard Nationalists shifting to market-driven economics since the mid-1990s, and relative economic gains under the new model. On global policy, India is likely to keep moving toward multilateral approaches, but given that alliances and use of force are perceived as near taboos across the board, Indian activism on the global stage is going to be much less than what other major powers, especially the United States, might expect from India.

Notes

1 · Barry Posen, *The Sources of Military Doctrine: France, Britain and Germany between the World Wars* (Ithaca, NY: Cornell University Press, 1984), 13.

2 · This characterization is from Daniel Markey, "Developing India's Foreign Policy Software," *Asia Policy*, 8 (July 2009), 73–96 (76–79).

3 · Interviews with current and former NSAB members, March 2011, New Delhi.

4 · C. Raja Mohan, *Impossible Allies: Nuclear India, United States and the Global Order* (New Delhi: India Research Press, 2006), 18–19.

5 · Somini Sengupta, "India Leader Struggles to Complete Nuclear Deal," *New York Times*, July 1, 2008.

6 · Sameer Surykant Patil, "India and the FMCT: Issues and Concerns," *CBRN South Asia Brief* (New Delhi: Institute of Peace and Conflict Studies, 2008).

7 · Indrani Bagchi, "Tharoor Plans to Revive MEA's Policy Planning," *Times of India*, September 21, 2009. Foreign policy in the MEA has been driven by territorial divisions, but as India's foreign policy begins to straddle several territorial divisions (e.g., Indian Ocean, climate change), institutional changes are needed. Tharoor, who has left the government, had held up the example of IORARC, a grouping that should have showcased India's interests in the Indian Ocean Rim but was basically allowed to lapse.

8 · On the differences within the Indian establishment on the United States–India nuclear deal, see Rajiv Sikri, "Nuclear Deal: The Road Ahead for India," *Rediff.com*, December 21, 2006, www.rediff.com/news/2006/dec/21sikri.htm. Rajiv Sikri, a career diplomat, resigned from the IFS in 2006. On the various controversies about the CDS issue, see Saurabh Joshi, "The Opposition to a CDS," *StratPost*, July 4, 2009, www.stratpost.com/the-opposition-to-a-cds.

9 · Someone perceived as having the confidence of Congress Party president Sonia Gandhi, for example, is likely to have an extra measure of influence in the current government and have his or her views heard.

10 · This case was best made by George Tanham. See George Tanham, *Indian Strategic Thought: An Interpretive Essay* (Santa Monica, CA: RAND, 1992). See also Chris Smith, *India's Ad Hoc Arsenal: Direction or Drift in Defence Policy* (New York: Oxford University Press, 1994); and Stephen P. Cohen and Sunil Dasgupta, *Arming without Aiming: India's Military Modernization* (New Delhi: Viking, 2010).

11 · The best case is made by C. Raja Mohan, *Crossing the Rubicon: The Shaping of India's New Foreign Policy* (New Delhi: Viking, 2003).

12 · Shekhar Gupta, "'Obama Does Not Have Much of an Option but to Make India Its Leading Partner' (Interview with K. Subrahmanyam)," *Indian Express*, October 26, 2010, www.expressindia.com/latest-news/Obama-does-not-have-much-of-an-option-but-to-make-India-its-leading-partner/702549/.

13 · Deepa Ollapally and Rajesh Rajagopalan, "The Pragmatic Challenge to Indian Foreign Policy," *Washington Quarterly*, 34, 2 (Spring 2011), 145–62.

14 · C. Raja Mohan, "Nehru's World View: More History and Less Politics Please," *Indian Express*, January 11, 2010, www.indianexpress.com/news/nehrus-world-view-more-history-and-less-politics-please/565669/0.

15 · K. Subrahmanyam, "Arms and the Mahatma: No Place for Pacifism in Security," *Times of India*, May 8, 1997, www.hvk.org/articles/0597/0138.html.

16 · D. Vasudevan, "Tharoor Criticises Nehru's 'Moralistic' Foreign Policy," *DNA: Daily News and Analysis*, January 10, 2010, www.dnaindia.com/india/report_tharoor-criticises-nehru-s-moralistic-foreign-policy_1332933.

17 · Ollapally and Rajagopalan, "The Pragmatic Challenge to Indian Foreign Policy."

18 · C. Raja Mohan, "Balancing Interests and Values: India's Struggle with Democracy Promotion," *Washington Quarterly*, 30, 3 (Summer 2007), http://twq.com/07summer/docs/07summer_mohan.pdf.

19 · Inder Malhotra, "Letters from the Darkest Hour," *Indian Express*, November 17, 2010, www.indianexpress.com/news/letters-from-the-darkest-hour/712359/0; and Inder Malhotra, "JN to JFK: 'Eyes Only,'" *Indian Express*, November 15, 2010, www.indianexpress.com/news/j.n.-to-jfk-eyes-only/711276/.

20 · For a discussion, see Pratap Bhanu Mehta, "Still under Nehru's Shadow? The Absence of Foreign Policy Frameworks in India," *India Review*, 8, 3 (July–September, 2009).

21 · Gideon Rose, "Neoclassical Realism and Theories of Foreign Policy," *World Politics*, 51, 1 (October 1998), 144–72.

22 · For a previous effort at such categorization, see Kanti Bajpai, "Indian Strategic Culture," in Michael R. Chambers, ed., *Asia in 2020: Future Strategic Balances and Alliances* (Carlisle, PA: Strategic Studies Institute, U.S. Army War College, 2002), 245–303; and Amitabh Mattoo, "Inching Closer to a Great Reconciliation," *Times of India*, January 21, 2010.

23 · Though some Indian military services, especially the Indian navy, do seek a larger "blue water" role normally associated with great powers, this is largely driven by bureaucratic and budgetary reasons because the navy is the smallest of the Indian military services. Moreover, there is little indication that such views have any resonance outside the navy. A recent Parliamentary Defence Committee report pointed out that the Indian navy has not yet reached capability targets set as far back as 1964.

24 · Standing Committee on Defence (2009–2010), Fifteenth Lok Sabha, *Ministry of Defence: Demand for Grants (2009–2010): First Report* (New Delhi: Lok Sabha Secretariat, December 2009), 9.

25 · Standing Committee on Defence (2009–2010), Fifteenth Lok Sabha, *Ministry of Defence: Construction of Roads in the Border Areas of the Country* (New Delhi: Lok Sabha Secretariat, August 2010).

26 · www.ipcs.org/pdf_file/news_archive/jul_04_militarynavy.pdf.

27 · N. V. Subramanian, "India Denies 'Cold Start' Plan," *Diplomat*, September 11, 2010, http://the-diplomat.com/indian-decade/2010/09/11/india-denies-cold-start-plan/.

28 · For previous attempts at such taxonomy, see Kanti Bajpai, "Indian Strategic Culture and the Problem of Pakistan," in Swarna Rajagopal, ed., *Security and South Asia: Ideas, Institutions and Initiatives* (New Delhi: Routledge, 2006), and Amitabh Mattoo, "Inching Closer to a Great Reconciliation," *Times of India*, January 21, 2010.

29 · Ollapally and Rajagopalan, "The Pragmatic Challenge to Indian Foreign Policy."

30 · Elsewhere, we have characterized this as the "Nationalist" perspective. See Ollapally and Rajagopalan, "The Pragmatic Challenge to Indian Foreign Policy."

31 · Vikram Sood, "Can You Hear Those Voices of America?" *Vikram Sood's Perspectives*, April 24, 2007, http://soodvikram.blogspot.com/2007/04/can-you-hear-those-voices-of-america.html#links.

32 · Manpreet Sethi, *Nuclear Strategy: India's March Towards Credible Deterrence* (New Delhi: Centre for Air Power Studies/Knowledge World, 2009), especially chapter 4.

33 · Thomas Mathew, "Signs of the Emerging Third Leg: Strengthening India's Triad," *Journal of Defence Studies*, 2, 1 (Summer 2008), 149–60.

34 · Kanwal Sibal, "Different Strokes," Observer Research Foundation, October 9, 2009, www.orfonline.com/cms/sites/orfonline/modules/analysis/AnalysisDetail.html?cmaid=17265&mmacmaid=17266.

35 · G. Parthasarathy, "There Is No Need to Be Defensive Every Time We Test a Missile," Rediff.com, March 7, 2001, www.rediff.com/news/2001/mar/07gp.htm.

36 · Rajiv Dogra, "In America We Trust? Not Very Likely," *Times of India*, March 20, 2011, http://timesofindia.indiatimes.com/home/sunday-toi/all-that-matters/In-America-we-trust-Not-very-likely/articleshow/7746283.cms.

37 · For an example of the former, see V. P. Malik and Gurmeet Kanwal, "Indo-US N-Deal: Overcoming the Last Hurdle," Observer Research Foundation, February 28, 2006, www.orfonline.com/cms/sites/orfonline/modules/analysis/AnalysisDetail.html?cmaid=2312&mmacmaid=257.

38 · "Mani Takes on Government for Rich-Poor Divide," *Times of India*, March 5, 2011, http://articles.timesofindia.indiatimes.com/2011-03-05/india/28658938_1_food-coupons-food-security-bill-social-security.

39 · P. Chidambaram, Peterson Institude, Washington D.C., September 25, 2007.

40 · Planning Commission Estimates, Government of India, Databook for DCH, March 28, 2011, 33–34, www.planningcommission.gov.in. For higher estimates by unofficial sources, see, for example, Oxford Poverty and Human Development Initiative's *Country Briefing: India, Multidimensional Poverty Index at a Glance*, July 2010, http://ophi.qeh.ox.ac.uk.

41 · In January 2010, India signed a Free Trade Agreement with ASEAN after ten years of negotiations, its first with a trade bloc.

42 · "PM Forms Group on Rajiv Plan for N-Arms World," *Outlook*, December 10, 2010, http://news.outlookindia.com/item.aspx?704585.

43 · This eclectic group includes Ramchandra Guha, Arundhati Roy, and Ashis Nandy.

44 · Lieutenant-General Vinay Shankar, "Steering India's Military Capabilities," *Indian Defence Review*, 23, 3 (July–October 2010).

45 · Bharatiya Janata Party, *Manifesto: Lok Sabha Election 2009*, www.bjp.org/index. php?option=com_content&view=article&id=137:manifesto-lok-sabha-election-2009&catid=50:election-manifestos&Itemid=549.

46 · Bharat Karnad, "Nuclear Morality," *Asian Age*, January 20, 2011, www.asianage.com/columnists/nuclear-morality-137.

47 · Brahma Chellaney, "India's Raw Deal with the United States," *International Herald Tribune*, August 8, 2005.

48 · See, for example, Prakash Karat, "Why the CPI(M) and the Left Oppose the Nuclear Deal," *Hindu*, August 20, 2007, www.hindu.com/2007/08/20/stories/2007082058071400. htm.

49 · On the Left's view on the United States–India nuclear deal, see Communist Party of India (Marxist), "Central Committee Resolution on Nuclear Deal," August 23, 2007, http://cpim.org/content/central-committee-resolution-nuclear-deal.

50 · Vinod Anand and Arun Sahgal, "Defence Capability vs. Defence Expenditure," *Vivekananda International Foundation*, March 8, 2011, www.vifindia.org/article/march/8/Defence-Capability-Vs-Defence-Expenditure. Both authors are former senior army officers.

51 · See, for example, Gurmeet Kanwal, "Why India Needs to Spend More on Its Defence," *Rediff.com*, March 22, 2011, www.rediff.com/business/slide-show/slide-show-1-budget-2011-why-india-needs-to-spend-more-on-its-defence/20110322.htm. Brigadier Kanwal, a retired army officer, currently heads the army's think tank in Delhi, the Centre for Land Warfare Studies (CLAWS).

52 · Brigadier Rahul K. Bhonsle (Retd.), "Transnational Terrorism: Challenges and Responses for India," *USI Journal*, 581 (July–September 2010), 338–46; and Gurmeet Kanwal, "Tackling Pakistan," *CLAWS*, December 8, 2008, www.claws.in/index.php?action=master&task=223&u_id=7.

53 · See, for example, "Revise 'No-First-Use' n-policy: Jaswant," *Indian Express*, March 16, 2011, www.indianexpress.com/news/Revise--no-first-use--n-policy--Jaswant/763040/; and Brahma Chellaney, "Nuclear Deterrent Posture," in Brahma Chellaney, ed., *Securing India's Future in the New Millenium* (New Delhi: Orient Longman, 1999).

54 · Bharat Karnad, "A Thermonuclear Deterrent," in Amitabh Mattoo, ed., *India's Nuclear Deterrent: Pokhran II and Beyond* (New Delhi: Har-Anand, 1999), 108–49.

55 · Brahma Chellaney, "The Wages of the Nuclear Deal," *LiveMint.com*, August 15, 2010, www.livemint.com/2010/08/15215312/The-wages-of-the-nuclear-deal.html.

56 · Rajiv Nayan, "India and the Fissile Material Cut-off Treaty: Policy Options," *Strategic Analysis*, 35, 1 (January 2011), 36–51; Bharat Karnad, "Nuclear Morality," *Asian Age*, January 20, 2011, www.asianage.com/columnists/nuclear-morality-137.

57 · For example, Bharat Karnad, *Nuclear Weapons and Indian Security: The Realist Foundations of Strategy* (New Delhi: Macmillan, 2002).

58 · This is not a judgment as to whether Hyper-Nationalists endorse such backing from the bloggers.

59 · See, for example, Harsh V. Pant, "India's Foreign Policy Comes of Age," *Rediff.com*, January 12, 2010, http://news.rediff.com/column/2010/jan/12/indian-foreign-policy-comes-of-age.htm.

60 · C. Raja Mohan, "PM, 'Vijay Diwas,' and the Nuke Sub," *Indian Express*, July 25, 2009, www.indianexpress.com/news/pm-vijay-diwas-and-the-nuke-sub/494012/0.

61 · Indrani Bagchi, "From Moral to Real: India on a Self-Building Path," *Times of India*, January 25, 2010, http://timesofindia.indiatimes.com/india/From-moral-to-real-India-on-a-self-building-path/articleshow/5496675.cms.

62 · C. Raja Mohan, "Jaswant, Jinnah and the South Asian Monroe Doctrine," *Indian Express*, August 16, 2009, www.indianexpress.com/news/jaswant-jinnah-and-the-south-asian-monroe-doctrine/502671/.

63 · Harsh V. Pant, "Tales of a Floundering Foreign Policy," *Business Standard*, July 25, 2010, www.business-standard.com/india/news/harsh-v-pant-talea-floundering-foreign-policy/402368/.

64 · C. Raja Mohan, "Rising India: Partner in Shaping the Global Commons," *Washington Quarterly*, 33, 3 (July 2010), 133–48.

65 · K. Subrahmanyam, "Non-alignment, Anyone?" *Indian Express*, July 6, 2007, www.indianexpress.com/news/nonalignment-anyone/203885/0.

66 · C. Raja Mohan, "Rising India's Great Power Burden," *Asia Report*, 7 (January 2010).

67 · K. Subrahmanyam, "Strategic Climate Change," *Indian Express*, December 28, 2010, www.indianexpress.com/news/strategic-climate-change/730141/0.

68 · Arundhati Ghose, "Enlightened Independence," *Outlook*, February 10, 2006, http://www.outlookindia.com/article.aspx?230143.

69 · New Powers for Global Change? Challenges for the International Development Cooperation: The Case of India, FES Briefing Paper 5, Friedrich Ebert Stiftung, March 2007, 2.

70 · The mechanism to circumvent the bilateral impasse emerged from the External Affairs Ministry in a rare show of innovative thinking. Interview with senior Indian government official, February 2010, Washington, DC.

71 · See, for example, Admiral Raja Menon, "The Importance of India's Strategic Rise in Asia," talk at the Asia Society, Washington, DC, October 7, 2010. See also Raja Menon and Rajiv Kumar, *The Long View from Delhi: To Define the Indian Grand Strategy for Foreign Policy* (New Delhi: Academic Foundation, 2010).

72 · K. P. Nayar (Diplomatic Editor), "Quiet Confidence: It Is Impossible to Be Ambivalent about the Navy Any Longer," *Telegraph*, November 28, 2008.

73 · The Indian navy was recognized by the UN for its antipiracy operations in the Gulf of Aden. As of mid-2010, the navy had escorted 1,000 ships from fifty countries through the Gulf of Aden. *Economic Times*, June 18, 2010.

74 · Ravi Ramamurti, "Made-in-India Multinationals," *India in Transition Series*, Center for the Advanced Study of India, University of Pennsylvania (October 9, 2008), http://casi.ssc.upenn.edu/iit/Ramamurti.

75 · Quoted in Sunila Kale, "Inside Out: India's Global Reorientation," *India Review*, 8, 1 (January–March 2009), 45.

76 · *McKinsey Quarterly*, April 2009.

77 · Arvind Subramanian, *Business Standard*, October 28, 2009.

78 · *McKinsey Quarterly*, April 2009.

79 · Bajpai, "Indian Strategic Culture"; and Mattoo, "Inching Closer to a Great Reconciliation."

80 · "Unjustified Concessions to MNCs," *Communist Party of India (Marxist)*, April 1, 2011, www.cpim.org/content/unjustified-concessions-mncs.

81 · "Stop Jaitapur Project," *Communist Party of India (Marxist)*, March 15, 2011, www.cpim.org/content/stop-jaitapur-project.

82 · "Iran Nuclear Programme: Submitted to the UPA-Left Parties Coordination Committee Meeting on 27 October 2005," *Communist Party of India (Marxist)*,www.cpim.org/node/1387.

83 · See, for example, Priyankar Upadhayaya's "Peace and Conflict: Reflections on Indian Thinking," *Strategic Analysis*, 33, 1 (January 2009), and Navnita Chadha Behera, "Re-Imagining IR in India," *International Relations of the Asia-Pacific*, 7 (2007).

84 · Amit Baruah, "A Test for India's Foreign Policy," *Hindu*, September 1, 2005, www.hindu.com/2005/09/01/stories/2005090105931100.htm.

85 · Sandeep Dikshit, "Japan to Take Part in India-U.S. Naval Exercises Again," *Hindu*, February 16, 2011, www.hindu.com/2011/02/16/stories/2011021665711500.htm.

86 · Paranjoy Guha Thakurta, "Energy Security: Mani Shankar Aiyar Slams UPA for Bowing to US," *Rediff.com*, October 1, 2010, http://business.rediff.com/slide-show/2010/oct/01/slide-show-1-maverick-mani-slams-upa-for-bowing-before-us.htm.

87 · Satish Chandra, "It's a Sellout," *Deccan Herald*, July 23, 2009, www.deccanherald.com/content/15317/its-sellout.html.

88 · Mohan, *Crossing the Rubicon*.

89 · Sanjaya Baru, "Foreign Policy Challenges and Priorities Facing the Next Government," *Center for Advanced Study of India*, March 29, 2009, http://casi.ssc.upenn.edu/iit/baru.

90 · Suresh Nambath, "BJP Says One Thing at Party Meet, Another in Private," *Hindu*, March 19, 2011, www.hindu.com/2011/03/19/stories/2011031965431300.htm.

91 · Rajiv Nayan, "Is NPT Membership as a Nuclear Weapon State an Option for India?" *Strategic Analysis*, 31, 6 (November 2006), 869–87.

92 · Mani Shankar Aiyar, "Towards a Nuclear-Weapons-Free and Non-Violent World Order," n.d., www.gsinstitute.org/pnnd/pubs/AIYAR_RajivGandhi.pdf.

93 · Brahma Chellaney, "Stop Chasing Illusions," *Times of India*, March 11, 2008, http://articles.timesofindia.indiatimes.com/2008-03-11/edit-page/27751486_1_anti-satellite-arms-race-missile.

94 · "CPI(M) Opposed to Signing CTBT Now," *Communist Party of India (Marxist)*, December 22, 1999, www.cpim.org/content/cpim-opposed-signing-ctbt-now.

95 · Ravish Tiwari and D. K. Singh, "Aiyar's Latest Revolt: UPA Depends on Israel, Is Ignoring Palestine Justice," *Indian Express*, September 25, 2010, www.indianexpress.com/news/aiyars-latest-revolt-upa-depends-on-israel-is-ignoring-palestine-justice/687661/0.

96 · Siddharth Varadarajan, "India's Anti-Iran Votes Were Coerced, Says Former U.S. Official," *Hindu*, February 16, 2007, www.hindu.com/2007/02/16/stories/2007021605671200.htm.

97 · C. Christine Fair, "India and Iran: New Delhi's Balancing Act," *Washington Quarterly*, 30, 3 (Summer 2007), 145–59, http://twq.com/07summer/docs/07summer_fair.pdf.

98 · M. K. Bhadrakumar, "Engaging China as a Friendly Neighbour," *Hindu*, April 10, 2008, www.hindu.com/2008/04/10/stories/2008041055661000.htm; and Siddharth Varadarajan, "Asian Interests and the Myth of Balance," *Hindu*, December 13, 2005, http://hindu.com/2005/12/13/stories/2005121301771000.htm.

99 · "Nuclear Crisis with China Cannot Be Ruled Out: Bharat Karnad," *oneindianews*, November 18, 2008, http://news.oneindia.in/2008/11/18/nuclear-crisis-with-china-cannot-be-ruled-out-bharat-karnad-1226991899.html.

4

Iran's Post-Revolution Foreign Policy Puzzle

Farideh Farhi and Saideh Lotfian

Analyzing domestic debates about Iran's foreign policy is difficult. Identifying the stakeholders, pinpointing their institutional affiliations, and understanding how different worldviews interact are elusive. Compounding the task further are shifting stances by participants, overgeneralized and bombastic rhetoric, and lack of institutionalization in a constrained and yet highly contested domestic political environment.

In the past three decades, advocates of certain policies have shifted positions and research institutions have become staffed by individuals with different viewpoints than those whom they have replaced. In some instances, even research centers have changed their institutional affiliations and have been moved from one branch of government to another.[1] Meanwhile some institutes have simply lost their significance or even personnel while others have mushroomed without much transparency about their affiliation or ideological tendencies.

Similar dynamics have been at play in the wider public arena. Even during the periods of high political repression, contending views regarding the scope and means of Iran's foreign policy have not disappeared in newspapers representing various political factions. However, closures of newspapers as well as subtle shifts of ideological positions either because of changed editors or changed views make the delineation of consistent points of view difficult.

Adding to the difficulty of understanding Iran's foreign policy debates, little literature or systematic theoretical work on international relations or foreign policy decision making has been produced inside the country. Unlike in China or the Soviet Union, literature on world politics in post-revolutionary Iran remains mostly descriptive and without articulation of a coherent model to follow. In the words of Mahmoud Sariolghalam, a professor of international relations at Shahid Beheshti University, one of Iran's prominent universities, "in a culture that values interaction far more than written expression, most Iranians heard about ideological interpretations of politics and international issues on state-run television, or at public sermons and Friday prayers."[2] Public pronouncements regarding the establishment of an alternative ideological model rarely go beyond pronouncements and are often mired in conflicting interpretations or undermined by practices of the new Islamic state, which has shown itself as, if not more, interested in survival and political consolidation as in ideational crusades.[3]

Given this situation, the general tendency in trying to understand Iran's foreign policy debates has been to pigeonhole them into preconceived patterns about trends, dynamics, and cycles in postrevolutionary societies. Along these lines, discussions of Iran's foreign policy tend to be dominated by analyses that attempt to understand policy output in terms of conflicts between pragmatists and ideologues located in Iran's various foreign policy–relevant state institutions. Others have emphasized postrevolutionary trends away from revolutionary ideals and toward a state-centered and national interest–based decision-making process for long-range strategic planning.

Ideologues or idealists—who presumably make the spread of Iran's revolution-inspired Islam the objective or preference of Iran's foreign policy—are often represented as expansionist and at war with the world order, while the pragmatists are portrayed as less confrontational in their approach. In identifying the opponents of idealism as pragmatists, a shift is made toward conduct and away from an analysis of objectives. Hence very little is discussed about whether the so-called pragmatists share similar foreign policy objectives or simply disagree in terms of methods of achieving those objectives.[4]

Even more problematic, at least in recent years, has been the direct linkage of pragmatism and ideological thinking to the country's existing domestic political cleavages. The reformists and centrists/moderates—at times identified as pragmatic conservatives—of the Iranian domestic politics are currently said to be pragmatic and open to negotiation with the United States. On the other hand, the hard-line conservative push for some sort of pan-Islamism or pan-Shi'ism and anti-Westernism underwrites their confrontationist foreign policy.

But such classifications are not sufficient for several reasons. First, these linkages do not necessarily hold historically. For instance, some contemporary reformists are former Leftists whose anti-imperialist fervor placed them squarely in the camp of the opponents of the normalized relations with the United States in the 1980s and even most of the 1990s. It is true that the move from being "Leftists" to "Reformists" in the domestic arena also entailed a reconsideration of former foreign policy positions, including a more favorable stance regarding relations with the United States. But given political constraints as well as political divisions among the Reformists, this foreign policy shift has never been fully articulated as a new principled position beyond the need to conduct a less confrontationist foreign policy everywhere.

Second, membership in any given political camp in the country does not necessarily translate into a unified position inside that camp regarding the objectives, scope, and means of foreign policy. Finally, by posing geopolitical concerns against ideological thinking not enough attention is given to the extent to which the ideological shift that occurred in 1979 frames debates regarding Iran's geopolitical predicament.[5]

There is undoubtedly some truth to the dichotomous division of Iran's foreign policy debates in all likelihood necessitated by the stark opposing choices faced by Iran during difficult times. These choices have included whether to continue or end the war with Iraq, whether to engage in critical dialogue with Western interlocutors, whether to cooperate with US forces to overthrow the Taliban regime in Afghanistan, and whether to negotiate over Iran's nuclear program. Indeed, with increased economic pressures on Iran, the bipolarity of public discourse has become accentuated, seemingly dividing the country into hard-line and reformist camps: one focusing on rejection, resistance, and heightened rhetorical challenge as a response to what is identified as Western "soft war" as well as economic war against Iran, and the other promoting dialogue, diplomatic maneuvers, some accommodation with the West, and eventually full integration in global geopolitics.

In this chapter, we will attempt to offer a more differentiated understanding of Iran's foreign policy discourse. We will acknowledge its essential bipolarity but we will also highlight variations based on disagreement on the scope and instruments of foreign policy. But before discussing variations, in the next section, we will argue that there is very little disagreement on Iran's potential significance in the international arena. In the words of Iran's current foreign minister, Ali Akbar Salehi, there is acknowledgment that "Iran has emerged and is rising."[6] Furthermore, we will argue that Iranian nationalism, as specified in the revolutionary emphasis on the idea of national sovereignty in the face of imperialism—identified as "global arrogance" in the country's Islamist discourse—is a shared framework that shapes most positions.

The combination of ideology and geopolitics creates a near consensus on the objective of securing both Iran *and* the Islamic Republic. Significantly, for the purpose of this project, it calls for a foreign policy that enhances Iran's strategic weight and role in the Middle East region while maintaining the country's Islamic identity in the face of resistance by global power wielders. But there are disagreements about the nature of that role and ways Islamic Iran might achieve its objectives.

Finally, we will argue that an overarching question hanging over these disagreements is the reality that the most powerful international player, which has significant presence and interests in the region, has had a long-standing policy of maintaining balance of power and preventing regional supremacy. Furthermore, in the post-September 11, 2001, environment, its policies have largely been in the direction of redefining the region's political-security order with a minimum role for Iran in its own immediate security circle. As a result, the "America question" or what kind of traditional or soft threats the United States poses for Iran's strategic ambitions and how to counter them plays a very large role in Iran's foreign policy discussions.

SHARED REVOLUTIONARY FRAMEWORK: COMBINING IDEOLOGY AND GEOPOLITICS

The nature of the Iranian revolutionary political system provided a new framework for the country's international ambitions and relations. Revolutionary Iran aspired for radical cultural and political independence, economic autarky, diplomatic and ideological mobilization against Zionism, and resistance against US interference in regional and domestic affairs. Furthermore, Islamic Iran rejected the idea that countries should be categorized according to economic or military power. Spiritual and moral sources were presented as sources of national power rather than economic indicators or technological innovation.

In short, at the rhetorical level, the new revolutionary state envisioned its initiatives as global in scope, ideational in means, and civilizational in objective. Inevitably, the Islamic Republic felt destined to change what was perceived to be an overbearingly hierarchical world order and this was not merely an abstract self-perception. It was formalized in the Iranian Constitution, which declares that the aim of the revolution is to bring about the victory of the downtrodden against arrogant powers.[7]

Yet two basic tensions that underwrite almost all foreign policy outlooks in the country complicate this vision. The first tension combines outright rejection or suspicion of the current international order and institutions with the expressed desire to improve Iran's position within the same order. The second tension combines the country's sense of importance as a regional or even global actor with a conflicting impulse that emphasizes the country's insecurities and strategic loneliness.

These tensions make Iran more of a "conflicted aspiring power" than a rising power. Some of these conflicted yearnings can be explained by Iran's recent history. Throughout the twentieth century and more so since the 1979 Revolution, Iran has not been a "comfortable" state as its legitimacy and even survival have continuously been challenged by domestic forces seeking an end to arbitrary rule, and external players perceived to have alternatively had Iran's containment, isolation, or at times destabilization and disintegration on their agenda. This lack of comfort has kept the general nationalistic emphasis on political sovereignty, military preparedness, Persian identity, and now Islamic identity.

Along with reaction to the shah's dictatorship, the Iranian Revolution was the historical outcome of defiance against foreign influence in Iran. Some revolutionaries saw the shah's relationship with the United States as a threat to national sovereignty and dignity, while others bemoaned the impact of Western consumerist values and commodities for the indigenous culture, religious values, and political integrity of the country.

The mind-set of the Iranian revolutionary leadership—which initially included Islamists, Marxists, and liberals—was more or less anti-imperialist and anti-Western. The Cultural Revolution that took place between 1981 and 1984, when the universities were forced to shut down, eventually marginalized the liberal and Marxist ideologies. The Islamist discourse then emerged as the only publicly allowed mode of nationalist expression. The Iran–Iraq war further provided the justification for this dominance in the name of national sacrifice and security.[8]

The official discourse in the 1980s was that Iran was defying the bipolar global system dominated by the consumerism and imperialism of the West and materialism of the East, and it was creating a new institutional order based on egalitarianism and religion-based ethics. It was claimed that it was only a matter of time and people's unity before such objectives were achieved. The divisive international system and its foundations were to be challenged and eventually reshaped by Muslims and those striving for cultural authenticity, justice, and salvation.

The revolutionary–internationalist ethos of the Iranian Revolution led activists and intellectuals to demand redefinition of the country's identity and redirection of relations with the whole world. In order to legitimize the monarchy, the Pahlavi state emphasized the ancient, pre-Islamic Persian heritage of Iran. It embedded the Iranian national self in a romantic discourse about the superior "Aryan" nation" linked to Indo-European roots and distinguished from the Arab-Semitic other.[9]

The revolutionaries, on the other hand, self-consciously, objected to this formulation as linking and ultimately expressing submission to Europe and the West at the expense of what a leading clerical thinker of revolution, Ali Mottahari, called "severance with neighboring Islamic nations." In his words, the decisions based on the "Aryan factor" will lead to "proclivity towards the Western world" while by choosing national foundation to be Iran's post-Islamic intellectual heritage "Arab, Turk, Indian, Indonesian . . . would become our friends, even kinsmen."[10]

It is important to note that this attempted redirection of Iran's foreign policy did not undermine Iran's sense of importance as a significant regional or at times even global player, although some by focusing on state capabilities rather than preferences offer a more realistic understanding of the country's potential role.[11] This sense of importance is undoubtedly partly generated out of the memory of Iran's imperial past, which as mentioned was particularly honed and celebrated during the prerevolutionary Pahlavi Dynasty. The Islamic Republic has neither been able nor willing to expunge it fully. As an ideological frame celebrated and heavily propagated during the previous regime, it has found and maintained a niche in a good part of the Iranian national psyche.[12] But Iran's geographic size and resources in the midst of a geopolitically and economically important region along with its perceived world-historical revolution have also accentuated this sense of importance.[13]

Still, coupled with this sense of importance is the conflicting impulse—at times bordering on paranoia—that emphasizes the country's insecurities and its strategic loneliness in a region in which Iran's distinctive cultural identity, combining both Persianness and Shi'ism, stands seemingly detached. The two other countries in the traditionally defined Middle East region with non-Arab identity and language—Turkey and Israel—have countered their isolation and insecurities through solid linkages with extra-regional players. Iran, on the other hand, for a variety of reasons—which include important cultural and resource endowment, geographical vastness and centrality, and century-long contentious domestic politics—remains both *insecure* and *aspiring for more,* a combination that frames debates regarding the objectives of Iran's foreign policy.[14]

This framing also existed in the prerevolutionary period. Iran's strategic alliance with the United States in the post-1953 coup period did somewhat allay the Iranian leader's insecurities. But this arrangement was neither lasting nor ultimately satisfactory even to the shah. On the one hand, he saw the alliance as an avenue for enhancing Iran's global standing and regional prominence. On the other hand, in an attempt to balance Iran's relationship with the United States, he tried to forge a significant relationship with the Soviet Union through the construction of a domestic steel industry. Ultimately, in his last days, even he became convinced that the United States was intent on replacing him. Perhaps had the United States not openly meddled in Iran's domestic politics, the way the British and Russians had done in the heydays of imperial rivalries, the situation might have been different.

Iran had sought in the United States a "third force" to counter the undue influence of the other two imperial powers. Indeed for a while the

American actions within the emerging Cold War environment effectively countered both egregious Soviet meddling and British control of the Iranian oil sector. But the coup and subsequent cultural and political alliance with the United States eventually challenged the historical desire for "cutting off the hands of foreigners."

This is a peculiarly Iranian formulation that openly posits external players as thieves, always seeking to extract resources and "concessions" (*emtiaz*) from Iran by manipulating domestic cleavages. One could even argue that Iran's not being directly colonized has made Iranian political discourse in some ways even more paranoid or sensitive about "hidden hands" intent on undermining the country's political independence in indirect ways.

It was this desire to counter external manipulation or perceived patron-client relationship between Iran and the United Kingdom first and then the United States that made "independence" (*esteqlal*) the slogan of the Iranian revolution along with "freedom" (*azadi*). And it is the same impulse today that has made the notion of "national sovereignty" the hallmark of Iran's self-identified "principled" stance on the nuclear issue. This does not mean that Iran's foreign policy has not been subject to vacillations based on genuine political disagreements about how to achieve "true independence" or enhance Iran's regional standing based on different understandings of threats Iran faces, national interest, and capabilities in the region and the world. It just explains why Iranian politicians of any point of view cannot be seen as "giving in" to external pressures.

In Iran, as in other countries in which there is contested political terrain, certain shared principles and fears create the boundaries outside of which significant political players cannot step if they wish to remain relevant and effective. Those seeking improved relations or accommodation with the global order always need to walk a fine line between being seen as promoting national interest and standing accused of engaging in "collusion" (*sazesh*) and giving in.

In the arena of foreign policy, ideology also comes to play in the way various players formulate shared principles in highly ideological or dogmatic ways particularly during times when the country perceives itself or is actually under threat or extreme pressure. In more recent years, some Iranian leaders such as the former nuclear negotiator and current Parliament speaker Ali Larijani have even openly discussed the use of ostentatious ideology in providing Iran with a "strategic weight" needed to make the country secure and fend off external antagonism.

Hence, more than thirty years after a revolution made in the name of "independence and freedom," the Islamic Republic continues to be contested at home. Its foreign policy debates on the one hand are shaped by a sense of victimhood or grievance, bordering on paranoia and distrust. Yet on the other hand it is also shaped by an elevated sense of the country's strategic importance and significance as an "indispensable actor" in the region, a "moral power" and an "independent force" in the world.

Events in the past decade—particularly the American invasions of Iraq and Afghanistan as well as increased US animosity and threats—have accentuated both senses of victimhood and importance. But they have also unleashed fierce debates about strategies to counter what is considered the attempted isolation, containment, "bullying," and even destabilization of the Islamic Republic. These debates, while related to discussions of Iran's regional or global influence or search for reliable partners to counter Iran's isolation, have at their core the issue of Islamic Iran's security in a highly unstable and insecure regional context, particularly in the post-2003 environment in which the Islamic Republic's most intractable adversary—the United States—has become an effective neighbor through its military presence in Iraq, Afghanistan, and several Persian Gulf states.[15]

These debates have also created a near consensus regarding the need—even the right—for Iran to pursue a bigger weight and role commensurate with its acquired postrevolutionary ideology, stature, and capabilities. Almost all players in the country see Iran's increased status to be due to its proximity to regional hot spots and deserved given Iran's history, geography, resources, and dynamic culture and religious ideology. To be sure, there is in the current public discourse an occasional articulation of sentiments rejecting even Iran's regional aspirations and calling for an inward-looking approach that promotes nonentanglement and taking care of the self. This sense was, for instance, articulated by some protestors in the post–June 12, 2009, election demonstrations with the slogan of "neither Gaza, nor Lebanon; only Iran."[16] The implication was that as a developing state Iran needs to take care of itself and not be the patron of other countries. However, these sentiments should probably be considered as expression of resentment against what is deemed to be the unnecessarily provocative rhetoric of the current president and policies rather than a well-articulated and coherent school of thought advocating Iran's introverted role.

Foreign Policy Perspectives

Acknowledging the lines outside of which Iran's foreign policy debates do not step, in the following section we will lay out three perspectives. We identify their proponents as *Islamic Idealists, Regional Power Balancers,* and *Global Power Balancers.* The last two categories are further divided into two, producing five distinct categories. We divide regional balancers into *offensive* and *defensive* realists and the global balancers into *rejectionists* and *accommodationists.*

The key to understanding foreign policy perspectives in Iran is to view them *not* as well-differentiated and fully articulated positions held by distinct groups of people. It is quite possible for key individuals to hold several positions at the same time or move from one position to another in reaction to the country's changed security environment. For instance, a look at any speech given by Iran's leader, Ayatollah Ali Khamenei, reveals his positioning as both a pan-Islamic idealist and an offensive regional power balancer. He has even been accused of being a global rejectionist. Former president Mohammad Khatami has also positioned himself as both an ecumenical idealist and a defensive regional power balancer. Political scientist Amir Haji-Yousefi argues that in his policies Mahmoud Ahmadinejad has shown himself to be both an offensive realist and a global accommodationist at the same time.[7]

It is for these reasons that in the following sections, attention will be mostly focused on positions and arguments made rather than individuals or institutions holding those positions. Even individual thinkers quoted as proponents of one position or another should not be considered as holding that position alone.

Islamic Idealists

The revolutionary idealism of Iranian foreign policy is often wrongly only associated with the early years of revolution and the idea of "export of

Islamic revolution."[18] In reality, the advocates of export of revolution quickly evolved and wed their announced desire for exporting the Islamic revolution with selective support for liberation movements for the sake of either national defense or regional balance of power. Today, pure revolutionary idealism maintains a weak presence in foreign policy debates mostly through calls for both Islamic unity and dialogue between the Muslim and non-Muslim world.

Since its creation, the Islamic Republic has pursued an official policy of Islamic unity based on bridging the gap between Shi'ism and Sunnism. To date, this ecumenical policy has been rather unsuccessful and one can even easily make an argument that it has not been tried in earnest. Nevertheless, this unity is propagated in official speeches and publications directed abroad as well as such institutional outlets as the Organization of Islamic Propaganda and Ministry of Culture and Islamic Guidance. This view of the need for Islamic unity in the face of "global arrogance" is also repeatedly mentioned by Iran's leader Ali Khamenei. For instance, criticizing the turning of the conflicts in the Persian Gulf region into a Shi'i–Sunni issue as a "service to the United States and enemies of the Islamic *Umma*," he identified the 2011 democratic movements in the Middle East as a movement of "peoples and Islamic *Umma* with Islamic slogans and in the direction of Islamic objectives."[19]

Along the same lines, the editors of *Taghrib*, the journal of the World Forum for Proximity of Islamic Schools of Thought, identify the coming together of the different schools of jurisprudence, theology, or thought within Islam and the unification of the ranks of Muslims against the enemies of Islam as "one of the most important goals of the Islamic Republic of Iran since its inception." They also identify this "noble aspiration" as dependent, among other things, on "avoiding division within the ranks of Muslims," and "putting a stop to the subjugation of Muslims and the dominance of foreign powers in Muslim countries."[20]

Beyond rhetorical commitment, this type of pan-Islamism continues to have advocates, particularly among reformist clerics. This is in the face of resistance by some of the traditional clergy in Qom who emphasize the Shi'i character of the 1979 Revolution instead of its pan-Islamic boast.[21] Two types of argument are generally made to make the case for Islamic unity. One focuses on the common need to maintain the cultural and religious identity of the Islamic World in the face of Western cultural, military, and economic expansion. The other concentrates on basic religious convictions to overcome nonessential differences.

Focused on Islamic identity, this view holds that Iran should define its interests in terms of coordination with Islamic countries through organizations such as the Organization of the Islamic Cooperation (OIC). This standpoint maintains that the Islamic Republic needs to be directly and actively involved in all issues related to the Islamic world. Furthermore, such a view contends that the interests of the Islamic Republic demand the establishment of an enduring link particularly with the Arab Middle East.[22]

Iran's Shi'ism, in practice and in theory, as well as Iranian nationalism is a challenge to this type of pan-Islamic idealism. The decentralized nature of Iranian clerical structure makes it difficult to maintain a consistent pan-Islamic posture as various high-ranking clerics find it hard not to insist on Shi'i superiority. In practice, too, the institution of the religious guide or leader, now occupied by Ayatollah Khamenei, makes it difficult to sustain the call for pan-Islamic unity because of the claim of Iran's leader to be the commander of the world's Muslims (*vali-ye amr-e muslemin-e jahan*),

The recent reformist formulation, under Mohammad Khatami's presidency (1997–2005), positing Iran as a champion of dialogue of civilizations, was an attempt to respond to these challenges by promoting Iran's historical and religious role in the pursuit of dialogue and not clash of civilizations. But it has suffered both because of increased animosity on the part of the United States as well as major changes in the region which have highlighted sectarian differences between Sunni and Shi'i communities, as demonstrated in the March 2011 events in Bahrain.

Regional Power Balancers

Regional power balancers consume the bulk of Iran's foreign policy discourse and should be considered the Iranian version of foreign policy realists even if, as mentioned above, the ideological framework within which they define Iran's role in the region and the world heavily emphasizes Iran's Islamism. Like their counterparts elsewhere, they emphasize the country's territorial integrity and security in interactions with other actors in the region and outside of the region. They also view capabilities (both ideational and material), leadership, and unity as the center of power and call for forming alliances to balance against security threats.

Again like realists elsewhere, their arguments have aggressive or offensive as well as defensive versions. But in the Iranian case, even the more aggressive version does not see Iran as a classic hegemonic or opportunistic power seeking to exert preponderance in its immediate neighborhood. Both versions define Iran's security policy along four lines: defense of territorial integrity, avoidance of international isolation, expansion of foreign trade and investment in order to promote development, and making the region less militarized.[23]

These broad objectives also bring agreement on a whole series of narrower security goals like securing vital waterways such as the Hormuz Strait, constant monitoring of foreign military forces in adjacent waters, combating international terrorism, preventing arms and narcotics smuggling, and expansion of defense cooperation with countries with similar views.

Finally, both versions see the United States and its allies in the region as engaged in the containment of Iran. But they disagree on the reasons for this containment, alliances that need to be emphasized, nature of security threats, and how to go about elevating Iran's status. In the offensive version, the old cliché that the best defense is good offense holds true. In particular, offensive power projection in as far away places as Latin America is promoted as a means of pressuring the United States to abandon its attempt to shape Iran's domestic politics as well as accept the country's actions and aspirations in its immediate perimeter in which the United States is an effective resident.

Offensive realists, prominent among defense officials as well as the current hard-line government, consider Iran as facing no or little physical security threat from its immediate neighbors. These realists call for restoring and emphasizing assertiveness to Iran's foreign policy, and most notably in regard to the country's nuclear enrichment program and its dealings with the West. They identify their main challenge to come from extraregional players, in particular the United States. To be sure, they consider talks of the United States and Israel attacking as mostly "psychological war" intended to undermine the confidence of the Iranian people in the survival of the Islamic Republic if it does not change its ways.[24] Still, they consider the American military presence in Afghanistan, Iraq, and the Persian Gulf as the most serious national security threat.

Even more of a threat is Washington's use of the nuclear issue not only to limit Iran's regional power—which they see as already impressive enough to make Iran an "indispensable regional player"—but also to reshape the Islamic Republic's politics away from Islamism. Unhappy with the ineffectiveness of the sanctions regime it has imposed on Iran and unable to attack Iran militarily because of involvement and extension of its military forces elsewhere, these offensive realists argue, the US strategy has turned to destabilization of Iran from within through the mechanism of a "soft war" that aims to divide the leadership as well as the population.[25] Iran's pushback, they argue, must be anything but complacent and take into account the nature of the threat as well the regional conditions faced by the issuer of the threat.

Their push for aggressive countermoves is based on two key beliefs: America's decline and strategic changes in the region in favor of Iran.[26] This combination, they argue, has begun a gradual transfer of power and influence in the region from America's camp to Iran's camp. In short, with the demonstrations of US failures and disappointments in the Middle East, they see the spread of Islamism or even democracy in the region as going hand in hand with the inclination of regional states to gravitate toward Iran.[27] Iran's strength, in turn, is manifested in its presence in "Lebanon, Iraq, Afghanistan, Palestine, and the oil market."

While the proponents of this view still seek—even if unsuccessfully—to maintain cordial relations with regional powerhouses such as Egypt and Saudi Arabia, they give even more importance to Iran's regional allies, such as Syria, and friendly factions such as Hezbollah and Hamas. They call for tying regional grievances to Iran's broader regional role and its nuclear program. Thus, for instance, by becoming especially vociferous on the Palestinian issue and the Israeli military assault on Lebanon in the summer of 2006, they endeavor to carve out a role for Iran on a broader regional scale.

They see such regional grievances, which to their minds have roots in long-standing injustices, as inseparable from Western efforts to retard Iranian development by depriving it of a raft of modern technologies, most prominently civilian nuclear technology. They argue that by speaking out on regional issues and contextualizing them to Iran's own embattled relationship with the West, Iran will improve its public diplomacy and will be able to garner and engender support among the masses of Muslim majority states.

Along the same lines, while focused on regional geopolitics and long-term national interests, promoters of an aggressive foreign policy argue that Shi'i ties, networks, and ideological kinships in Lebanon and Iraq can and must be utilized as instruments to form alliances, project power (enhance Iran's strategic weight at least temporarily), and make clear the regional costs of external powers trying to make Iran insecure.

Emphasis on the alliance with Hezbollah in Lebanon, in particular, is seen as necessary in order to check Israeli threats as well as enhance Iran's standing vis-à-vis the United States. Here Shi'ism is not promoted as a preferred state ideology—in fact, as mentioned above, pan-Islamism is rhetorically supported—but tapped implicitly as a lever of influence or more accurately as an opportune instrument to pursue national interest and security.

In this sense, the use of Shi'i Islam as an instrument of foreign policy is inconsistent with the global message of Islamic unity or dialogue of civilizations promoted by revolutionary idealists. But by intervening, or even seeming to intervene, in matters beyond Iran's immediate neighborhood (Iraq and Persian Gulf), the intent here is to make a case for the *interconnection* of Iran's security and stability and regional security and stability in the broader Middle East. The intended message is that regional tranquility and Iranian security go hand in hand.

From this point of view Iran's greater involvement in Middle Eastern affairs is not a matter of ideological solidarity but strategy. Although eager to spread its views, Iran must also extend its influence and networks further afield in order to engage the enemy in forward defense, so as to avoid fighting near its borders. Given Iran's limited military capabilities, this Iranian version of credible deterrence is less concerned about this projection of power resulting in retaliation with unacceptably high casualties and damage. Rather it explicitly wants Iran's enemies to worry about the costs of attacking and destabilizing Iran for the security of not only the Persian Gulf but also the Middle East and Southwest Asia.

In addition, Iran's presence in the greater Middle East is viewed as a bulwark particularly since the absence of any peace process and fading prospects of a two-state solution has created a vacuum for Iran to fill. The controversial enhanced US military presence in the region and blatant disregard of the concerns of many Arabs and Palestinians, offensive realists argue, have provided fertile ground for Iran's rejectionist stance to have resonance with citizens of many Arab countries. The aligning of the sentiments of the "Arab Street" with Iran's positions on the Israeli–Palestinian conflict creates limitations for the leadership of Arab countries allied with the United Sates and forces them to check their anti-Iran rhetoric as well as actions.

Within Iran's highly contested domestic environment, the proponents of an aggressive foreign policy go as far as accusing the proponents of a more defensive posture as promoting a "passive" foreign policy oblivious to the "malicious" intents of Iran's enemies to undermine the Islamic Republic and negligent in the use of all levers of power available to Iran, including ideology and regional networks. For instance, in criticizing the foreign policy of the previous reformist administration of Mohammad Khatami, Ali Bagheri, the current director of foreign policy and deputy secretary of the Supreme National Security Council, states:

> The reformist government stepped into international relations with the slogan of détente, which means the approach of accepting the dominant global order. This view in foreign policy, which awaits to see what share the dominant political order has for it [sic] so that it can act on that basis, is a passive approach and what America and Westerners want. This is why the dominant order doesn't have any problems with this interpretation of the Islamic system and even supports the governance of such a view in the Islamic Republic. But the view that believes in the Islamic Revolution not only being a part of the Islamic Republic but also given birth by it, while having complete understanding of the mechanisms of the dominant order, rejects its policies and approaches on principle and places the promotion of national interest at the helm of its foreign policy. On this basis the discourse of *reducing threats* instead of *reducing tensions* becomes what shapes the Islamic Republic of Iran's foreign policy. This discourse endeavors through preventive and proactive initiatives to not allow any potential or actual threat to take place against the country's interests. It is on the basis of a passive approach that the opponent who is your enemy even designs a

scenario to confront you with tensions so that you would give up your sovereign rights. So you can see that during the tenure of the reform government, when the West told them [sic] either suspend your nuclear activities or we punish you via the Security Council, since the discourse of détente was dominant in foreign policy and entry [of Iran's case] into the Security Council was an example of tension, the enemy was easily allowed to interfere in the country's sovereign mechanisms without any justification or rational and legal reasons. And on this basis even with pride suspension of nuclear activities was accepted and in justification it was said that we did not allow the [Iran] file to go to Security Council. But they never referred to the technical, scientific, political costs and credibility loss for the country and people.[28]

Defensive realists, accused of passivity, respond by questioning the offensive realists' optimism regarding the decline of American power at least in the short run. Even if they acknowledge the argument regarding the decline of America's power at this juncture, they argue that offensive realists leave two questions unanswered: "First, will American power diminish before it can damage Iran? Second, will the end of American dominance coincide with the appearance of a new unipolar power or with the creation of a multipolar world system? If the latter, will Iran be prepared for a multipolar environment?"[29]

Accusing the offensive realists of pursuing a more adventurist foreign policy than a proactive one, they argue against the fallacy of seeing Iran's security situation as a zero-sum game against the United States since their notion of security is broader and includes domestic stability and economic security or development. They argue that Iran's improved regional standing must be found in mending relations in the region, which had been severely strained after the 1979 revolution and the subsequent Iran–Iraq War.

Following the pattern laid out during Akbar Hashemi Rafsanjani's presidency (1989–1997), in the wake of the end of Iran–Iraq War, these defensive realists argue for a policy of détente and confidence-building toward key regional players such as Kuwait and Saudi Arabia while continuing to maintain strong ties with allied state actors such as Syria and nonstate actors such as Hezbollah of Lebanon.

Focusing on the limitations imposed by key international players on Iran's foreign policy choices, their argument essentially concerns what might be feasible and more flexible policies. They do not see Iran's involvement in the broader regional issues such as the Israeli-Palestinian conflict as serving the long-term interest of Iran.[30] Furthermore, they see it as dangerous and unduly provocative in the short term. As such, they do not believe in the use of ideological Shi'ism in making inroads in the broader Arab world. This view, while acknowledging Iran's strong security interests in the immediate neighborhood, including Iraq, Afghanistan, and the Persian Gulf, does not consider Iran's extensive involvement in issues related to Palestine, Lebanon, Syria as in line with the country's long-term strategic interests. While emphasis on issues such as the Israeli–Palestinian conflict may be deemed useful tactically in countering immediate security threats but in the long run, they argue, it will lead to conflict with important players in the region such as Saudi Arabia—a country with which Iran in a strategic shift opted to improve relations in the mid-1990s—and Egypt and ultimately the United States. Accordingly, they argue, Iran's national interest necessitates that issues such as the Israeli–Palestinian conflict be spearheaded by leading Arab countries such as Egypt and Saudi Arabia.

Defining security in terms that include the economic well-being and development of the country, these defensive realists also promote a regional—and more technocratic—approach that is reflected in Iran's *20-year Outlook Document*, produced in 2005. This document sets Iran's aspiration as one of becoming a fully advanced country, rising to the "number-one rank in economic, scientific and technological progress" among twenty-eight nations in the Middle East and Southeast Asia.[31] The widely publicized document calls for achievement of fast-paced and sustainable economic growth, creation of durable employment opportunities, enhancement of factor productivity, active presence in regional and international markets; development of a diverse, knowledge-based economy free of inflation and blessed by food security, and establishment of a market environment conducive to domestic and international business entrepreneurship. By 2025, Iran is promised to be a nation with an Islamic and revolutionary identity, offering a guiding light for the Islamic world while engaged in effective and constructive interaction with the rest of the global community.

All this, it is argued, is made impossible by the policies promoted by offensive realists, which are not only counterproductive and dangerous but also costly and merely reactive or in opposition to the policy of containment pursued by the United States. In the words of Nasser Hadian and Shani Hormozi:

> It should be cautioned, however, that *Counter Containment,* as a reactive strategy, has proved quite costly. Its pursuit has involved increasing political, diplomatic, economic, and social costs for the country, and has, as a result, proved contentious....While the government officially denigrates sanctions as ineffective and of marginal impact on the Iranian society and economy, pursuit of the *Counter Containment* strategy has involved, inter alias, active search for alternative sources for substitution regardless of cost; reliance on imports and domestic substitution at the expense of quality; coalition-making with like-minded countries in order to balance and challenge the U.S. power and pressure; building up of defense, intelligence, and security infrastructures in a number of countries for deterrence purposes or possible retaliatory action in case of external (U.S. or Israeli) military adventure; allocation of substantial resources for public diplomacy and psychological warfare geared to refuting the current prevalent tarnished image at the international level and for promoting an alternative image of Iran—the Islamic Republic—among Muslims and "oppressed people" of the world.[32]

They hold that it would be a mistake to adopt an inflexible belligerent attitude because the risks of such a posture far outweigh the benefits. Dehgani Firuzabadi asserts that Iran does not seek conflict with the international community. Yet in pursuit of its idealistic foreign policy goals, it occasionally has to adopt a more confrontational foreign policy. Unless key values and interests are at stake, the Iranian government should avoid conflictive situations in view of the fact that they will "prevent Iran from optimizing its domestic resources" while using opportunities to improve its power position.[33] In short, in order for Iran to attain its sustainable development goals, "the country must not be seen as a threat to international peace and stability."[34] The alternative foreign policy that can be pursued, it is argued, is one that strives to be viewed as nonthreatening by the international community and other regional players through engagement and participation in international organizations, treaties, and events in order to appear as a less rogue state and more like a status quo power. Confidence building, avoidance of provocative language and acts, improvement of relations with neighbors as well as key international players are promoted as the best route for countering security threats and most effective security doctrine in the long term.

It is important to note that forging regional and international bonds is also valued by offensive regional power balancers. But, given the concerted US attempt to limit Iran's choices and pressure Iran, quite a bit of contemporary Iranian debates are about bonds that could or should be forged either to extend Iran's influence or counter efforts to isolate it. In fact, discussions abound where to look for these bonds: East or West? Neither East nor West? Russia? Europe? China? Non-Aligned Movement? Islamic countries? The Third World? Persian Gulf or Central Asia? Latin America or Africa?

It is also significant that the debates regarding Iran's possible alliance have shifted significantly over time with changing international circumstances and Iran's failure to form solid alliances in order to counter external pressure. To just give one example, the defensive realist argument calling for enhanced political and economic bonds with Europe as a means to counter American pressures eventually lost potency with the European refusal to take a distinct position from the United States on Iran's nuclear file. This argument was promoted by some members of the Foreign Ministry affiliated Institute for Political and International Studies as well as the Expediency Council–affiliate Institute for Strategic Research in the late 1990s and particularly after the United States invasion of Iraq. Those promoting this type of rapprochement or confidence building with Europe eventually lost the argument, inside the country because of their inability to deliver change in the behavior of external actors.

Similar dynamics are currently at play with the Iranian disappointment over Russia's support for UN sanctions. The offensive realists' calculation and promise that Russia would not abandon Iran has served to reduce the influence of the argument, which advocated closer relationship with Russia. With this backdrop and history of disappointment a discursive shift to China as a possible ally has faced skepticism from the start buttressed by the Russian and Chinese opposition to the elevation of Iran's observer status at the Shanghai Cooperation Organization (SCO).[35]

Still some offensive realists, including Ahmadinejad, continue to believe that Iran's leaning toward a powerful Asia can help resolve Iran's lack of strategic partnership. Both Russia and China are deemed as powerful balancers.

Defensive regional power balancers, while acknowledging the need for ties with both Russia and China for economic and military reasons, find those ties lacking in their ability to solve Iran's strategic concerns. The key to why this is so must be found in the way both Russia and China look at Iran. Focusing on Russia, for instance, Jahangir Karami argues:

> [The Russians] do not see much authenticity in Iran's independent action and see Iran as a Third World country that is repeating the Soviet's revolutionary ways and is important for causing some headaches for the United States in international relations. But this situation should not create costs for Russia since Russia has more important priorities in its immediate periphery (commonwealth countries), Europe, the United States and the East and Iran is within [Russia's] fifth priority (the Middle East). Hence the Russians expect that whenever they indicate to Iran to end its anti-systemic activities that it would do it so that they would not be faced with a difficult choice. In other words, the two sides have unrealistic expectations of each other. Iran wants Russia more for macro level international relations (confrontation with the US) and Russia wants relations with Iran at bilateral and regional level.[36]

Karami goes on to argue that Iran's Eastern policy is confronted with more basic problems beyond the Russian or Chinese attitudes and expectations regarding Iran. Generally, Karami argues, a country should delineate its national interest and then place its foreign policy and its direction at the service of these interests. But due to the hostile relationship with the United States, the Islamic Republic "has gradually reached a situation in which the shadow of an enemy has covered its interests and these interests are defined in a passive way." Hence in every issue, instead of giving attention to what its national interests are, it has to give attention to America's position and frantically work to create an international front to counter the US pressures. But, according to Karami, the reality is that the creation of such a front against the United States is not possible at this point:

> Of course one can think of common interests regarding particular, limited, and short-term issues with countries and at times even act on that basis but China,

India, or Russia under no circumstances are willing to pay the costs of such important confrontations....If the intent of Eastern policy is relations with Eastern countries, it is very good, useful, and necessary. But the basic reality is that these relations cannot be substitute for other relations.[37]

Global Balancers and the America Question

The global balancers are also realists, again within the frame of the ideological shift that has occurred since the revolution, in so far as they seek to maximize the Islamic Republic's security and chances of survival. But their emphasis on Iran's relationship with the United States places them in a different category than regional balancers. This is not to say that the latter does not give attention to Iran's "America Question." As mentioned above, the history and reality of animosity and regional competition with the United States and its allies in the region make the question of Iran's disposition toward the United States a key issue for almost everyone focused on security and power.

The globalists' distinction is the tying of the Islamic Republic's status to the resolution or lack of resolution of the conflict with the United States. On the one hand, there are those who see the Islamic Republic's status and identity intricately tied to its *rejectionist* stance against any kind of relations or accommodation with the United States. On the other hand, there are those who see Iran's crisis-free and secure status in the region tied to some sort of *accommodation*, functional relations, or even a new geopolitical arrangement with the United States and, consequently, better integration in global geopolitics. In their call for accommodation and integration they come close to defensive regional balancers. But they see the path to the acceptance of Iran as a legitimate regional powerhouse through the resolving of Iran's America question first. Defensive regional balancers, on the other hand, see piecemeal cooperation in areas of mutual interest (e.g., Afghanistan, arms, and drug trade) as the means to reducing US hostility. In short, while defensive regional balancers entertain the possibility of "selective engagement," accommodation-oriented globalists see the Islamic Republic's security in "comprehensive" engagement.[38]

The global rejectionists, on the other hand, find their point of reference in an adversarial United States that is unable for ideological and geopolitical reasons to come to terms with the existence of an independent and globally influential Islamic Republic. While regional balancers on both stripes may entertain the possibility of selective cooperation with the United States on regional issues of mutual interest (e.g., Afghanistan), the global rejectionists find Iran's global import as well as survival of the Islamic Republic in diligent resistance. In the words of Ali Saeidi, the representative of the office of the leader to the Islamic Revolution's Guard Corps (IRGC), "there is no other way for safeguarding the revolution than resistance against the United States."[39] These rejectionists do not seem indifferent to the implication of economic sanctions and other punitive measures, but they use fundamentally different logic and are willing to gamble on big returns in relation to certain foreign policy issues.

For instance, Manouchehr Mohammadi, a former deputy foreign minister claims that the Islamic Republic has endured all foreign pressures and has changed threats into opportunities to become independent, self-sufficient, and freed from all the restrictions imposed by the *estekbar* (global arrogance). He concludes that if the enemy had not posed such a threat to Iran's national security, Iran would not have been able to "become an emerging global power in the international arena."[40]

Those globalists who focus on the need for a functional relationship with the United States, on the other hand, see the latter as the main producer of wealth and power in the globe and think that Iran, as a rising regional power, is in need of Western technology and investment in order to grow economically. Accordingly, it should interact with the United States in order to fulfill its preferred political and security role in the region. Improved integration in the global and regional economy, in other words, is posited as the key to Iranian security and not the pursuit of hard power (conventional or nuclear). In the words of Mohsen Aminzadeh, former deputy foreign minister for Asia and Oceania:

> Those with nuclear weapons capability are not necessarily more powerful than the ones without. In the past century, when military capability was considered the main basis of power, this was true. But today such a view has no meaning. Pakistan has accomplished a nuclear weapons test. But this test has done nothing to enhance Pakistan's position in the world. Instead it has created problems for this country. If India had not tested, Pakistan would not have tested either, given the great problems associated with [nuclear testing]. India's nuclear testing

did not lead to its enhanced [global] position either; rather it has implied a kind of extremist and baseless competition. If India's standing in the world is improving, this is due to her rapid economic, scientific, industrial progress and her political and social situation. This is also true of Japan, South Korea, Malaysia, Australia and other countries that do not have nuclear weapons...The Cold War and its military competition is over. Military balance no longer has the same strategic position as before and having [nuclear] weapons does not bring immunity for us. The Soviet disintegration showed that a superpower armed to the teeth with the best arms, if without superior economic and social indicators, will move towards total disintegration and military capability can be of no help.[41]

Their argument emphasizes the improbability of building a regional coalition between Iran and the Arab world as a counter to American hegemony essentially because of the ideological nature of the Islamic Republic and its stated objective of support for Muslim and liberation movements, on the one hand, and the nature of structure of power in the Arab world on the other hand. In addition, like the defensive realists, they argue that Iran's entry into sensitive Middle Eastern issues, such as the Arab–Israeli problem, complicate the relationship between Iran and the United States, and this complication in turn poses problems for development trends in Iran. Finding a way to strike a comprehensive bargain with the United States is offered as a means to reduce tensions with other regional players as well as enhance Iran's regional standing.[42]

In recent years, after the US invasions of Iraq and Afghanistan, a variation of this accommodationist view has come to the fore. It can be considered as an attempt to join an offensive realist point of view with the idea of comprehensive negotiation with the United States. The argument is based on the "reality" that the post–September 11 global importance of Iran derives from the security issues of a region in which Iran is a main player. According to Kayhan Barzegar,

Although Iran was important before the September 11 events and during the Cold War, but the increase in Iran's role and influence after September 11 and the Iraq crisis is not comparable to the previous period. The increase in the importance of Iran's role is due to the placement of Iran in a politico-security environment which has vital importance for the global order. The fight against al-Qaeda terrorism, preventing the proliferation of weapons of mass destruction, and resolution of regional crises in Afghanistan, Iraq, Lebanon, and Palestine are issues that are currently the main headlines in international security. The Islamic Republic has an impact in all the issues that are important to the region. Essentially, the high maneuverability of Iran in Middle Eastern issues and also Iran's nuclear program and the decision to maintain an independent nuclear fuel cycle provided the context for a strategic dialogue between the Iran and the United States and possible negotiations between the two sides in the region based on equal political positions.[43]

This argument does not see Iran's improved standing in the region as derivative of improved relations with the United States. In fact, it sees the potential of improved United States–Iran relations as being embedded in Iran's already enhanced regional standing in the post–Iraq War period. It is nevertheless a globalist argument in so far as it prioritizes relations with the United States and calls for comprehensive engagement. Iran's improved standing in the region, Barzegar argues, should become the basis for the settlement of all outstanding issues between the United States and Iran. In short, the nuclear issue that in recent years has dominated United States–Iran interactions should not be seen as separate from various regional crises, such as Iraq and Afghanistan, and the ongoing tensions and disputes surrounding the Arab–Israeli conflict (where the role of Hezbollah is significant). It should also not be seen as the only chip with which Iran can bargain:

> Settling the nuclear issue, acknowledging Iran's status as a regional power, and incorporating it into the region's security architecture would allow Iran to work in coordination with the United States, as opposed to playing the roles of strategic adversaries, to bring greater security to the region. If the crisis is resolved and the U.S. military presence is wound down to a level at which Iran's security fears are attenuated due to the essentially defensive character of Iranian foreign policy, Iranian and U.S. regional aims and goals could move toward coexistence instead of mutual exclusivity.[44]

The argument made here is in reality intended to convince opponents of accommodation both in Iran and the United States that comprehensive engagement can turn a losing game into a win–win one for both sides.

Along the same lines, reminding the United States that the demand for the suspension of Iran's nuclear program is a nonstarter, Sadeq Kharrazi, former deputy foreign minister, also warns Iran's rejectionists as well as offensive realists about the loss of opportunity to engage with the United States in the light of recent democracy protests and changes in the leadership in the region:

> Iran is entitled, as a member of the NPT, to fully benefit from its rights, and the possibility of reversing Iran's peaceful nuclear program is out of the question. On the other hand, Iran has to be responsive to the legitimate demands of the international community through its interaction with it. If both parties exercise their political will, reaching an understanding should not be impossible. The recent developments in the Middle East and the awakening of democracy and freedom, and the confrontation of tyrants in these countries, have increased the necessity of reaching an understanding with Iran on its nuclear issue. The West believes that the situation in the Middle East is so fluid that any change in the region could only create a more ambiguous future. Therefore, it is willing to resume talks with Iran. Iran should take advantage of this situation, and gain the necessary points to move the negotiations forward in accordance with its nuclear policy stance to reach a conclusion. Paying excessive attention to the need in the West to negotiate with Iran should not lead to a loss of opportunity in the situation. Otherwise, everyone will be a loser in this equation.[45]

CONCLUSION

Iran's foreign policy perspectives offer little doubt that Iranian Islamist leaders of all viewpoints strive for both security and a greater role in regional and global affairs. In addition, revolutionary-inspired Islamic nationalism in the face of what is deemed Western intransigence or bullying is effectively the thread that runs through almost all politically acceptable positions inside Iran. In this sense, revolutionary Islamic ideology envelops the understanding of regional and global geopolitics and Iran's aspirations. It also makes priorities of safeguarding Iran's territorial integrity, preserving the Islamic Republic's security and survival, countering its attempted isolation, and improving its standing in the region and, by implication, the world.

But there is quite a bit of contention regarding how Iran might achieve these objectives and whether it should see its rise in regional or global terms or through integration or resistance. International pressures and threats have increasingly marginalized the integrationist and economically focused perspectives, strengthening the views that emphasize resistance and opportunistic challenges of global powers. In this sense Iran's decision-making environment is becoming more securitized, centralized, and uniform based on the heavy-handed demands of a state worried about its survival while at the same time touting its global relevance on Islamic terms.

The implications of the debate between promoters of detente or accommodation and those in favor of an aggressive or confrontational foreign policy have been profound for Iran–US relations. Those in favor of a foreign policy intent on reducing tensions have been unable to deliver a less acrimonious relationship with the United States, thus strenthening the hands of those in favor of a more aggressive and confrontational foreign policy. Meanwhile advocates of a confrontationist or offensive foreign policy, now in charge, have had to face criticism: while their approach may have had some short-term yields—made possible by the opportunities provided to Iran by events in Iraq and Afghanistan—it has not only bordered on adventurism but more important, has been in conflict with the broader frames of Iran's ambitions as outlined in Iran's *20-Year Outlook Document*, which emphasizes Iran's regional dominance as a technological and economic power.

At its core Iran's foreign policy, reproducing its domestic politics, remains conflicted, lacking consensus regarding how to implement its leadership's aspired rise. Faced with the prospect of a prolonged policy of containment exercised by the United States, Iran's ascendant confrontationist stance may end up being the biggest obstacle to the country's achieving the status of a rising power.

Notes

1 · The most prominent example of such an institutional move is the Center for Strategic Research, which was established in 1989. It was affiliated with the office of the president until 1997, but with the change in presidency it was annexed as the research arm of the Expediency Discernment Council. In short, it remained close to former

president Akbar Hashemi Rafsanjani and is currently headed by Iran's former nuclear negotiator Hassam Rowhani. The affiliate research center with the office of the president is now the Center for Strategic Studies headed by former first vice president Parviz Davoudi.

2 · Mahmoud Sariolghalam, "Iran: Accomplishments and Limitations in IR," in Arlene B Tickner and Ole Waever, eds., *International Relations Scholarship around the World* (New York: Routledge, 2009), 163. According to Sariolghalam, in the universities in particular the field of international relations has not produced an alternative based on Islamist thought mostly because the subfield continues to be taught by scholars educated in the West and their students. It is the acknowledged failure to produce "Islamic models" that has led to yet another attempt at Islamizing humanities and social sciences in the past year after the contested June 2009 presidential election.

3 · The decision on the part of an influential faction within the Iranian government to authorize a secret arms-for-hostage deal with the Reagan administration (known as the Iran–Contra Affair in the United States) is often cited as an example of the conflict between ideology and practice in Iran. Another example is the Iranian decision to take sides with Armenia in its conflict with the predominantly Muslim Azerbaijan over the disputed territory of Nagorno-Karabakh.

4 · Lack of attention to the so-called pragmatists' objectives and focus on their less confrontational approach ends up ignoring, for instance, the ambitious objectives of the former reformist president Mohammad Khatami whose project of "dialogue of civilizations" effectively posited Islamic Iran as a significant global player.

5 · For a criticism of the problems of posing ideological and geopolitical concerns as opposite objectives of Iran's foreign policy, see Seyyed Jalal Dehghani Firuzabadi, "Nazariye-ye elsami-ye siasat khareji; Chaharchubi baraye tahlil-e siasat-e khareji-ye jomhuri-ye eslami-ye iran" (Islamic Theory of Foreign Policy: A Framework for the Analysis of the Islamic Republic of Iran's Foreign Policy), *Faslname-ye Beynolmellali-ye Ravabet-e Khareji*, 3, 1 (Bahar 1390/Spring 2011), 7–47. Dehghani Firuzabadi argues for placing the concept of *"maslehat"* at the core of understanding Islamic foreign policy. *Maslehat* is usually translated as either interest or expediency in English, but according to Dehghani Firuzabadi, it should be distinguished from interest because it entails worldly and otherworldly as well as material and spiritual interests. *"Maslehat* in the Islamic Republic's foreign policy is defined on the basis of the understanding of domestic material and spiritual potential and power, urgency and importance of the issue or situation, and international conditions and environment." This expanded notion of interest, which is based on "multi-layered rational decision making," allows for explanation of decisions such as acceptance of cease-fire with Iraq in 1988 based on the urgency to protect Islam and the Islamic Republic of Iran. On the other hand, it helps explain Iran's support for some Islamic movements (such as in Lebanon and Palestine) and not others (such as in Chechnya and China).

6 · *Khabaronline*, March 22, 2011, www.khabaronline.ir/news-136326.aspx.

7 · According to the preamble of Iran's Constitution, "With due attention to the Islamic content of the Iranian Revolution, the Constitution provides the necessary basis for ensuring the continuation of the Revolution at home and abroad. In particular, in the development of international relations, the Constitution will strive with other Islamic and popular movements to prepare the way for the formation of a single world community (in accordance with the Qur'anic verse '*This your community is a single community, and I am your Lord, so worship Me*' [21:92]), and to assure the continuation of the struggle for the liberation of all deprived and oppressed peoples in the world." Hamid Algar, *Constitution of the Islamic Republic of Iran* (Berkeley, CA: Mizan Press, 1980).

8 • Farideh Farhi, "The Antinomies of Iran's War Generation," in Lawrence G. Potter and Gary G. Sick, eds., *Iran, Iraq, and the Legacies of War* (New York: Palgrave, 2004), 101–20.

9 • Arshin Adib-Moghadam, *Iran in World Politics: The Question of the Islamic Republic* (New York: Columbia University Press, 2008), ch. 1. For a more elaborate discussion of the use of the Aryan discourse under the Pahlavi monarchy, see Reza Zia-Ebrahimi, "Self-Orientalization and Dislocation: The Uses and Abuses of the 'Aryan' Discourse in Iran," *Iranian Studies*, 44, 4 (July 2011), 445–72.

10 • Morteza Mottahari, *Islam and Iran* (Beirut: Dar al Ta'aruf, no date), 22, quoted in Adib-Moghadam, *Iran in World Politics*, 46.

11 • An elevated sense of Iran's role can be seen in the words of very different Iranian leaders as reflected in the shah's boast in making Iran the "fifth" military power in the world and the current president Mahmoud Ahmadinejad's declaration of Iran's readiness to "manage" global affairs.

12 • It is noteworthy that overt reference to Iran's imperial past has even made a comeback during the second term of Ahmadinejad, who is also known for his overt Shi'i millenarianism. His senior advisor, Rahim Esfandiar Mashaei, has been accused of promoting "Iranian Islam" by traditionalist clerics and conservative competitors who object to his celebration of pre-Islamic relics and traditions for the sake of gaining popularity in preparation for the next presidential elections in 2013. *Mehrnews*, August 9, 2011.

13 • Seyed Jalal Dehqani-Firouzabadi, "Manabe' melli-ye siasat khareji-ye jomhuri-ye eslami-ye iran" (National Resources of the Islamic Republic of Iran's Foreign Policy), *Faslname-ye Siasat*, 39, 3 (Fall 1388/2009), 221–45. Firouzabadi argues that Iran's foreign policy, like foreign policies of other countries, is influenced by several variables but the role of neither ideology nor geography can be ignored. He also reiterates the close linkage between domestic and foreign policy.

14 • A question was posed regarding possible international alliances that Iran can be placed within so as to prevent the United States from threatening it as easily as it has done in recent years. In response, Iran's former foreign minister and a current advisor to the leader on foreign policy, Kamal Kharrazi, said: "It is very unlikely for Iran to be part of such alliances since the nature of our state…is unique.…This does not rule out the possibility of regional cooperation.…But alliances are different since they usually come about when there is linguistic, ethnic, historical, and cultural homogeneity between countries or those which have strong and complementary economic and political bondage. Neither case is true about Iran. Countries which wish to join in a coalition should be at a balanced level of active power so that they could form a larger alliance. We do not know of any such country to join in a coalition with the Islamic Republic of Iran and this is why I always find it difficult to imagine Iran's alliance with another country." "On Iranian Foreign Policy with Dr. Kamal Kharrazi," *Discourse: An Iranian Quarterly*, 3, 4 (Spring 2002), 2–3.

15 • Saideh Lotfian, "Pendar az tahdid va siasatha-ye amniati-ye jomhuri-ye eslami-ye iran" (Threat Perception and Security Policies of the Islamic Republic of Iran). *Faslname-ye Siasat-e Khareji*, 3,1 (Bahar 1390/Spring 2011), 175–207.

16 • There is no reason to believe that this new form of political expression will be accepted by those in charge of Iran any time soon. Rahimpoor Azghady, a member of the influential Supreme Revolutionary Cultural Council, reminded the slogan creators that Iran's foreign policy formulation must be based on Islamic criteria [according to Article III, Section XVI,

of the Constitution]. For that reason, Iranians must pay attention to the moral commitment to all Muslims around the world. He scolded the protestors by declaring that "if we are honorable, we should not say 'neither Gaza, nor Lebanon', [because] we cannot be indifferent to the killings of Muslims or non-Muslims." He even went as far as saying that this slogan is contrary to the Constitution, Islam, and *Shari'a* (Islamic law). He warned that if the Iranians abandon the anti-imperialistic rhetoric, Iran will not survive and Iranians will be destroyed. See "Emam (rah) ta lahze-yi ke zendeh bood, ba mostakberan tanesh dasht (Imam had tension with the arrogant powers until his last moment)," *Kabarnameh Shora* (The Council's Newsletter), 15–16 (October–November 2009), 22–25.

17 ∘ Amir M. Haji-Yousefi, "Iran's Foreign Policy during Ahmadinejad: From Confrontation to Accommodation." Paper presented at the 2010 Annual Conference of Canadian Political Science Association held in Montreal, Canada.

18 ∘ Kazem Sami, a leader of the Revolutionary Movement of Iranian people and the first postrevolution Minister of Health, during his campaign in the first presidential campaign said: "Our foreign policy should be Islamic and international. We must defend all the world's oppressed against the oppressors. Not exporting the revolution…is nonsense babble." *Kayhan*, January 22, 1980.

19 ∘ *Farsnews*, March 21, 2011.

20 ∘ *Al-Taghrib:A Quarterly Journal of Islamic Unity*, 2, 3 (Winter 2008). For the mission and activities of the World Forum for Islamic Schools of Thought, see www.taghrib.ir.

21 ∘ For a discussion of different views on Iran's pan-Islamic project, see Wilfried Buchta, "The Failed Pan-Islamic Program of the Islamic Republic: Views of the Liberal Reformers of the Religious Semi-Opposition," in Nikki R. Keddie and Rudi Mathee, eds., *Iran and the Surrounding World* (Seattle: University of Washington Press, 2002), 281–304.

22 ∘ In naming the Iranian calendar year 1386 (beginning on March 21, 2007) the Year of Solidarity, Ayatollah Khamenei suggested a shift from "unity" to "solidarity." According to Gharayagh Zandi, this is a more precise meaning of Islamic idealism since Islamic solidarity is in "pursuit of cohesion and increasing interaction among Islamic countries that can both provide grounds for Islamic unity or the formation of Islamic community." Davoud Gharayah Zandi, "Conceptualization of Islamic Solidarity in Foreign Policy of the Islamic Republic of Iran," *Iranian Journal of International Affairs*, 20, 1 (Winter 2007–08), 69–91.

23 ∘ Lotfian, "Threat Perception and Security Policies." These security objectives explain the Islamic Republic's principled objection to the presence of all foreign forces in the region.

24 ∘ See Farideh Farhi, "What to Do about U.S. Sanctions and Israeli Threats: Iran's Muted Nuclear Debate," *Middle East Brief*, 61 (April 2012). Crown Center for Middle East Studies, Brandeis University.

25 ∘ In the words of an editorial in *Tabnak*, a website closely associated with the former commander of Islamic Iran's Guard Corp (IRGC), Mohsen Rezaie, "The thought room of Westerners—led by America and Israel—who see all their belongings from North Africa to the Persian Gulf blown away by the wind, see their tactic for passing through these difficult conditions in showing muscle in the Occupied Territories and intensifying their destructive activities against the Islamic Republic of Iran along with increasing economic sanctions." March 24, 2011, www.tabnak.ir/fa/news/155139.

26 ∘ Comments on the imminent US defeat and the departure of its military forces from the Middle East are abundant in Iran's more hawkish political circles. Some analysts have predicted that the US administration will be confronted with the escalation of regional crises in such a way that would diminish its ability to deal with perilous security threats.

As a result, Washington's need for cooperation with Iran will increase, and under such circumstances, the level of US conflict with Iran will be gradually reduced. See Seyed Hamid Mowlana and Manuchehr Mohammadi, *Siasat-e khareji-ye jomhori-ye eslami Iran (Islamic Republic of Iran Foreign Policy in Ahmadinejad Government)* (Tehran: Dadgostar, 2008), 119.

27 · In the words of Ayatollah Khamenei, "In a 32-year combat with the arrogant powers, the Islamic Republic of Iran has not only not surrendered to the oppressive global order but has also progressed and the opposing camp, spearheaded by the United States, in comparison to past years has also encountered weakness and defeat." *Farsnews*, April 4, 2011, www. farsnews.com/newstext.php?nn=9001141258.

28 · Interview with Ali Bagheri, originally published in the special issue of *Hamshahri* on March 19, 2011, and reproduced in *khabaronline*, www.khabaronline.ir/news-138272.aspx.

29 · Abbas Maleki, "Iran's Nuclear File: Recommendations for the Future,"*Daedalus* (Winter 2010). Abbas Maleki was deputy foreign minister for Research and Education and director of the Foreign Ministry's Institute for Political and International Studies between 1989 and 1997.

30 · It is tempting to say that the presence of many former diplomats at the Center for Strategic Research, affiliated with the Expediency Council, currently makes this center a bastion of defensive realism. The problem with this clear categorization is that changed regional circumstances and American refusal to accommodate any Iranian demands in negotiations may have led to a change of view among many of the diplomats who were intensely involved in negotiations with the European Union over Iran's nuclear program during the Bush administration. It is probably more accurate to say that these debates are reproduced within most institutions in Iran.

31 · For the Persian text of the document, see *Cheshmandaz-e Jomhoouri Eslami Iran dar Ofoq-e 1404* (Tehran: Jamal-al-Haq, 2006). The document also envisions Iran to be a nation with an Islamic and revolutionary identity by 2025, offering a guiding light for the Islamic world while engaged in effective and constructive interaction with the rest of the global community. For a commentary on this document, see Mohammad Jafar Javadi-Arjomand, "Sanad-e chemanadaz-e 1404 va siasat-khareji-ye jomhuri-ye eslami-ye iran dar dastyabi beh qodrat-e bartar-e mantaqwh" (Outlook Document of 1404 and the [Role of] the Islamic Republic of Iran's Foreign Policy in Attaining Superior Power in the Region," *Faslname-ye Siasat*, 39, 1 (Spring 1388/2009), 67–90.

32 · Nasser Hadian and Shani Hormozi, "Iran's New Security Imperatives," *Iran Review of International Affairs*, 1, 4 (Winter 2011), 13–55.

33 · Jalal Dehgani Firuzabadi, "Foreign Policy Requirements for National Development in Iran's 20-Year View," *Iranian Journal of International Affairs*, 1 (Spring 2005), 83.

34 · Ibid., 84.

35 · For a critique of the Ahmadinejad government's unrealistic security-oriented expectations from SCO, see "Shanghai Cooperation Organization and Practical Capacities for Iran: An Interview with Mohsen Shariatinia," *Iran Review* (May 23, 2011).

36 · Jahangir Karami, "Iran va russiyeh: Mottahed sharqi ya tahdid-e jonubi?" (Iran and Russia: Eastern Ally or Southern Threat?), *Faslname-ye Beynolmellali-ye Ravet Khareji*, 2, 7 (Fall 1389/2010).

37 · Ibid.

38 · Hadian and Hormozi, "Iran's New Security Imperatives."

39 · *Tabnak*, October 27, 2010, www.tabnak.ir/fa/pages/?cid=127543.

40 · Manouchehr Mohammadi, "The Sources of Power in Islamic Republic of Iran," *Journal of Foreign Policy,* 5, 22 (Summer 2008), 240.

41 · *Iran Daily,* September 23, 2003.

42 · The best-known articulation of a comprehensive bargain—a road map for improved relations—came in Iran's May 2003 negotiation proposal to the United States. Among other things, it called for the American abolition of economic sanctions and recognition of Iran's legitimate security interests in return for full transparency in Iran's nuclear program, coordination of activities in Iraq, suspension of material support for Palestinian opposition group, and action on making Hizbollah a political organization. This proposal was reportedly written by the then Iranian ambassador to Paris, Sadegh Kharrazi, and approved to be passed along by both President Khatami and Leader Khamenei with the latter having some reservations. The proposal can be found in Trita Parsi, *Treacherous Alliance* (New Haven, CT: Yale University Press, 2007).

43 · Kayhan Barzegar, "Iran's Foreign Policy Strategy after Saddam," *Washington Quarterly,* 33, 1 (January 2010), 173–89.

44 · Ibid.

45 · Seyed Sadeq Kharrazi, "A Year of Nuclear Diplomacy," *Iranian Diplomacy* (April 4, 2011), www.irdiplomacy.ir/index.php?Lang=en&Page=21&TypeId=&ArticleId=10870&BranchId=43&Action=ArticleBodyView.

5

Hugging and Hedging

Japanese Grand Strategy in the Twenty-First Century

NARUSHIGE MICHISHITA AND RICHARD J. SAMUELS

After decades of accepting US supremacy in Asia as the foundation of its foreign and security policies, finding the right distance between the United States and China is the most important strategic choice facing Japan today. "Getting it just right" with these two powers will require both military and economic readjustments. There is a great deal at stake in Tokyo's recalculation. Japan, China, and the United States are, after all, the three largest economies in the world, together accounting for nearly 40 percent of global production. Each has a deep—and deepening—stake in the other two. The United States and Japan are China's top two trade partners. The United States and China are Japan's top two trade partners. And Japan and China are the top two US trade partners outside of the North American Free Trade Agreement (NAFTA). In security terms, the United States remains the world's only hyperpower, but China's rapid (if opaque) military modernization is shifting regional dynamics. For its part, Japan annually spends over $50 billion on defense, no trivial sum despite its self-imposed cap on spending at 1 percent of GDP. Japan has an impressive navy and air force and has openly debated possessing strike capabilities. Even the nuclear option reportedly has been discussed among members of the National Diet.[1] In short, each of the three is a bona fide current or potential "great power"—namely, each has the ability to exert its economic, military, cultural, and diplomatic influence on a global scale in ways that could alter the regional and global balances.

The Japan–United States alliance is still the bedrock of Tokyo's national security strategy, one that for generations has been stable and unassailable under the so-called Yoshida Doctrine by which Japan has provided forward bases for US forces that provide it protection. But the Yoshida Doctrine, designed for a bipolar world, has been dissolving without a clear replacement strategy for a multipolar one. Japan's next grand strategy has been under debate for some time now, and both China and the United States are central to the discourse. Indeed, however close Tokyo remains to Washington, a rising China and a United States in relative decline are today at least equals in Japan's strategic calculus. Some in Japan openly fret about a Washington–Beijing "G-2" condominium. Others insist that Japan must do more to pre-pare for the (coming) day when the US capabilities slip below its commitments. There are also those who insist that unless Japan accommodates to Chinese power, it will lose influence in the region and globally. Still others are con-cerned that rivalry with China is unavoidable. Some wish to maximize Japa-nese sovereignty, some its prosperity, and others its status in world councils. Because the debate is often so clamorous, the possibility that improved rela-tions with China might be compatible with sustained close relations with the United States is often lost in the noise.

As this volume emphasizes, grand strategies are a function of both the struc-tural constraints of the international system and the choices made amid the tumult of domestic politics. From a Realist perspective, states act rationally to maximize security or power on the international level only to the extent that they can contain domestic political entropy.[2] Because democratic politics are fueled by contested preferences and values, they are notoriously unruly and domestic political interventions are common. Thus, explanations for the strategic behavior of nation-states require that analysts fully incorporate political dynamics below the level of the international system as well as in the structure of that system itself. This chapter, therefore, assesses the shifting discourse on Japanese grand strat-egy with both domestic political struggles and international relations in mind.

CURRENT SETTING FOR THE DEBATE

In recent years Japan has witnessed epochal transformations. The most strik-ing have been domestic. In August 2009, Japanese voters repudiated more than a half century of single party dominance by the Liberal Democratic Party (LDP). It elected the Democratic Party of Japan (DPJ), which ran on a platform of thoroughgoing change. The DPJ "manifesto" called for political control of Japan's "mandarin" bureaucracy, more transparent budgeting and an end to wasteful government spending, local autonomy, fuller national strategic thinking, enhanced social policies, and an end to Tokyo's subordination to Washington. DPJ leaders were embraced by voters with an overwhelming majority of seats in the House of Representatives. Japan's fabled "one and a half party system" had given way to viable two-party democracy for the first time ever.

DPJ dominance did not last long, however. Before the House of Councillors election in July 2010, the DPJ-led coalition fell apart over Prime Minister Hatoyama's mishandling of the US base issue and voter concerns over a political finance scandal in which party secretary general Ozawa Ichirō was embroiled. Less than a year after its unprecedented landslide victory in the lower house, the DPJ failed to gain a majority in the upper house, even with the help of its remaining coalition partners. The DPJ now governed with a "twisted Diet," and had to make concessions to opposition parties to pass legislation.

Changes have been just as real—and only slightly less dramatic—in the international relations of East Asia, where the tectonic plates of national power have shifted perceptibly in both the military and economic realms. Despite the increasing dependence of the United States on Asian finance and on commodity trade, an Asian regional trade and financial system has been debated without US leadership or, in some important cases, even without US participation. In 2004, the Chinese completed a historic free trade agreement (FTA) with ASEAN that became operational in January 2010 and the Japanese—"making up for lost time"—found themselves in the midst of what one scholar has labeled an "FTA frenzy."[3] Japan concluded Free Trade Agreements with Singapore (2002) and with Mexico (2004), and has nearly a dozen "economic partnership agreements" with ASEAN and other regional states.[4] Its "on again–off again" negotiations with the Republic of Korea (ROK) were resumed in June 2008, and a trilateral meeting of senior economic bureaucrats in Seoul in January 2010 stimulated informed speculation that a PRC–Japan–ROK free trade bloc is under construction.[5] Indeed, in May 2010, the "Plus Three" economic powerhouses of East Asia announced the launch of a Joint Study for a trilateral free trade agreement (FTA) and the establishment of a secretariat in Korea in 2011.[6] In one scholar's judgment, these "bilateral and region preferential FTA agreements are the building blocks to genuine, ground-up, and made-for-and-by Asians institutionalism," a process that she says "will affect not just [Washington's] relationship with [its] most important ally in Asia, but also [the US] role in shaping the geopolitics of the region."[7] A former Bush administration official agrees, suggesting that Washington is blithely un-aware of how fast the ground has shifted beneath its own feet in Asia:

> The United States still has its head in the sand about the degree to which Asians—including some of its closest allies—are groping for their *own* solutions to regional problems.... Most pan-Asian institutions will move forward regardless of American views and preferences.[8]

Although Washington has sought membership in (and would de facto become a leader of) some new regional economic institutions like the Trans Pacific Partnership (TPP), Asia's new regional economic architecture is still a work in progress. Economic ministers meet annually to discuss trade promotion, industrial standards setting, information technology, skills training, disease control, environmental protection, and small business development. Even though each of these various formulations is underde-veloped as compared with the European Community or NAFTA, it has led some analysts to predict that new economic institutions "will eventually redraw the regional-institutional and political map of Asia—one in which the U.S. may be an outsider."[9] Even if this is too extreme an expectation, the recent emergence of active economic diplomacy that has not been US-led reflects the relative decline of US influence in the region.

Although the institutional trajectory on the military security side is even less clear, there are comparable dynamics in play. Transformation of the US military posture has been under way—albeit in fits and starts—for nearly a decade. In October 2004, the United States and South Korea reached an agreement to reduce the number of US troops by 12,500, to approximately 25,000, by 2008. In Japan, the transfer of the 3rd Marine Expeditionary Force headquarters from Okinawa, and other efforts to consolidate US forces based in Japan were negotiated with the LDP government in 2005–2006.

These suggestions were stymied in 2010, when the Hatoyama government and the Obama administration failed to agree on how to implement this agreement.[10]

Still, most in Tokyo and Washington continue to expect redeployment of US forces in the region. Fewer US troops, especially near key hotspots, are seen by some as a sign of declining US commitment to the region's security and stimulate apprehension by some of abandonment. Some commentators raised fears that America was "marching out of Asia," while others celebrated the prospect.[11] These dynamics became part of Japan's national security strategy in 2010. In a report to the prime minister that would later form the basis of the 2010 National Defense Program Guidelines, a distinguished panel of experts addressed directly the relative decline of the United States and suggested several implications for Japanese policy, including the "deterioration of public goods provision," a "trend toward multipolarity," and an expectation that the United States would demand higher levels of security contributions by its allies. And, in what seems to be a euphemism for a *weakening* in US deterrent power, the experts spoke of "*changing* US deterrence."[12] Let us turn, therefore, to this evolving security discourse.

MODELING THE DISCOURSE

Moments of national consensus on grand strategy, as in the mid- and late-twentieth century, have punctuated a long and vigorous debate on how Japan should provide for its national security.[13] As in other countries examined in this volume, Japan's discourse has been buffeted by debates among "regionalists," "nationalists," "nativists," "autonomists," "liberals," and "internationalists," inter alia. Each has contributed important ideas that have been incorporated into Japanese security thinking at one time or another. For example, the ideas of Mercantile Realists who first argued that Japan would be safest as a small maritime trading nation in the early twentieth century inspired the Yoshida Doctrine.

But even if these various ideas have connected across time, changes in world order have filtered how each is applied to policy. As a case in point, late-nineteenth-century Asianism, often expressed as opposition to the state, morphed into militarized opposition to the West by the 1920s. By the

1960s, Asianism was common ground for autonomists on both the left and the right, and today, as expressed by some in the ruling DPJ, Asianism is both a realist and a liberal strategy: it is designed to compensate for declining US power at the same time that it seeks to capture full economic benefit from China's dramatic economic growth.

In the political realm, Japan's left and right long have shared a belief that the United States–Japan alliance diminishes Japanese sovereignty. Thus, the national security debate has not always strictly reflected ideological, or even party, lines. For example, the LDP supported the US alliance unconditionally but was divided on how to deal with Asia, while DPJ has been more unified on regional integration than on the alliance. It ought to be no surprise, then, that the contemporary discourse about Japanese grand strategy is filled with strange—and shifting—coalitions. Heirs to prewar nativism share antipathetic views of the US alliance with heirs of the old left. Today's small Japanists and big Japanists agree that the alliance matters, but disagree fundamentally on how much Japan should pay for its maintenance—and whether part of that cost should include Japan's becoming "normal." The deck is reshuffled yet again on the issue of accommodation with China.

These divisions led coauthor Samuels to represent the security policy preferences of contemporary Japanese scholars, commentators, politicians, and bureaucrats along two axes.[14] The first is a measure of the value placed on the alliance with the United States. At one extreme is the view that the United States is Japan's most important source of security, and must be embraced tightly. On this account, US bases in Japan are necessary in order to keep Washington committed to Japan's defense. At the other extreme is the view that in a unipolar world, the United States is unbalanced and therefore unconstrained; Japan must keep its distance to avoid becoming entangled in American military adventures. This entanglement is made all the more likely by the presence of US bases. This first axis, then, is a surrogate measure of the relative value one places on the dangers of abandonment and entanglement. Those with a high tolerance for the former are willing to keep a greater distance from the United States than are those with a higher tolerance for the latter.

Those with a high tolerance for entanglement are not all status quo–oriented, however. They are divided by the second axis—the willingness to use force in international affairs. As the introductory chapter to this volume anticipates, this division reflects differences over the means of foreign policy. Support for revision of Article 9 of the constitution, for Japan to assume a more proactive, even global, defense posture and for the dispatch of SDF abroad are all measures of where one stands on this second dimension. Some who support the US alliance, then, are more willing to deploy the SDF to "share alliance burdens" than are others who prefer that Japan continue to limit itself to rear area support. The former, some of whom wish Japan to become a great power again, are associated with the idea that Japan should become "normal." In the view of these "Normal Nation-alists"—essentially the "regular nationalists" identified in the introductory chapter by Henry Nau—the statute of limitations for Japan's mid-twentieth-century aggression expired long ago; it is time for Japan to step onto the international stage as an equal of the United States. The latter, "Mercantile Realists," are not multilater-alists or economic liberals. They believe that Japan must remain a small power with self-imposed limits to its right to belligerency and that Ja-pan's contributions to world affairs should remain nonmilitary. Among those who prefer Japan to keep a greater distance from the United States, are "Autonomists" who, like the nativists in China and Russia, would build an independent, full-spectrum Japanese military that could use force, and "Pacifists" who eschew the military institution altogether. All four groups seek security for Japan, but each closely associates security with different values: "Autonomists" seek security with sovereignty and dignity; "Pacifists" seek security with peace and isolation; "Normal na-tion-alists" want security with equality and a more robust role in the in-ternational community; and "Mercantile Realists" have sought security with prosperity (see Figure 5.1).

This model defines clear policy spaces for important groups in the Jap-anese security discourse. But because these groups are themselves divided by party and other policy preferences, it also raises questions about whether any one of them on its own could consolidate power long enough to impose its preferred grand strategy for Japan. It has long been clear that public support for constitutional revision is limited and therefore that the preferences of "Normal Nation-alists" would butt up against a public more focused on economic and social issues and weary of Japan's

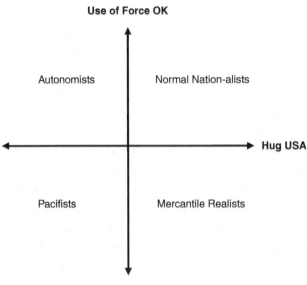

Use of Force OK

Autonomists   Normal Nation-alists

◄——————————————————► **Hug USA**

Pacifists   Mercantile Realists

Figure 5.1

"culture wars."[15] Indeed, LDP policy makers themselves also realized that relations with an emergent China, Japan's largest trade partner, could not be allowed to deteriorate further, and began to repair Sino–Japanese relations immediately after Prime Minister Koizumi retired. Support for the "Mercantilist" position was also limited, however. It seemed that these prosperity seekers had exhausted the patience of the Japanese public with their inability to find a growth path independent of Washington. Since these groups together formed the core of the governing LDP, it was apparent by 2007 that change was in the offing. Meanwhile, the "Pacifists" seemed an anachronism to many, and the "autonomists" were far too hawkish for most Japanese voters.

It was clear, then, that Japan would begin to find a more effective balance between its neighbors and its security partner. Samuels described this groping for a more robust approach to security as a "Goldilocks Consensus"—an effort to "get it just right." This recalculation, now well under way, comprises multiple hedges: a hedge against US decline and Chinese aggression, a hedge against entanglement in US adventures and abandonment by a still needed partner, and a hedge against predation and protectionism in economic affairs. Each of Japan's post-Koizumi prime

ministers—starting with the surprisingly accommodating Abe Shinzō—
acted like Goldilocks by deferring to China on particularly irritating dis-
plays of Japanese nationalism, such as refraining from prime ministerial
visits to the Yasukuni Shrine. When power was transferred to the DPJ in
2009, Japan's Goldilocks behavior accelerated, receiving considerably more
attention in the press and generating predictable, and therefore avoidable,
frictions with Washington.

Even if North Korean and Chinese actions blunted some of the DPJ's
enthusiasms, Japan is still feeling its way toward a new security posture in
an era in which China is at least as important economically and militarily
as the United States. The migration of Japan's grand strategy from one
centered on becoming normal in military terms in alliance with the United
States to one centered on becoming normal in more comprehensive
terms—by getting relations with the two greatest powers on earth "just
right"—is a tricky business. It requires great skill from diplomats and
policy makers who must convince domestic audiences and the international community that collective goods will continue to be provided. It
likewise demands more fine-grained examination by analysts. Toward that
end, we adjust the original model to account more fully for the nascent
view—and for some, merely a hope—that a positive sum relationship between improved relations with China and sustained alliance with the
United States is possible.

(RE)MODELING THE DISCOURSE

Specifically, it seems to us that it would be particularly useful to array relations with the United States against relations with China.[16] In doing so, we
use familiar issues—military and economic, each in turn—to locate familiar groups in slightly different orientations to one another. By redimen-
sioning the debate, we are able to examine more closely how Japanese
hedging and hugging can be mutually reinforcing as the discourse evolves.
We also note that the use of force may not be as decisive as posited in the
original model. We begin with Japan's relationship with the United
States.

Adjusting the Distance from the United States

The original postwar deal engineered by Prime Minister Yoshida, Japan's iconic Mercantile Realist, involved a trade-off of economic and military benefits between Washington and Tokyo. The United States would provide two kinds of goods to Japan: It would protect Japan with extended nuclear deterrence (the so-called nuclear umbrella) and it would provide access both to the US market and technology for Japanese firms. In exchange, a pragmatic Japan would be a loyal ally in the larger Cold War competition. It would prosper without remilitarizing and would provide an "unsinkable aircraft carrier" for forward deployed US forces to deter and contain communist expansion.

So long as this mercantilist wing of the LDP was in power, it would collude with pacifists to keep the normal nationalists (most of whom were also in the LDP) from revising—or even reinterpreting—the constitution. The mercantilists were more concerned about electoral backlash from Japan's antiwar public than about responding to pressure from the United States to "share the burden" in providing global security. They therefore (self-) imposed constraints on Japanese military power. These constraints took many forms, including the adoption of three nonnuclear principles—no manufacture, deployment, or introduction of nuclear weapons. Defense spending would be limited to 1 percent of GDP, the export of arms would be banned, and the military use of space foresworn. In addition, in the process of consolidating its power during the 1960s–1970s, this pragmatic mainstream of the LDP refused to acquire what it considered "offensive weapons" such as long-range bombers, aircraft carriers, intercontinental ballistic missiles, and aerial refueling capabilities that would extend Japan's military reach. They would construct a "reliable and warm-hearted" military and keep their political rivals out of power.[17]

But the LDP's revisionists, whose progeny we now label "normal nation-alists," had not been completely shut out of power. In the 1950s, Hatoyama Ichirō and Kishi Nobusuke represented (and implemented) a harder line on national security. Nakasone Yasuhiro likewise did so in the 1980s. Hatoyama reserved for Japan the right to preempt the imminent use of force in 1956, while Kishi established the next year that nuclear weapons were not unconstitutional. Nakasone demonstrated that the 1 percent limit on defense spending could be breached, that dual-use technology could be exported, and that Japan could engage in the military use of space (by participating in Ronald Reagan's "Star Wars" program). But it was not until the 2000s that the "normal nation-alists" would consolidate power. Under the leadership of Koizumi Junichirō and his successor, Abe Shinzō, this next generation of revisionists would press for revision of the constitution, enhance Japan's military capabilities by acquiring weapons that earlier had been deemed unconstitutional, dispatch troops for the first time to a foreign country in which there were active combat operations, elevate the Defense Agency to ministry status, engage in de facto collective self-defense, and relax the arms export ban. In short, despite vigorous opposition from the pacifists and mercantilists, they moved to eliminate (albeit incrementally) many of Japan's self-imposed restraints on the military.[18]

These shifts were facilitated by enhanced threats from China and North Korea. Each group perceived these threats differently, of course. But the normal nation-alists were in power and Kim Jong Il seemed heaven sent by those who wished to enhance Japan's defense capabilities. With Kim admitting to the abduction of Japanese, testing missiles inside Japanese air space, openly developing and then testing nuclear weapons, and defying his neighbors—including China—there was no need to overinflate a "China threat." North Korea would suffice as justification for Japanese acquisition of sea-based missile defense platforms, new destroyers, and assault ships, and for participation in the joint ballistic missile defense program with the United States.

This cooperation notwithstanding, there have been persistent irritants to the United States–Japan military relationship. The central problem has been the issue of Japanese sovereignty. For many Japanese, sovereignty is diminished by the continued presence of US troops on the archipelago more than sixty-five years after Japan's unconditional surrender. The US military has exclusive right to over 300 square kilometers of land, three-quarters of it in Okinawa, Japan's southernmost prefecture.[19] Every Japanese political party, from the Communists to the LDP, has called for a reduction in the "base burden" if not for outright elimination of the facilities altogether. Even former defense officials rail against US extra-territorial privilege: former JDA director general Ohno Yoshinori declared "the Occupation-era base structure" to be the single most difficult problem for the future of the United States–Japan alliance, adding that a new Status of Forces Agreement (SOFA) should be negotiated.[20] Journalist Ina Hisayoshi reflects the widely held (and less restrained) judgment that the conduct of the US military in Japan "resembles that of an occupying force."[21]

In 1960, Prime Minister Kishi arranged for a revision of the treaty to reduce the extraterritorial privileges of US forces. Article Six of the revised treaty provides "the use of facilities and areas in Japan" by the US armed forces "for the purpose of contributing to the security of Japan and the maintenance of international peace and security in the Far East."[22] The accompanying Status of Forces Agreement stipulates responsibilities for the maintenance of facilities and legal jurisdictions in the event of accidents or crimes by US military personnel (both have occurred with uncomfortable frequency). Local government officials have even less jurisdiction vis-à-vis base issues than does the central government. Associations of governors and mayors from the fourteen prefectures that host US bases have pressed the case for greater local jurisdiction, particularly regarding search and seizure powers and environmental standards.

Although both the security treaty and the SOFA have been altered through side agreements that give the Japanese government somewhat greater latitude, neither has ever been formally revised. Nor has the 1996 bilateral agreement to resize US forces in Okinawa ever been implemented.[23] At no time in the history of the postwar alliance has the base issue not been characterized by extreme displeasure—either of local residents who put up with base pollution and crime, or of alliance managers who spend endless hours finding ways to co-opt opposition and maintain the status quo.[24] In the 2009 election campaign, the DPJ declared its opposition to the 2006 agreement negotiated by Tokyo and Washington on the relocation of Futenma, a marine helicopter base in the middle of densely populated Ginowan City. In the party's widely circulated 2009 "Manifesto," the first item under the heading "Diplomacy" called for a more equal relationship with the United States and for a reexamination of the US base structure in Japan.[25] Given this campaign promise, and given that the DPJ victory depended upon a coalition with a small, but insistent Socialist Party centered in Okinawa, the government led by Hatoyama Yukio made a beeline for the base relocation issue immediately upon taking office. It began questioning decisions on the realignment of US forces as well. US opposition notwithstanding, the DPJ elevated the sovereignty issue and seemed determined to put more space between Japan and the United States than had heretofore seemed possible.

Hatoyama pressed hard on this issue but failed to produce positive results. Instead, his ill-prepared and disorganized attempt to find a new destination for the Futenma marine air base generated tension between Washington and Tokyo, and reignited Okinawans' once becalmed opposition to the 2006 decision to relocate the base to Henoko, a less populated area in Nago City further to the northeast. In May 2010, amid mounting frustrations on both sides, the two governments decided to settle the issue by re-agreeing to the original 2006 deal.[26] Taking responsibility for his bungled attempt, Hatoyama resigned and Kan Naoto became prime minister.

This would have been merely a return to the status quo ante had the relationship not become so frayed by the controversy, and had relocation of US marines to Guam not been delayed by opposition in Guam and by Congress.[27] In the event, Washington announced that base construction could not be completed by 2014 as scheduled, and the completion date might be put off by three to five years.[28] Agreement by the two governments that relocation to Guam was dependent on tangible progress made by Japan toward completion of the replacement facility further complicated the process and the relationship.[29] In 2011, when Noda Yoshihiko succeeded Kan to become the third DPJ prime minister in two years, the base issue was even further from resolution.[30]

The economic relationship—never entirely satisfactory to some on either side—has also faced many challenges. After a decade of double-digit Japanese growth and the consolidation of Japanese prosperity, the period from the late 1960s to the mid-1990s was particularly fractious. Japanese trade surpluses mushroomed in what was perceived in Washington as at US expense. Tokyo and Washington found themselves in an incessant series of negotiations on market access across the board: textiles, rice, apples, semiconductor chips, retailing, direct investment, copyright laws, fighter jets, dual-use technology transfer, automobiles, lawyers, satellites—the list seemed endless and the national interests seemed irreconcilable. These bilateral "frictions" defined the perspectives of an entire generation of business elites and alliance managers who came to believe that different forms of capitalism bred of different values could undermine even the most carefully crafted international relationships and rules of the economic road.[31] Many veterans of these trade wars—former business executives, junior government officials, and backbench politicians—are now senior DPJ leaders or their advisors.

That road was paved with new institutions, including the evolution of the General Agreement on Tariffs and Trade (GATT) into the World Trade Organization (WTO). But, while the nations of Western Europe moved forward with their European Union, and while the United States, Canada, and Mexico lurched forward with their North American Free Trade Agreement (NAFTA), no comparable regional economic bloc emerged in Asia. This has now begun to change, as have the prospects for enhanced transparency in the military realm. Let us turn, then, to examine shifts in the distance between Japan and China on the economic and military dimensions in our effort to remodel the discourse on Japanese national security.

Closing the Distance with China

It is an understatement to point out that Japan's relations with China are complex and very much in flux. Much of the complexity comes from the perceived mismatch between Sino–Japanese economic and political–military relations—what was often referred to as "hot economics and cold politics" during the 2000s.[32] Although China became Japan's largest trading partner in 2006 and although an enormous volume of Japanese technology has flowed into Chinese-based factories, competition for regional leadership, territorial disputes, and military competition have complicated efforts to reconcile the two nations.

The most fundamental element in this complexity—the Sino–Japanese analogue to the United States–Japan base issue—derives from history and how to interpret it. In this regard, no burr under the bilateral saddle has been more unsettling than prime ministerial visits to the Yasukuni Shrine in central Tokyo. Even though Article 20 of the Japanese constitution expressly separated church and state, Yasukuni has remained Japan's de facto official war memorial. Virtually every postwar prime minister, regardless of political orientation, visited Yasukuni while in office—including Yoshida Shigeru (ten times).[33] In October 1978, however, the priests at Yasukuni secretly enshrined fourteen Class A war criminals, including General Tōjō Hideki. By honoring—rather than just mourning—fallen soldiers, and by identifying more than 1,000 "martyrs of *Shōwa*" who in their view were "cruelly and unjustly tried as war criminals by a shamlike tribunal of the allied forces," Yasukuni became a lightning rod for disputes over historical memory after Prime Minister Koizumi began a series of annual visits to the Yasukuni Shrine during his long tenure from 2001 to 2006. Yasukuni now had come to be about far more than soldiers' souls; it had become a political litmus test of one's view of the colonial experiences of China and Korea and, by implication, of the bilateral past and future as well. Okada Katsuya, who became Japan's foreign minister in 2009, declared in 2005 that these visits "sabotaged" Japan's relations with its neighbors. Each of Koizumi's successors—LDP and DPJ alike—understood the problems that Yasukuni visits were causing in Sino–Japanese relations. Almost immediately upon assuming office, each visited Beijing and promised to discontinue the visits.[34] Even before assuming office, Prime Minister Noda made headlines—and attracted considerable apprehension from Beijing— by reaffirming his view that the fourteen designated Class A war criminals enshrined there were not war criminals under the Japanese law in the first place, and that their status had already been rehabilitated in 1956 based on the San Francisco Peace Treaty.[35] Still, he followed his predecessors' path and steered clear of shrine visits.

History—and, especially, government-approved textbooks that chronicle it—have deeply affected Sino–Japanese relations. Indeed, most of Japan's neighbors have been frustrated by the frequency with which Japanese aggression during the Pacific War has been understated—or even denied. As a result—and despite repeated official apologies—Japan and its neighbors have never found the "deep reconciliation" achieved by France and Germany.[36] Instead, they have battled endlessly, and without closure, on the basic facts of the last century. Joint study teams of Korean and Japanese historians issued a report that merely sustained different interpretations of the past. Meanwhile, Chinese and Japanese historians who began meeting in 2006 at the initiative of Prime Minister Abe and President Hu Jintao, missed their targeted deadline in 2008 for a final report on the thirtieth anniversary of normalized relations. But by late 2009, after the shift to a DPJ government, the Chinese press began reporting that fundamentals of a common narrative may be in the offing.[37] Reports in January 2010 that Prime Minister Hatoyama was prepared to visit Nanjing, where he would atone for Japan's aggression and, it was hoped, take a giant step toward laying the bilateral history issue to rest, were unrealized.[38]

As noted, China and Japan, which had competed for regional economic leadership in the 1990s–2000s, also now seemed ready to engage substantively on the issue of economic institution building. Much had changed in the economic relationship. China has been Japan's most important trading partner since 2007. The trade volume between the two countries increased from 9 trillion yen, or one-tenth of Japan's total trade, in 2000 to 22 trillion yen in 2009, or more than one-fifth of Japan's total trade. In contrast, Japan's trade with the United States has declined from 23 trillion yen— one-quarter of Japan's total trade volume to 14 trillion yen, just over one-eighth of Japan's total trade volume in the same period.[39] Japan's foreign direct investment in China started to increase significantly in 2001, and in 2009 Japan overtook Singapore to become the third largest investor there.[40] Moreover, because so many Japanese firms manufacture products in China for export to the still significant US market, China's importance as Japan's economic partner will continue to grow in the foreseeable future.

These shifts and the resulting bilateral discussions over new regional institutions—what Henry Nau referred to in his introductory chapter as a regional scope, institutional means, and collective goods-oriented policy— predated the ascendance to power of the DPJ. But the DPJ's long commitment to an East Asian Economic Community—however vaguely defined—accelerated the process. The DPJ government began closing the distance between China and Japan on the economic front. The logic was compelling to many in both countries, for the two economies had been complementary for some time. Japan provides China with technology and capital, while China provides Japan with cheap production and an export platform. Both have an abiding interest in a vibrant regional economy. More than 10 million Chinese work in Japanese firms, a number that continues to grow as Japan redirects its direct foreign investment toward China and away from the United States. One government researcher calls for a Sino–Japanese free trade agreement and insists that "if the comparative advantages of both countries can be realized through trade, China's advancement will not be a threat to Japan but rather a win–win game for both sides."[41] Likewise, an "ASEAN Plus Three" regional order integrating the economies of Japan, China, and Korea with those of Southeast Asia is a central feature of Chinese diplomacy and an "ASEAN Plus Six" alternative that includes Australia, New Zealand, and India is championed by Japan.[42] As Mike Mochizuki has suggested, there are many in Japan who see China as "a potential partner in establishing an attractive global economic balance of power."[43]

The military picture is less clear. Chinese leaders remain wary of prospects for the Japanese military—and vice versa. Even those Chinese who believe that stable Sino–United States relations are possible in the long term are divided over the role of the United States–Japan alliance. At best, they credit it with serving as a "cork in the Japanese bottle," and at worst they view it as a "cover for Japanese military modernization."[44] They are wary of Japan's sympathy toward Taiwan, which, after the Korean peninsula, is the most volatile flash point in East Asia. And they are even more concerned about Japan's plan to reorient its defense.[45] Chinese suspicions have been exacerbated by competition for resources in adjacent sea beds, further raising the stakes and the tensions for both nations, despite the fact that both countries are energy importers, and that each therefore benefits considerably from global resource development, from stability in the sea lanes, and from the efficient use of resources.

So, while there are ample incentives for cooperation, more than a few boulders remain strewn along the road to Sino–Japanese rapprochement. Perhaps the largest are territorial: sovereignty of the Senkaku Islands, located near both Taiwan and Okinawa, and an agreed international border in the East China Sea. The former dispute remains the more dangerous because it is more militarized, while recent Sino–Japanese summits have addressed the latter in potentially productive ways.[46] In Japan, public debate of a "China threat" intensified in the early 2000s, when the discourse became "less restrained and compromising" and accounts of Chinese intentions became increasingly "visceral."[47] By then, the Self Defense Forces had already begun to incorporate Chinese military power as a factor in its defense plans.[48] And in 2005, the Foreign Ministry and the JDA characterized the modernization of Chinese military capabilities as a threat for the first time.[49]

As we shall examine below, it would get worse in 2010, after a Chinese trawler rammed a Japan Coast Guard cutter in waters claimed by Japan near the Senkaku/Diaoyu Islands. First, however, the relationship enjoyed a thaw. After Koizumi retired in 2006, Japan was eager to close the distance with China. In August, Chinese minister of defense Cao Gangchuan visited Japan to meet Defense Minister Kōmura Masahiko. Within eight months, a Chinese destroyer made a port call in Tokyo for the first time and a joint statement was issued calling for promotion of a "Mutually Beneficial Relationship Based on Common Strategic Interests." Mutual visits by high-level defense officials and port calls by naval warships would now take place on a regular basis. In June 2008, an MSDF destroyer visited Guandong Province to deliver blankets and emergency food and sanitary supplies for the victims of the Sichuan earthquake.[50] At the same time, a bilateral agreement was reached on joint development and participation of Japanese enterprises in the development of the Shirakaba (Chinese name: Chunxiao) oil and gas field in the East China Sea, which China had already started developing.[51] This was followed by new rounds of bilateral security dialogues in 2009.

The shift in power in Japan after the August 2009 election contributed further to this apparent Sino–Japanese rapprochement. Although the election was not fought on foreign and security policy issues, the DPJ manifesto was clear: Its candidates promised that a DPJ government would establish a more equal relationship with the United States and that to do so, it would show "will" toward Washington in the first instance by revisiting deals struck on Okinawa bases and US military realignment. The party also promised to adjust policy toward Asia—and began tilting Japan toward the continent. Foreign Minister Okada and his Chinese counterpart, Yang Jiechi, agreed in late 2009 to cooperate in the construction of an East Asian Community and to cooperate on food safety, energy resources, and other issues. This was all rather imprecise, but the rebalancing seemed most energized in December 2009 when then DPJ power broker Ozawa Ichirō took a

600 person entourage to China—including more than 120 DPJ Diet members. And, as if to drive home the point that change was truly under way, a "final, final" decision on relocation of the Futenma marine air strip was postponed during the Tokyo visit of PRC heir apparent Xi Jinping who, at DPJ insistence, was allowed to meet the emperor on short notice. Then, in January 2010, the Hatoyama administration canceled the logistic support operations the SDF had been conducting since 2001 in the Indian Ocean to help US and other forces fighting in Afghanistan. Michael Green refers to this as "the greatest period of political turmoil and confusion in the United States–Japan alliance since the mutual security treaty was signed in 1960."[52]

But Tokyo's rebalancing between Beijing and Washington soon ran into difficulties. The disconnect between the economic and military components has revealed contradictions in Japan's grand strategy and especially in the tactical shifts required for its implementation. In September 2011, Prime Minister Noda indicated that the plan for an "East Asian Community" would not be a priority of his administration given the nation's more immediate diplomatic tasks. He wrote, "We do not have to set out a grand vision, such as [the creation of] an East Asian community, for now."[53]

Coping with the Emerging Contradictions

Given the post–Cold War transformation of the international environment and the relative power shift taking place between the United States and China, maintaining the distance from the United States while closing it with China made grand strategic sense for Japan. But Tokyo's military, economic, and diplomatic policies vis-à-vis Washington and Beijing have not been well coordinated.

Fortunately—at least from the perspective of alliance supporters—most US and Japanese policy makers continued to appreciate the importance of the bilateral alliance at a time when China is becoming stronger militarily and more assertive diplomatically. Washington's 2010 *Quadrennial Defense Review Report* discussed in some detail the "anti-access and area denial capabilities" that China has been developing. The report contended that a "joint air–sea battle concept" must be developed to address "how air and naval forces will integrate capabilities across all operational domains—air, sea, land, space, and cyberspace—to counter growing challenges to U.S. freedom of action."[54] It also acknowledged that undertaking such a mission requires strong support from regional allies, most notably Japan. In the same vein, while pointing to a "changing global power balance," Japan's 2010 National Defense Program Guidelines emphasized America's singular importance in contributing to global peace and stability.[55]

Alliance drift was sharply halted in 2010 owing largely to China's military in the region. On two separate occasions in April, Chinese military helicopters flew dangerously close to Japanese destroyers engaged in surveillance activities in the East China Sea, engendering formal Japanese government protests. A month later Beijing was widely reported to have declared the South China Sea to be an area of "core national interest," although many analysts believe it not to have been a formal statement of national policy.[56] The September collision of a Chinese fishing boat with a Japan Coast Guard patrol boat in Japanese territory near the Senkaku/ Diaoyu Islands attracted the most attention. After Chinese crew members were detained by the Japanese authorities and the captain was arrested, the Chinese government reiterated its position that these islands belonged to China, and made a set of demands, including for apologies and reparations, that attracted international attention. Harassing the Japanese ambassador in Beijing, cutting off exports of rare earth metals, arresting Japanese businessmen, and canceling ministerial meetings all struck the Japanese public as heavy-handed and unbecoming of a "responsible" stakeholder. In one intense week of diplomacy, Beijing seemed to many in Japan and elsewhere to undercut a long and determined effort to build confidence in Japan and around the region. This incident touched off anti-Japanese fervor in China and a reciprocal nationalism in Japan that portend more rough seas ahead. In late 2010, Japanese public opinion had turned against China in higher numbers than at any time since the survey was started in 1978.[57]

These developments—and others involving North Korea—drove Japanese leaders to reconsider the wisdom of alienating Washington's affections. The post-Hatoyama DPJ shifted direction sharply and increased its commitment to the alliance. By January 2011, for example, Prime Minister Kan delivered a policy speech identifying the United States–Japan alliance as the "lynchpin of Japan's diplomacy"—a position indistinguishable from

LDP policies he once opposed—and his foreign minister, Maehara Seiji, signed a deal with US ambassador John Roos to maintain the current level of Host Nation Support for another five years.[58]

The devastating chain of earthquakes, tsunami, and nuclear radiation disasters in March 2011 significantly enhanced the legitimacy of both the SDF and the US alliance. In the largest deployment of Japanese military personnel since the Pacific War, 100,000 soldiers were quickly mobilized to deal with the search, rescue, and eventual reconstruction campaign. The Japanese public welcomed the soldiers, as well as the US forces deployed to support them. Within hours of learning of the earthquake, President Barack Obama expressed his "sadness," promised extensive financial and humanitarian assistance, and declared the alliance "rock solid." At Japan's request, Washington immediately redirected the USS *Ronald Reagan* and its carrier task force from the waters around South Korea toward the affected Japanese coast. Supported by American personnel and equipment from as far afield as Singapore, those forces engaged with the SDF in their first ever full-scale joint rescue and relief operations. The deployment of helicopters from the Futenma marine air base in Okinawa was also well received. From the Japanese people's view, the alliance had never worked so smoothly. For them, the alliance had always been a vague concept; now, for the first time, it seemed a concrete and useful cooperative framework.

At the same time, the Chinese government and people also acted quickly and generously. Prime Minister Wen Jiabao reminded the nation that Japan had come to their aid after the 2008 Sichuan earthquake. He expressed sympathy for the Japanese people, promised $4.5 million in aid, and dispatched personnel to assist in the relief and recovery efforts. The Chinese government also provided relief supplies, including fuel. For their part, Chinese netizens shucked the jingoistic excesses of past years and regular citizens responded generously with fund-raising efforts of their own.

Thus, we have observed considerable movement on two axes in the formulation of Japan's post-Yoshida consensus on grand strategy. After beginning to openly confront the United States on issues of particular resonance with the Japanese public, for example, sovereignty and bases, Tokyo returned to its more traditional posture vis-à-vis its alliance partner when, in 2010, China seemed more the dragon and less the panda. Arrayed against one another, Japan's relationships with the world's two most powerful nations define spaces for several kinds of national security strategies, and provide a finer-grained set of distinctions than the original model (Figure 5.2).

Several of these quadrants are quite familiar from the original model, particularly those who would maintain Japan's distance from the United States and those who would discount military security in favor of economic gains. As in the original model, there are those who distrust foreign entanglements, preferring instead that Japan acquire and sustain an independent military capability. These "autonomists" see no reason to hedge their bets on the rise of China or on the decline of the United States. In their view, Japan should regain full sovereignty and provide for itself in a "self-help" world. They would model Japan on India and would, in a sense, "self-hedge"—what realist international relations theorists call "internal balancing."[59] They would pursue autarchic economic policies and an autonomous military posture. This group includes pacifists as well as Gaullists—an indication that the preference for autonomy is independent

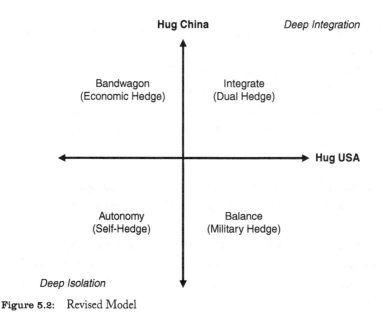

Figure 5.2: Revised Model

of a preference for the use of force, contra the original model. Liberal values are not particularly important to either of these groups, but independence is. Both would build fences and dig moats to preserve their version of Japan as a "small but shining nation."[60] In order to preserve a pure and orderly Japan, advocates of this view on the right such as Tokyo governor Ishihara Shintarō, former Air Self-Defense Force chief of staff Tamogami Toshio, Kobayashi Yoshinori, a popular nationalist cartoonist, and journalists Sakurai Yoshiko and Nishibe Susumu, argue for equidistance from Washington and Beijing—emphasizing *distance*.

For example, General Tamogami has insisted:

Although Japan and the United States are allied politically, their economic interests are often in conflict. This means that Japan keeps losing its economic interest as it always obeys U.S. will. It is therefore necessary for us to be assertive with the United States to protect our own interests. But still, there is a limit to our assertiveness, so long as we are dependent on the United States for our defense. Therefore, we have to become a truly independent nation by strengthening our military and intelligence capabilities.[61]

Ms. Sakurai, although less radical than Tamogami, also reflects this position:

When the number of U.S. forces is reduced through the force realignment process there will be a huge military vacuum.... Considering Japan's national interests, Japan would have to fill the vacuum. In this sense, the call by Prime Minister [Abe] for an amendment of the Constitution and a possible change to the current policy on collective self-defense, was of extreme importance. If [this succeeds] Japan would be able to fill the vacuum and securing itself autonomously.[62]

Inada Tomomi, an LDP Diet member, has publicly advocated that Japan should possess nuclear weapons and should introduce conscription:

Japan should explore possessing nuclear weapons as a national strategy, not just as a matter for discussion...[and should consider] creating a system in which all young people will belong for a time to the Self-Defense Forces as an educational experience.[63]

Joining in this group from the left are politicians such as Social Democratic Party chief Fukushima Mizuho, although her party has taken less of a hard line toward Chinese provocations of Japan. The preference of this group for a political and military isolation of Japan could reduce the ability of Japanese firms to compete in global markets. The domestic consequences would likely include social alienation and economic lethargy.

Those advocating a China–Japan economic condominium, such as Terashima Jitsurō, Ozawa Ichirō, and Waseda University professor emeritus Mori Kazuko, prefer a strategy of what we call bandwagoning. They discount the Chinese military threat and emphasize the benefits from a robust bilateral economic relationship with the new global economic giant. In August 2009, Terashima argued:

> The statistics showing economic relations with other countries matter in formulating foreign and security policies. Trade with China, which accounted for only 3% of Japan's total amount of trade in 1990, rapidly increased to represent as much as 20.4% this year, whereas the percentage of Japan-U.S. trade declined from 28% to 13.7%... these numbers are symbol of a change in Japan's position in the international arena.[64]

For his part, the once powerful former DPJ leader, Ozawa Ichirō, who led the highly visible mission of DPJ Diet members to Beijing mentioned above, famously suggested that the US military presence in Japan should be limited to the 7th Fleet in Yokosuka.[65]

By hedging economically and bandwagoning with Chinese market power, that is, by rebalancing Japan's strategic portfolio, proponents of this position would try to prevent predation and stave off technological decline. They would contribute to the construction of a China-centered East Asian economic bloc, acting as China's regional ally and discount the costs of alienating Washington. The main risk they face is betrayal by China. Still, they imagine Beijing will generally be a responsible stakeholder in regional stability and, as their top short-term objective is prosperity, they feel it imperative not to "miss the China bus." Their longer-term objective would be to create a China–Japan condominium, the global impact of which would be the acceleration of the post-Washington economic consensus and the global multipolarity they see as already under construction.

Like the self-hedgers described earlier, these economic hedgers are heterogeneous. Acting on the expectation that China is the future and the United States is the past, a small number of them highly discounts the risk that Tokyo would swap subordination to Washington to subordination to Beijing. In that (admittedly extreme) case, liberal democratic values would also be subordinated and Russia would be a more appropriate model than India. But while most continue to be wary of Chinese hegemony, all believe that Sino–Japanese relations should take priority over those between Japan and the United States. For example, DPJ vice president Yamaoka Kenji has reportedly argued that "a better relationship with China could be a deterrent vis-à-vis the United States on security matters." He also has insisted that "The most realistic way to go is to make the Sino-Japan relationship solid first, and thereafter solve the problems between Japan and the U.S."[66]

"Balancers" are attentive to direct military threats from China and less enamored with the economic benefits to be derived from closer relations with China. If those who bandwagon would hedge by integrating with China economically, those who balance China would hedge militarily, by maintaining a robust alliance with the United States. Leading politicians like the LDP's former defense minister, Ishiba Shigeru, and the party's former foreign minister, Maehara Seiji, Tokyo University professors Kitaoka Shinichi and Kubo Fumiaki, former diplomat Okazaki Hisahiko, former president of the National Defense Academy Nishihara Masashi, president of Takushoku University Watanabe Toshio, and the vice chairman of the Research Institute for Peace and Security (RIPS) Watanabe Akio all believe that Chinese power is apt to be assertive and should be met with containment and deterrence through an expanded network of alert states—including Australia and India. Ishiba said as long ago as 2005 that "Chinese defense capabilities are by far stronger than what is necessary for its own defense. No country intends to attack China today. I, therefore, have to bring the objective of its rapid military expansion into question."[67] The future foreign minister, Maehara Seiji, then DPJ president, concurred in 2006, stating that there was "no change in my perception that China's military power constitutes a real threat [to Japan]."[68] Earlier, Maehara had stressed to a Washington audience that

China's rapid economic growth and strength has allowed it to maintain a growth rate of more than 10% in military spending for nearly 20 years. Some say that amount is perhaps 2 or even 3 times the Chinese government's official figures. Nonetheless, it continues to strengthen and modernize its military power. This is a very real concern. . . . We see movements by China to ignore the sovereignty and maritime rights of other nations, and to establish vested interests by creating a fait accompli through the development of natural gas and oil in the East China Sea. A Chinese nuclear-powered submarine has even made an incursion into Japan's territorial waters. It is important that we not just wait and see, but take a firm response to these kinds of actions.[69]

Former prime minister Tony Blair's Great Britain may be the most relevant foreign model for this group of military hedgers who argue for enhancing Japan's capabilities and reinterpreting the constitution to allow Japan to defend its US ally. They prefer the global status quo in which Washington remains the dominant player in the system, and imagine that Japan will be safest when aligned with Washington as the system becomes bi- or multipolar. Economically, they tend to embrace liberal free trade, using it as both policy guide and leverage in international negotiations. Their short-term objective is to buy time for the revitalization of Japan.

We label the final group "integrators." These are the "Goldilocks" strategists who discount the contradictions we have identified and who believe that Japan can—and should—have it both ways. They believe Tokyo can "get it just right" and that better economic relations with Beijing need not be purchased at the price of diminished relations with Washington. Their dual hedge would protect Japan from economic predation by integrating with the Chinese economically and would protect Japan from Chinese coercion by maintaining a healthy alliance with the United States. They would, in short, wield an economic sword and a military shield.[70] Representative thinkers and strategists in this group are policy intellectuals like Soeya Yoshihide and Shiraishi Takashi, as well as former diplomats like Tanaka Hitoshi and Yabunaka Mitoji, each of whom has identified benefits from rebalancing Japan's foreign and security policy. Soeya, for example, has argued that

it will be necessary for Japan to engage more actively in efforts to construct a regional community in Asia. Japan should do so without changing the basic

framework of its Japan-U.S. relationship-centered foreign policy, and by advocating "human security" as the objective of its global diplomacy. Japan is certainly in a position to propose an alternative to the current process in which
China has taken leadership role. However, Japan will never be able to be a superpower that could compete with China. Its diplomacy, therefore, should be
more focused on cooperation with other middle powers like South Korea,
Southeast Asian countries, Australia, and New Zealand, in order to get their
support for its initiatives.[71]

For his part, Tanaka has laid out a "four story security structure" for Asia.
The first floor would comprise

> a mosaic of multiple bilateral security arrangements such as Japan-U.S., U.S.-
> ROK, and U.S.-Australia alliances. The second floor would be made up of a
> framework for confidence building among Japan, U.S., and China. The third
> floor would consist of multilateral regional security frameworks, the best ex-
> ample of which is the six-party talks. The fourth floor would be composed of
> non-traditional type of security cooperation in disaster relief, anti-piracy activi-
> ties, or anti-terrorism operations.[72]

These strategists, including former foreign minister Okada Katsuya, former
deputy chief cabinet secretary Furukawa Motohisa, and other senior DPJ
leaders, are confident that China's rise can be peaceful and fear China's
betrayal and US decline in equal measure. In contrast to the military hedgers, these dual hedgers are well aware that the United States and China are
getting closer to each other politically and economically and hope to establish a Concert of Asia that sustains equidistance among the three great
powers. They view Japan as a middle power, modeled on Germany, which
will be able to maintain the US alliance while pursuing protection against
Chinese mercantilism through economic integration. They would deploy
liberal economic policy as leverage, while using Washington to protect
them as they fix the failed fiscal and security policies of their predecessors. Their short-term objective is to seize the opportunity to help design,
build, and board a "G-3 bus" in order to avoid either dominance by a
Washington–Beijing–G-2 condominium or subordination to a new Chinese regional hegemon. Should they achieve (and sustain) such a position,

they are likely to have engineered a power shift to East Asia and will have secured new possibilities for growth and innovation in the region.

While each of these four idea spaces has occupants, their advocates in the Japanese foreign policy establishment are not evenly distributed. In a 2011 survey of the views of some fifty Japanese international affairs scholars and diplomats about the future of Japanese diplomacy, nearly half the respondents were, by our measures, "balancers." Seven could be characterized as "integrators." While there were even fewer "autonomists" and "bandwagoners," about one-quarter of these experts claimed that Japan should further promote its relationships multidirectionally rather than focusing on either the United States or China.[73]

This is an abstract caricature of real—and quite robust—strategic positions, all of which are in play within the Japanese grand strategic discourse. Indeed, it is a debate that is very much in play within the ruling DPJ itself. Within its first year of power we saw economic hedgers cede power to military hedgers within the party, while dual hedgers continued to strategize on the margins. We conclude by speculating on how Tokyo's rebalancing its relationships with Washington and Beijing will combine to illuminate a path for Japan's Goldilocks.

CONCLUSION

In this chapter we have examined the Japanese foreign and security policy discourse and identified four distinct schools of thought, each with a different structural preference for the United States–Japan–China strategic triangle. We call those who would hedge against Chinese regional economic dominance "bandwagoners." They prefer Sino–Japanese ties that are closer than either United States–Japan or Sino–United States ties. Those who would hedge against Chinese military power we labeled "balancers." They prefer a strategic environment in which United States–Japan ties remain more intimate than either Sino–United States or Sino–Japanese ties. The strategic preference of the "self-hedgers"—a group that comprises "autonomists" on the left and right—is for both Sino–Japanese and United States–Japanese ties to be closer than Sino–United States ties, with each more distant than they are at present. Finally, we identify a group of "dual hedgers" who wish for a fuller integration of United States–Japanese–Chinese relations. These strategists prefer the sort of "equilateral" strategic triangle first openly described by Ozawa Ichirō in 2006.[74]

These models also vary by what Henry Nau called "scope conditions" in his introduction to this volume. As he argued, foreign and security policies conform to leaders' preferences for how involved their nation should be in world affairs. Some prefer isolation, others global engagement—or even global leadership. We observe that the scope conditions of Japanese foreign policy have been in constant flux—usually in ways that have been consistent with the power and preferences of the schools of thought we have identified. During the Cold War, when the Mercantile Realists were in power, Japan's security perimeter stopped at the homeland's shores. After the Cold War, Japan's leaders slowly expanded the scope to the larger Asian region. After 9/11, Japan was governed by military hedgers like Koizumi Junichirō, who famously declared a global role for Japan. Soon, however, the scope of Japan's security ambitions was trimmed back to the region. This retrenchment occurred for several reasons, not least because successive Japanese leaders—even those in the LDP—wished to correct for Koizumi's excesses vis-à-vis China. Japan faced a rising China, a more belligerent North Korea, and the possibility that US decline would require greater investment in collective goods than Japan was prepared to provide.

In the short term, the military hedgers, who had been temporarily eclipsed by the rise of the economic hedgers, seem to have been the primary beneficiary of these developments. But in the long term, they will be constrained by fiscal and demographic pressures and risk Japan's isolation in the event of a Sino–United States condominium in the region. The economic hedgers who were briefly ascendant were surprised by China's bellicosity. Their return to power will depend on the emergence of a responsible and moderate China willing to accept liberal political and economic values. The self-hedgers who had won the hearts and minds of some voters on the base and sovereignty issues, define Japan's scope most narrowly. But they lost credibility when the United States expressed its willingness to defend Japan in the event of Chinese aggression in the Senkaku/Diaoyu Islands.[75] In the event of a failure by the United States to fulfill its promise, their position on Japanese national security policy likely will prevail. The group most flexible about the appropriate scope for Japanese foreign and security policy is the dual hedgers. By balancing enthusiasm with caution vis-à-vis both Beijing and Washington, they leave some room for global involvements, but focus primarily on regional dynamics. The greatest risk faced by these strategists is the premature loss of US support.

We have argued that ideas matter, and we have mapped them across the full range of Japan's security discourse. Still, in the course of this analysis we have been struck by how much more often Japanese security and foreign policy has been shaped by structural than by ideational or domestic political factors. We have seen how ideas about Japanese grand strategy vary and how domestic politics has affected policy choices, but we note how ideas and local politics have often acted as filters and tools, rather than as drivers, of policy. For example, while ideas about sovereignty and about enhancing equality in the alliance relationship led the Hatoyama administration to renege on an existing agreement on the relocation of the Futenma marine air base, miscalculations by North Korea (its sinking of an ROK naval vessel and artillery fire onto Yeonpyeong Island in 2010) and by China (escalation of tensions in the Senkaku/Diaoyu dispute) drove Japanese policy back to the status quo ante—one that privileged the alliance with the United States. Likewise, while human rights and democracy, values cherished by the DPJ, have been pursued as tools in Japan's China diplomacy, the DPJ abandoned an equally idealist preference of "no first use" of nuclear weapons after determining that the United States was firmly opposed to the idea.[76] And even the stated preference dealing with democracies when relaxing the arms export ban has been strained by the desire by the Japanese government to find ways to cooperate with Vietnam in this area.[77] Structure does not always trump values and ideas, of course, but we have observed that more often than not Japanese foreign and security policy decisions are taken in the cold, harsh light of such prosaic issues as the shifting balance of power—especially when the more realist dual hedgers or military balancers, rather than the more idealist autonomists or economic balancers, are in power.

We note in closing that schools of thought are not only always in collision at home. They also collide across national borders in ways that enable us to draw policy implications from our analysis. In the case at hand, for example, we can imagine very different paths of the bilateral alliance between the United States and Japan in the event that different groups govern each

country at the same time. Specifically, we would expect particularly insalu-
tary consequences for the alliance in the event that bandwagoners govern
in Tokyo at the same time that nationalists govern in Washington. In that
case, it is easy to see how the US position in Asia could be marginalized,
the rise of China accelerated, and how construction of a new regional security architecture would become the order of the day. On the other hand,
should Japan's balancers come to power at the same time as US internationalists, the result—ceteris paribus—would surely be a strengthened
alliance and a more robust US presence in East Asia.

Notes

Part of this research was completed while coauthor Samuels was a visiting scholar at the
Graduate Research Institute for Policy Studies in Tokyo. The authors wish to acknowledge
with gratitude the research assistance of Fukushima Mayumi and Yokoyama Saharu.

1 · *Asahi Shimbun*, October 19, 2006, and *Akahata*, February 5, 2011.

2 · Jack L. Snyder, *Myths of Empire: Domestic Politics and International Ambition* (Ithaca, NY:
Cornell University Press, 1991); Gideon Rose, "Neoclassical Realism and Theories of Foreign
Policy," *World Politics*, 51, 1 (October 1998),144–72; Randall Schweller, *Unanswered Threats:
Political Constraints on the Balance of Power* (Princeton, NJ: Princeton University Press, 2006).

3 · Saadia Pekkanen, "Japan's FTA Frenzy," unpublished paper, Seattle, Jackson School of
International Affairs, University of Washington, 2005. Christopher Dent speaks of the
"isolation avoiding" behavior of regional economies and the need to "make up for lost time"
(pp. 10–11) after the 1997–1998 financial crisis. For his analysis and a detailed snapshot of the
region-wide FTA "spaghetti bowl," see Christopher M. Dent, "Free Trade Agreements in
the Asia Pacific a Decade On: Evaluating the Past, "Looking to the Future," *International
Relations of the Asia-Pacific* (January 11, 2010), http://irap.oxfordjournals.org/cgi/reprint/
lco22vi (accessed January 14, 2010).

4 · www.mofa.go.jp/policy/economy/fta/index.html (accessed January 11, 2010).

5 · *Nihon Keizai Shimbun*, January 14, 2010; Development Research Center of China,
National Institute for Research Advancement of Japan, and Korea Institute for International Economic Policy of Korea, eds., "Joint Report and Policy Recommendations on Sec-
toral Implications of a China-Japan-Korea FTA," November 2004, www.nira.or.jp/past/
newse/paper/joint4/report.html (accessed January 13, 2009); also see "Fortress Asia: Is a
Powerful New Trade Bloc Forming?" *Time Magazine* (September 7, 2009), and "Three-Way
FTA," *Japan Times*, October 13, 2009.

6 · John Ravenhill and Ralf Emmers, "Asian and Global Financial Crises: Implications
for East Asian Regionalism," www.eurasiareview.com/201009208358/asian-and-global-
financial-crises-implications-for-east-asian-regionalism.html.

7 · Pekkanen, "Japan's FTA Frenzy," 5, 17.

8 · Evan A. Feigenbaum, "Clinton's Missed Opportunity in Asia," Council on Foreign
Relations, January 13, 2010, http://blogs.cfr.org/asia/2010/01/13/clinton%e2%80%99s-
missed-opportunity-in-asia/ (accessed January 14, 2010. Emphasis in original), 1.

9 · Pekkanen, "Japan's FTA Frenzy," 19.

10 · Eric Heginbotham, Ely Ratner, and Richard J. Samuels, "How Japan Is Changing and What It Means for the United States," *Foreign Affairs* (September/October 2011), 138–48.

11 · Susan V. Lawrence and David Lague, "Marching Out of Asia," *Far Eastern Economic Review* (August 26, 2004); for a Japanese military analyst's view of the problems that may accompany transformation, see Ohnori Ugaki, "Bei Taiheiyōgun Toransufōmeeshiyon no Zenbō" (The Full Picture of the Transformation of US Pacific Forces in the Pacific), *Gunji Kenkyū* (December 2004), 38–49. For an unruffled perspective from a military analyst, see Sakaguchi Daisaku, "Zainichi Beigun Saihen to Nichibei Sogo Izon Kankei e no Eikyō" (The Realignment of US Bases in Japan and Its Influence on US-Japanese Mutual Dependence).

12 · See Council on Security and Defense Capabilities in the New Era, "Japan's Vision for Future Security and Defense Capabilities in the New Era: Toward a Peace-Creating Nation," August 2010, 51–52, www.kantei.go.jp/jp/singi/shin-ampobouei2010/houkokusyo.pdf, emphasis added.

13 · This argument is elaborated in Richard J. Samuels, *Securing Japan: Tokyo's Grand Strategy and the Future of East Asia* (Ithaca, NY: Cornell University Press, 2007).

14 · Samuels, *Securing Japan*.

15 · J. Patrick Boyd and Richard J. Samuels, "Prosperity's Children: Generational Change and Japan's Future Leadership," *Asia Policy*, 2 (July 2008).

16 · Here we follow the lead of Shiraishi Takashi. See Takashi Shiraishi, "Tōajia Kyōdōtai no Kōchiku wa Kannō Ka?" (Is It Possible to Create an East Asian Community?) *Chūō Kōron*, January 2006, 118–27.

17 · "White Paper," Japan Defense Agency, Tokyo, 2002.

18 · For a brief history of this "salami slicing," see Samuels, *Securing Japan*.

19 · For the most comprehensive treatment of contemporary base issues, see Sheila Smith, "Shifting Terrain: The Domestic Politics of the U.S. Military in Asia," East-West Center Special Report No. 8 (Honolulu: East-West Center, March 2006).

20 · Interview, January 26, 2006.

21 · Hisayoshi Ina, "Implementing the SACO and Revising the SOFA," in Akikaku Hashimoto, Mike Mochizuki, and Kurayoshi Takara, eds., *The Okinawa Question and the U.S.-Japan Alliance* (Washington, DC: Sigur Center for Asian Studies, 2005), 42.

22 · The full text of the treaty is at www.mofa.go.jp/region/n-america/us/q&a/ref/1.html. A former director general of the Defense Facilities Administration argues vigorously that Article Six is the source of continued extraterritorial privilege for US forces. See Shimaguchi, 16.

23 · For more on this agreement of the Special Action Committee on Okinawa (SACO), see Akikaku Hashimoto, Mike Mochizuki, and Kurayoshi Takara, eds., *The Okinawa Question and the U.S.-Japan Alliance*. Washington, DC: Sigur Center for Asian Studies, 2005, and Sheila A. Smith, "Shifting Terrain: The Domestic Politics of the U.S. Military Presence in Asia," East-West Center Special Report No. 8 (Honolulu: East-West Center, March 2006).

24 · For a particularly insightful analysis of recent developments by former US alliance managers, see Michael Finnegan, *Managing Unmet Expectations in the US-Japan Alliance*. NBR Special Report #17 (Seattle, WA: National Bureau of Asian Research, November 2009).

25 · *Minshutō no Seiken Seisaku: Manifesto*, Tokyo, July 27, 2009, 22.

26 · "Joint Statement of the U.S.-Japan Security Consultative Committee," Secretary of State Clinton, Secretary of Defense Gates, Minister for Foreign Affairs Okada, and Minister of Defense Kitazawa, May 28, 2010, www.mofa.go.jp/region/n-america/us/security/scc/joint1005.html.

27 · www.yomiuri.co.jp/dy/national/T100723005957.htm.

28 · *Kyodo Tsūshin*, May 31, 2010.

29 · "Joint Statement of the U.S.-Japan Security Consultative Committee," May 28, 2010.

30 · Heginbotham, Ratner, and Samuels, "Tokyo's Transformation."

31 · James Fallows, "Containing Japan," *The Atlantic* (May 1989). See also Chalmers Johnson, *MITI and the Japanese Miracle: The Growth of Industrial Policy, 1925–1975* (Stanford, CA: Stanford University Press, 1982).

32 · Injoo Sohn, "East Asia's Counterweight Strategy: Asian Financial Cooperation and Evolving International Monetary Order," United Nations Conference on Trade and Development Conference G-24 Paper Series, No. 44, March 2007, 6.

33 · See Bungei Shunjū, ed., *Nihon no Ronten: 2006* (Issues for Japan: 2006) (Tokyo: Bungei Shunjū, 2005), for the list of postwar visits by Japanese prime ministers.

34 · David Kang and Ji-Young Lee, "Japan's New Government: Hope and Optimism," *Comparative Connections*, October 2009.

35 · Asia Japan Watch, *Asahi Shimbun*, August 30, 2011; "Prospectus of Inquiry into the Understanding of the 'War Criminals' and Prime Minister [Koizumi]'s Visit to the Yasukuni Shrine" (in Japanese), presented by Yoshihiko Noda, Inquiry No. 21, October 17, 2005; and "Prospectus of Inquiry into the Interpretation of Article 11 of the San Francisco Peace Treaty and the Commemoration of the 'Class-A War Criminals'" (in Japanese), presented by Yoshihiko Noda, Inquiry No. 308, June 6, 2006.

36 · Yinan He, *The Search for Reconciliation: Sino-Japanese and German-Polish Relations since World War II* (New York: Cambridge University Press, 2009); Jennifer Lind, *Sorry States: Apologies in International Politics* (Ithaca, NY: Cornell University Press, 2008).

37 · *People's Daily Online*, December 24, 2009.

38 · *Yomiuri Shimbun*, January 7, 2010.

39 · "*Bōeki Aitekoku Jōi 10 Kakokuno Suii (Yushutsunyu Sōgaku: Nen Beesu)*, www.customs.go.jp/toukei/suii/html/data/y3.pdf.

40 · *Gaimushō Ajia Taiyōshūkyoku Chūgoku-Mongoruka, Saikin no Chūgoku Jōsei to Nitchū Kankei Heisei 21 Nen 7 Gatsu*, 6–7, www.mofa.go.jp/mofaj/area/china/pdfs/kankei.pdf#02; JETRO Sekai Bōeki Tōshi Hōkoku 2010 Nenpan, 6–7, www.jetro.go.jp/world/gtir/2010/pdf/2010-cn.pdf.

41 · Chi Hung Kwan, "Why Japan Should Pursue an FTA with China: The Need to Prevent a Hollowing-out of Domestic Industry," RIETI online column, 2004, www.rietri.go.jp/en/columns/a01_0122.html, p.1.

42 · Yoshihide Soeya, *Nihon no "Midoru Pawaa" Gaikō: Sengo Nihon no Sentaku to Kōsō* (Japan's "Middle Power" Diplomacy: Postwar Japan's Choices and Conceptions) (Tokyo: Chikuma Shinsho, 2005), 219–22.

43 ° Mike M. Mochizuki, "Japan: Between Alliance and Autonomy," in A. Tellis and M. Wills, eds., *Confronting Terrorism in the Pursuit of Power: Strategic Asia, 2004–2005* (Seattle, WA: National Bureau of Asian Research, 2004), 122–23.

44 · Private correspondence, Peking University professor, January 2010.

45 · *China Daily*, December 20, 2010.

46 · James Manicom, "Hu-Fukuda Summit: The East China Sea Dispute," *China Brief*, 8, 12 (June 6, 2008); M. Taylor Fravel, "Explaining Stability in the Senkaku (Diaoyu) Islands Dispute," in Gerald Curtis, Ryōsei Kokubun, and Wang Jisi, eds., *Getting the Triangle Straight: Managing China, Japan, U.S. Relations* (Washington, DC: Brookings Institution Press, 2010), chapter 7.

47 · Chikako Kawakatsu Ueki, "The Rise of the 'China Threat' Arguments," PhD dissertation, Department of Political Science, Massachusetts Institute of Technology, Cambridge, MA, 2006, chapter. 6, 10–11, 14.

48 · Bōeichō Bōeikenkyūsho Senshibu, ed., *Sakuma Makoto Ōraru Hisutori*, Vol. 2 (Sakuma Makoto: Oral History, Vol. 2) (Tokyo: Bōeichō Bōeikenkyūsho, 2007), 135–36.

49 · See the Joint Statement of the US-Japan Security Consultative Committee, February 2005, www.mofa.go.jp/region/n-america/us/security/scc/joint0502.html.

50 · Ministry of Defense, *Defense of Japan 2009* (Annual White Paper), 308–9.

51 · Ministry of Foreign Affairs, *Diplomatic Bluebook 2009* (Tokyo: Ministry of Foreign Affairs, 2009), www.mofa.go.jp/POLICY/other/bluebook/2009/html/h2/h2_01.html.

52 · Michael J. Green, "The Democratic Party of Japan and the Future of the U.S.-Japan Alliance," *Journal of Japanese Studies*, 31, 1 (2011), 91.

53 · Yoshihiko Noda, "Waga Seiken Kōsō: Ima Koso 'Chōyō' No Seiji wo" (My Vision for Government: Toward Moderate Politics), *Bungei Shunjū* (September 2011), 52.

54 · US Department of Defense, *Quadrennial Defense Review Report*, February 2010, 31–34.

55 · "Heisei 23 Nendo Ikō ni Kakaru Bōei Keikaku no Taikou ni Tsuite" (Japan's 2010 National Defense Program Guidelines), 2.

56 · *Japan Times*, May 9, 2010.

57 · In December 2010, an annual opinion poll on foreign affairs conducted by the Cabinet Office of Japan showed that the number of Japanese who said they did not have friendly feelings toward China jumped 19.3 points to 77.8 percent, a record high. See www8.cao.go.jp/survey/h22/h22-gaiko/2-1.html.

58 · *Yomiuri Shimbun*, January 21, 2011, and *Asahi Shimbun*, January 24, 2011.

59 · Kenneth N. Waltz, *Theory of International Politics* (Reading, MA: Addison-Wesley, 1979).

60 · Masayoshi Takemura, *Chiisakutemo Kirari to Hikaru Kuni* (Tokyo: Kobun-sha, 1994).

61 · General Tamogami's personal blog—June 21, 2010, http://ameblo.jp/toshio-tamogami/entry-10569269913.html.

62 · Ms. Sakurai's personal blog—January 18, 2007, http://yoshiko-sakurai.jp/index.php/2007/01/18/post_498/.

63 · *Akahata*, February 5, 2011.

64 · http://business.nikkeibp.co.jp/article/topics/20090820/203028/.

65 · *Mainichi Shimbun*, February 25, 2009.

66 · http://panther.iza.ne.jp/blog/entry/1593580/ and www2.asahi.com/senkyo2010/special/TKY201007090380.html.

67 · November 10, 2005, www.ja-nsrg.or.jp/forum2005-6/f2005-6.htm.

68 · *Kyodo Tsūshin*, January 10, 2006.

69 · December 8, 2005, http://csis.org/files/media/csis/events/051208_maehara_engremarks.pdf.

70 · The earliest identification of this group was Heginbotham and Samuels, "Tokyo's Transformation." The model was further articulated in Samuels, *Securing Japan*.

71 · Soeya, *Japan's "Middle Power" Diplomacy*, 217.

72 · March 17, 2010, http://info.yomiuri.co.jp/yri/y-forum/yf20100317.htm.

73 · Japanese Institute for International Affairs, ed., *Kokusai Mondai* (Tokyo: International Affairs, April 2011).

74 · *Sankei Shimbun* July 5, 2006; according to Ozawa, "Relations between Japan, China and the US should be structured as 'an equilateral triangle,' with Japan being the linchpin of these relations."

75 · *Asahi Shimbun*, November 1, 2010.

76 · In a policy speech at the Japan National Press Club on February 1, 2010, then foreign minister Okada Katsuya stated: "I advocated 'no first use' in the past, but now I am no longer saying this," www.jnpc.or.jp/files/opdf/444.pdf.

77 · Interview, Japanese national security specialist, January 25, 2011.

6

Russia's Contested National Identity and Foreign Policy

Andrew C. Kuchins and Igor Zevelev

Russia's tumultuous history sets a very unique background for the study of internal debates over the newly independent Russia's foreign policy orientation by comparison with the other cases in this book. Russia's history as a political entity stretches back for more than a thousand years, but unlike China, India, Iran, and Japan, Russia today is in a more circumscribed geographical position than at any time since the seventeenth century. The Russian case is unusual because even though it is emerging as a Great Power, its status, unlike the other countries, is largely diminished from what it was as the superpower Soviet Union of the second half of the twentieth century.

Like Russia, China, India, and Iran all share imperial histories of greatness, but it has been at least two centuries since any of them would have been described as a "Great Power." Russia's status in the international system, and the international system itself, has experienced particularly wide swings over the past forty years. In the 1970s the system was bipolar, and the Soviet Union was viewed as a rising power. The system remained bipolar in the 1980s, yet Moscow's view of itself and the view of others (notably China and the United States) shifted quickly, and Russia became seen as a struggling and declining power. With the Soviet collapse at the end of 1991, the system was transformed from one of bipolarity to unipolarity, and Moscow's status transformed overnight from superpower to recipient of humanitarian assistance. Over the past decade, however, the international system seems to be shifting with increasing rapidity to genuine multipolarity as Russia unexpectedly surged economically and simultaneously regained confidence as an international Great Power; but the country was hit hard by the crisis of 2008 that caused more damage to the Russian economy than to any other G-20 country.

Despite this wild roller-coaster ride, certain elements of Russian national identity and core foreign policy goals and the parameters of debate over them find their roots and continuity deep in Russian history.[1] One is the enduring belief that Russia is a Great Power and must be treated as such. Two, international politics is essentially a Darwinian or Hobbesian competition in which "realist" and "neo-realist" state-centric power politics is the dominant paradigm. Three, from Peter the Great 300 years ago to Putin/Medvedev today, Russia continually faces challenges to "catch up" to the economic, technological, and military achievements of its rivals in order to survive. Four, strategies over how best to achieve catch-up growth constitute and contextualize contested aspects of Russian national identity that often link the nature of the domestic economic and political order with foreign policy priorities and orientation. Five, the central debate today and going back at least 200 years revolves around the West: to what extent Western liberalism is an appropriate model for Russia and how closely Moscow should ally with the West, or certain partners in the West, to achieve its goals.

Analysis of competing schools of thought in the Communist Party of the Soviet Union about Moscow's role in the world was a mainstay of the Sovietological profession during the Cold War decades.[2] Several generations of experts were trained in the West, especially the United States, and millions of research dollars allocated in the attempt to better understand the primary adversary, the USSR. Similarly, the Soviet Union devoted priority attention during the Cold War to training several generations of international relations experts, principally through the Academy of Sciences system with growing resources especially in the 1960s–1980s. Soviet policy debates became most lively and open during the brief years of Gorbachev's Perestroika and glasnost and revolved around the core questions of Moscow's relationship with the West and the role of the West in facilitating Soviet Union's domestic economic and political reform agenda.

For the purposes of this chapter, we will categorize the leading schools of thought and policy practitioners in Russia in 1992–2011 into three groups: (1) pro-Western Liberals; (2) Great Power balancers; and (3) Nationalists. Vigorous and lively debate among Russian experts and government officials about Russia's foreign policy course evolved in the 1990s primarily over Moscow's relationships with the West and newly independent states of the former Soviet Union as pro-Western Liberals quickly lost political ground to different strains of Great Power balancers and Nationalists.[3] Still, from the period of 1993–2002, Russian foreign policy orientation was dominated by a combination of pro-Western Liberals and Great Power balancers. As Russia's resurgence gained momentum from 2003 to 2008, the policy tilted toward a combination of Great Power balancing and Russian Nationalist strains. The definitive statement during this period was Putin's scathing anti-United States speech delivered at the Werkunde Security Conference in Munich in February 2007.[4] Russian confidence, however, was again shaken by the shock of the global economic crisis of 2008 and its exposure of Russian vulnerabilities. Once again, Russia's foreign policy orientation and its path of modernization are being openly contested with no clear answer evident.

As this volume argues, worldviews affect foreign policy and foreign policy events affect worldviews. Countries debate their worldviews and identities.[5] Collective national identities are not simple sums of individual ones. National identities are formulated and maintained by the elites. Collective identities are never "out there," but the result of a dynamic intellectual discourse and a political struggle that never ends. Identity is a provisional and fluid image of ourselves, as we want to be, limited by the facts of history. Historic sources of identity are a tool kit. People construct, negotiate, manipulate and affirm a response to the demand for a collective identity.[6] Various Russian foreign policy schools of thought have been active players in the country's discourse on what Russia is and should be in the future.

For the purposes of this study, the external face of Russian identity that is projected into the international arena has to be deconstructed into several components: scope of ambition, projected desired image, preferred type of power used in international relations, perception of the main trends on the world arena, and vision of the main international organizations. These components conform to the general parameters of foreign policy—scope, ends, and means—emphasized in the introductory chapter of this study.

MAIN SCHOOLS OF THOUGHT: PRO-WESTERN LIBERALS, GREAT POWER BALANCERS, AND NATIONALISTS

The analysis of foreign policy views and programs of various political parties, groups, leading think-tanks, and prominent experts leads to the conclusion that there are three major perspectives on the main trends on the global arena and desirable Russian foreign policy.[7] These perspectives are

Table 6.1: *Who Are the Major Domestic Groups?*

MAJOR GROUPS	IMPORTANT SUBGROUPS	POLITICAL REPRESENTATION	INFLUENTIAL INSTITUTIONS
Pro-Western Liberals		Non-parliamentary parties and movements, including Yabloko; The Party of People's Freedom and Solidarnost movement	INSOR; Liberal Mission; Carnegie Moscow Center; partly—Academy of Sciences institutions (IMEMO, ISKRAN)
Great Power balancers	Former pro-Western liberals	Most of the government's executive branch; parliamentary parties: United Russia and Just Russia	United Russia's "clubs"; Council on Foreign and Defense Policy; The Institute for Social Forecasting; partly—MGIMO and Academy of Sciences institutions
Nationalists	Neo-imperialists; proponents of regional domination; ethnic nationalists	Parliamentary parties: CPRF and LDPR	Many independent intellectuals; Historic Perspective Foundation; Institute for the CIS Countries

related to the way Russian national identity is constructed in different discourses.[8] The findings are summarized in Table 6.1.

The three groups are more or less ideal types. Some schools of thought might include the features of other perspectives, and there is natural affinity among some subgroups belonging to different major clusters. These affinities might serve as the basis for intellectual and political coalition building on concrete foreign policy issues.

Intellectual sources and theoretical foundations of political outlooks of all three major groups (pro-Western liberals, Great Power balancers, and different strains of Nationalists) may be divided into endogenous and external. For at least a century and a half, the debate over Russian identity and its role in the world was focused primarily on Russia's relation and interaction with the West. The roots of this Western-focused discourse can be traced back to the nineteenth-century debates between Slavophiles and Westernizers. Slavophiles emphasized the unique character of Russian civilization, based on Slavic Orthodox communitarian traditions, and they were opposed to alien Western civilization. In contrast, Westernizers argued that Russia should emulate and learn from the West.

Liberals

Modern Russian pro-Western liberals' roots are within the Westernizers' intellectual tradition. They usually advocate collective security, globalization, membership in WTO, among others. In the terms of international relations theory, this group combines aspects of liberal institutional and realist thinking. Some pro-Western Liberals of the early 1990s described their goals not just as integration with the West but as assimilation on the terms of the West. This was the core foreign policy goal of the Yeltsin government in its first year when Yegor Gaidar was acting prime minister. Russia should subordinate its foreign policy goals to those of the West since the hope, and even expectation for many, was that Russia would soon become a fully Western country. Becoming part of the West greatly overshadowed traditional Russian images of itself as a Great Power, and sovereignty and the role of the state were also diminished by the goal of transformation into a market democracy.

It was not long into the 1990s that this most liberal pro-Western wing lost traction in Russian politics and emphasis on Russian sovereignty, a greater role for the state, and the goal of reemerging as an independent Great Power gradually came to predominate in Russian policies as well as policy debates. This shift represented a move from right to left on the spectrum in the introductory chapter of this book. Today the liberals' views have been so marginalized that in Laruelle's categorization they are associated with strictly opposition politicians who have no significant influence in Russian politics, or what some call the "a-systemic" opposition.⁹ Leaders include Mikhail Kasyanov, Boris Nemtsov, Vladimir Ryzhkov, as well as Garry Kasparov and others.

Another subgroup consists of those Russian thinkers and policy makers who argue that the West constitutes the set of the most important international partners, especially Europe, and deeper integration with Western economic and political institutions is a goal, but there is no desire to define Russia's national interests as subordinate to those of the "West." Alexei Arbatov and Dmitry Trenin are two voices that represent this subgroup. Arbatov primarily concerns himself with traditional balance of power issues but his view of the West as that of a complete in-group allows for a different reading of Russia's strategic interests. The current global system is indeed lacking and does not accurately reflect Russia's strategic interests. As opposed to Great Power balancers, the West is not perceived as a direct threat, but the international status quo does need to be adjusted to make room for Russia as a Great Power. This is different from the more traditional balancers' perspective which sees Russia's international status as an inverse proportion of Western influence in the world. Arbatov notes that although the capability of Russia's military is indeed much less than the military power of the United States, this is not the true source of Russia's security risks. Instead, it is the possibility of unstable regimes and extremists that pose the greatest threat, and these should be addressed in concert with other world powers including the United States, the European Union (EU), Japan, and China.¹⁰

Dmitry Trenin has insisted that the only rational option for Russia is to fully stress its European identity and engineer its gradual integration into a Greater Europe. This may be a project requiring several generations. Meanwhile, Trenin argued for "building Europe" within Russia's own borders, demilitarizing its relations with the West, nourishing its partnership with NATO, and making accession to the European Union a long-term policy goal.[11] In his later works, Trenin admitted that Russian leaders gave up these European dreams and returned to the familiar road of great-power policy.[12] In *Post-Imperium: A Eurasian Story*, Dmitri Trenin more recently argued that Moscow needs to drop the notion of creating an exclusive power center in the post-Soviet space. Like other former European empires, Russia has no choice but to reinvent itself as a global player and as part of a wider community.[13]

Vladislav Inozemtsev is another example of this increasingly hard to identify ideological trend. He argues that Russia is a society that was built on Western culture and any current drift toward China that is couched in identity rhetoric must be corrected through dramatic military and economic cooperation with the West. His argument boils down to this: "Russia as part of the West, but on its own (only slightly different) terms." That is, Russia should become a part of the "Broader West."[14] He rejects the idea of Russian historical determinism that precludes modernization and reform. Moreover, he asserts that geopolitical strategizing is a twentieth-century phenomenon that will soon become inapplicable.[15] It is the same as EU being Western but not subordinate to the United States. Many modern Russian liberals look at the West as a developmental model and mostly disregard civilizational and cultural arguments of assimilation or opposition. The West remains a complete in-group and the dominant policy preference is cooperation, but no longer assimilation. The goal is to see Russia legitimately assume the role of a Great Power through economic modernization.

Great Power Balancers

While this school of thought bears much in common with realism, for the purposes of our analysis, we term this broad group "Great Power balancers" because their interpretation of the dynamics of the international system is more state-centric and focused on Russian national interests in the context of the balance of power. Great Power balancers are well represented politically and have a foremost influence on the government. The founding father of the Great Power school of thought in Russia is Evgeniy Primakov, who was an academic as well as both prime minister and foreign minister of Russia at different stages of his career. Primakov, both for his ability as a statesman and for his straight-forward realist conception of international affairs, is most likened to Henry Kissinger in the United States. Russian Great Power balancers may be called broader defensive realists advocating maintaining sphere of influence on the territory of the former Soviet Union and striving to contain American global preeminence.

An important faction within Great Power proponents group includes former pro-Western Liberals who were disappointed with the Western policies toward Russia—in particular, the enlargement of NATO—and moved to a more assertive Great Power stance in the mid-late 1990s. Russian liberal internationalists dreamed of a "common European home" and were against NATO expansion. By the mid-1990s, many influential Russian foreign policy experts started to argue that by embracing the ideology of liberalism and democracy, Russia seemed to confine itself to the second-ary role of a country "in transition" in the international arena. Many in the Russian foreign policy community thought that transitional countries are always led, judged, praised, and punished for progress or lack of it by other international actors. Absence of an equal partnership with the United States and other Western countries led to adjusting Moscow's overarching concept of international relations. Kozyrev's pro-Western liberal approach reflected in the line "Russia is joining the civilized world" was replaced by Primakov's view of Russia "as one of centers of power in a multipolar world" when the latter was appointed foreign minister in 1996.

One version of the Great Power balancers' approaches is "the indepen-dent foreign policy path" that Vyacheslav Nikonov articulated in 2002. The argument held that while principles of the Washington Consensus were not nearly as universal as had been hoped, there were still many universal values that Russia had in common with the West.[16] These could be com-bined in a new global concert framework—one that would more accu-rately reflect the new balance of power in which Russia could pursue its separate path, but this independent national self-image is not so different from Russia's Western rivals. Nikonov is the ultimate insider intellectual, and his analytical framework steeped in traditional realism is at the heart of mainstream Russian thinking in international relations. In drawing on Russia's constructive role in the nineteenth-century concert of powers after the Congress of Vienna, Nikonov's framework nicely meets both the credibility and efficacy tests of Clunan's aspirational constructivism.[17] This system of balance is both power-based and civilizational. Sergey Karaganov, an influential head of the Council on Foreign and Defense Policy, is another representative of this group, although Karaganov is more inclined to promote Russia's European orientation.[18]

Great Power balancers do not reject Western experience and are effectively in favor of learning from the West. Their notion of Russia's modernization relies in some respect on the historic tradition established by Peter the Great. They would like to import Western technology, attract direct foreign investment, and compete successfully with the West. The existence of "polarity" on the global arena is taken for granted and never perceived as simply one of possible analytical lenses. They strive to play the Great Power game not just on the regional stage, as most Nationalists do, but on the global stage—in G-8, G-20, UNSC, and other groups. Nevertheless, unlike current Chinese policy, Russian policy based primarily on Great Power balancers' views, seems to approach global economy with its guard up.

In 2008–2010, the "civilizational" approach became popular among the proponents of the Great Power status for Russia. Some interpretations of the "Russian civilization" make Great Power proponents closer to the pro-Western Liberals by emphasizing the unity between Russia and the West, while some other understandings of the matter unite Great Power proponents with the neo-imperial strain of Nationalists. Ideologically, the concept of civilization has proved to be attractive to the Russian authorities. In the nineteenth century, it was usually Nationalist conservatives—above all, philosophers Nikolai Danilevsky and Konstantin Leontiev—who spoke about a special Russian civilization. The late Samuel Huntington, a conservative, thought in similar terms. Neo-imperialist ("Eurasianist") Alexander Dugin has long been arguing that Russia is not a country but a civilization. The idea of civilizations is hardly compatible with liberal concepts of globalization and the universality of democratic values.[19]

To date, the Russians have formulated two possible approaches to Russia's civilizational affiliation. One was set forth by President Dmitry

Medvedev in his speech in Berlin in June 2008: "The end of the Cold War made it possible to build up genuinely equal cooperation between Russia, the European Union and North America as three branches of European civilization." Russian foreign minister Sergei Lavrov, however, said that the adoption of Western values is only one of two basic approaches to humankind's development. In his words, Russia advocates a different approach, which suggests that "competition is becoming truly global and acquiring a civilizational dimension; that is, the subject of competition now includes values and development models." In his letter to a Latvian Russian-language newspaper in the summer of 2009 Lavrov used the term "Greater Russian civilization." In this interpretation, the world may look to be driven by Great Civilization balance of power rather than Great Power balance of power. The more civilizationally oriented the balance becomes, the more likely the competition is to become more intense or Cold War–like compared to a nonideological Great Power balance.

In a more recent articulation of this thesis, Foreign Minister Lavrov in Washington put the accent on the three wings of European civilization working more closely together.

> I think for us…the European civilization, which was spread by the Americans, I mean by those who emigrated to America westward, and was spread by the Russians over centuries eastward, thus creating this famous space from Vancouver to Vladivostok—I think it's in our best interest to make sure what we are competitive in the modern world, in the modern polycentric world. And from this point of view, we have to be united. We have to join resources and join intellectual, inventive, creative capacity.[20]

What is notable about this formulation is the stated import of deeper integration among the three wings of European civilization to maintain and strengthen their competitiveness globally, and the implication that the three should not compete against each other but rather cooperate to better compete against others. Suffice it to say that the foreign minister and other Russian political figures do not speak in this manner in Beijing and most other places outside the famed belt from Vancouver to Vladivostok.[21]

Indeed, there is an impression that many in Russia, including the Russian authorities, do not see much contradiction between these two approaches and view them not as mutually exclusive but as complementary. One approach is intended for the West, while the other is intended for neighboring states and fellow Russians abroad. On the one hand, the concept of Russia as a separate large civilization allows it to easily parry criticism of its undemocratic polity. On the other hand, it lets Russia interpret the "Russian question" in the modern, twenty-first-century spirit: "The Russian civilization is our state together with the Russian World, which includes all those who gravitate to Russian culture." In this context, the nationalist "divided nation" idea sounds archaic.

In 2009, the Russian Orthodox Church joined in discussions about Russia as the center of a special civilization. Patriarch of Moscow and All Russia Kirill began to pose not as the head of the Orthodox Church of Russia and Russian people but as a supranational spiritual leader of "Holy Russia," which comprises Russia, Ukraine, Belarus, Moldova, and—on a broader scale—all Orthodox Christians. Continuing in a way Konstantin Leontiev's Orthodox conservative tradition, the patriarch has obviously set out to preserve the East Slavic civilization, while respecting the present political borders and existing cultural differences. The latter circumstance is a new aspect in the policy of the Russian Orthodox Church. During his visit to Ukraine in August 2009, Patriarch Kirill often addressed his congregation in the Ukrainian language and called Kyiv "the southern capital of Russian Orthodoxy," rather than just "the mother of Russian towns."

For Patriarch Kirill, Orthodoxy cannot be reduced to "Russian faith" only. This is a major change from the previous years when Orthodox hierarchs were favorably disposed toward the nationalist "divided nation" concept, which, of course, looks much more parochial than the idea of spiritual leadership of an entire civilization. Symbolically, Patriarch Kirill has ordered that the flags of all states within the Moscow Patriarchate's jurisdiction be put on display in his Throne Room, instead of just the flag of the Russian Federation. In 2009, the Russian Orthodox Church showed itself as a major participant in the discourse on Russian identity and on Russia's relations with neighboring states and the rest of the world.

From a certain perspective, the Great Power balancers may be close to the Eurasianist view of Russia as a unique Great Power with a mission, but in this framework the state's purpose is tied less to a concrete historical self-image of a great and unique culture and path. Aspirations become focused not on an intangible messianic cultural status, but on international status and prestige that is achieved through a traditional balance of power strategy focused on territory and empire. For this group, using Clunan's terminology, the West is neither a complete out-group, nor is it a complete in-group. It is a reference point and serves as a goal to reach and ideally surpass either through competition or cooperation as the situation dictates. This formulation of identity is still relatively close to seeing Russia as being defined by an innate cultural difference and often this is used as an explanation for a lack of international prestige or failure to completely assimilate with the West. Within this framework, the concept of a separate path also exists, but without the messianic overtones that the Nationalist or Eurasianist self-image implies. This group includes, first of all, Vladimir Putin. Vladislav Surkov, a former first deputy chief of staff of the president of the Russian Federation and a top aide to Vladimir Putin, also belongs to the group. Vladislav Surkov is widely seen as the main ideologist of the Kremlin. Within the United Russia Party, they call themselves the social conservatives.[22]

Nationalists

The group broadly defined as "Russian Nationalists" may be especially averse to United States and Western interests. It includes at least three subgroups, namely, neo-imperialists, proponents of Russia's regional domination on the post-Soviet space, and ethnic Nationalists. Many of them challenge the boundaries of the Russian political community, but draw different conclusions regarding desirable foreign policy under given circumstances.[23]

The essence of the neo-imperialist project was to restore a state within the borders of the USSR. The most influential party that effectively backed neo-imperialism throughout the 1990s was the Communist Party of the Russian Federation. The essence of the domination project is state-building within the borders of present-day Russia accompanied by subjugation of other successor states and the creation of a buffer zone of protectorates and dependent countries around Russia. The essence of an ethno-nationalist program is to unite Russia with the Russian communities in the near abroad and build the Russian state within the area of settlement of ethnic Russians and other Eastern Slavs. This would mean the reunification of Russia, Belarus, part of Ukraine, and northern Kazakhstan. Advocates of both ethno-nationalism and neo-imperialism argue for redrawing political borders, but along different lines.

Unlike most ethno-nationalists who often cherish traditional preindustrial values, neo-imperialists and dominators are modernizers, albeit twentieth-century style. They favor a strong army, big cities, and industrial development. Vladimir Zhirinovsky, founder and the leader of the Liberal Democratic Party of Russia (LDPR), vice chairman of the State Duma, in his own distinctive style, dismissed the image of a Russia of "small villages, forests, fields, accordion player Petr and milkmaid Marfa" as a writers-assisted communist plot aimed to partly compensate for the suppression of Russian nationalism.[24] His is the Russia of historic might, world influence, and impressive richness. Zhirinovsky sided with painter Ilya Glazunov, who created images not of a country of drunken peasants but of an "empire with shining palaces of Petersburg, great historical traditions and achievements, thinkers of genius and the leading culture."[25] In 2010–2011, Zhirinovsky's rhetoric included much more ethno-nationalist xenophobic overtones. It was a reflection of a growing popularity of this perspective.

The dominance outlook might be viewed as very similar to a neo-imperialist approach. Principles for a Russian policy of dominance over the "near abroad" were developed initially by the then Presidential Council member Andranik Migranyan in the early 1990s.[26] In more policy-oriented and moderate terms, this project was advocated by the former chairman of the Committee for International Affairs and Foreign Economic Relations of the Russian Supreme Soviet, Yevgeniy Ambartsumov. Dominance rhetoric was also present in some statements, articles, and reports of Russian foreign minister Andrey Kozyrev from 1993.[27] In 1996–2010 the most vocal advocate of the policy of hegemony and domination was Yuri Luzhkov; he was mayor of Moscow and relied heavily on the political expertise of Konstantin Zatulin, who until April 2011 was the first deputy chairman of the committee of the State Duma for the CIS Affairs and Relations with Compatriots.

The modern Russian ethno-nationalism is a radical departure from the mainstream Russian tradition shaped by imperialist and liberal perspectives.

The founding founder of ethno-nationalism as a consistent worldview in modern Russia is Aleksandr Solzhenitsyn. Solzhenitsyn was arguably the first giant figure in Russian intellectual history to challenge the imperialist tradition and condemn centuries-long empire-building as detrimental to the Russian people and wasteful of the country's resources; he considered empire-building a misdirection of human energies that deprived Russians of their national character. The magnitude of Solzhenitsyn's rebellion against tradition can be truly appreciated if it is put into the context of several centuries of intellectual discourse that allowed Nikolai Berdyaev, a leading philosopher of the first half of the twentieth century, to call Russia "providentially imperialist."[28] Paradoxically, in this context, Solzhenitsyn, although speaking out against the Westernization of Russia, looks like a radical Westernizer. He effectively argues for building a Russian nation-state along the path of nation-building in nineteenth-century Europe. During World War I, Nikolai Berdyaev contended that "our nationalism always makes an impression of something non-Russian, extraneous, sort of Germanic....Russians are almost ashamed of their Russianness."[29] Solzhenitsyn has not been ashamed of being a Russian. He has been more concerned with preservation of his people, which was almost ruined, according to him, by the self-imposed burden of an empire. Solzhenitsyn called Russia a "torn state" arguing that 25 million Russians found themselves "abroad" without moving anywhere from "the land of their fathers and grandfathers," thus creating "the largest diaspora in the world."[30]

Like most ethno-nationalists all over the world, the theorists belonging to this school of thought in Russia adhere to the Romantic tradition stipulating that "people" is a mystical collective entity with its own soul and fate.[31] According to Russian historian, Natalia Narochnitskaya, nation is a "successively living entity bound by spirit, world-view, common perceptions of good and evil, and historic emotions."[32]

Russian ethnic nationalism is not a well-organized political force at the moment, yet it may rise quickly. The deep economic crisis of the 1990s and the difficulties faced by Russians in neighboring states created prerequisites for political mobilization around this issue. The inflow of migrants to big Russian cities during the last decade has provoked a rise in xenophobia and in the activities of extremist groups. However, Russian ethno-nationalism has not become a serious force in Russia yet and it does not have any significant impact on the country's policy toward neighboring states. Supranational aspects of Russian identity in various forms (imperial, Soviet, civilizational, and universalist) continue to play a significant role.

The term "nation" traditionally has a strong ethnic, not civic, connotation in Soviet and post-Soviet academia, public opinion, and politics. As it has often happened in European history, common culture may at some point be perceived as a natural political boundary, which can become a springboard for demands to unite all Russians under one political roof. One cannot say that such ideas were advocated by fringe politicians only. The largest contribution to the development of this idea have been made by Natalia Narochnitskaya, Viktor Aksyuchits, as well as such politicians like Vladimir Zhirinovsky, Gennady Zyuganov, and Sergei Baburin. There were several attempts in the period from 1998 to 2001 to embody such ideas in legislative initiatives. The State Duma discussed several bills, including On the Ethnic and Cultural Development of the Russian People; On the Right of the Russian People to Self-Determination and Sovereignty in the Entire Territory of Russia and to Reunification in a Single State; and On the Russian People, but none of them was adopted. Reality put very different tasks on the agenda, and the pragmatism of the Russian elite prevailed over ideological constructs of individual political groups each time.

After the establishment of tough presidential control over parliament in 2003, the issue of the divided Russian nation and its right to reunite was marginalized. Nevertheless, the Communist Party included a thesis on the divided Russian people in its program and reiterated its commitment to this idea at its 13th Congress in 2010. The program of the Liberal Democratic Party still contains a demand to recognize Russians as a divided nation. Some members of the ruling United Russia party, especially Konstantin Zatulin, keep repeating that the Russian people are "the largest divided nation in the world." Numerous websites and the Nationalist part of the blogosphere actively popularize these ideas. Possible democratization in the second decade of the twenty-first century may return the issue of separation of the Russian people on the political scene. We cannot exclude the emergence of political parties, built around this idea. The experience of Israel, Austria, Hungary, and other countries shows that sometimes even small Nationalist parties gain disproportionate weight, as alliance

Table 6.2: *Beliefs about Self and the World*

MAJOR GROUPS	INTELLECTUAL SOURCES AND THEORETICAL FOUNDATION	PROJECTED DESIRED IMAGE OF RUSSIA	PREFERRED TYPE OF POWER	THE VIEW OF MAIN GLOBAL TRENDS	PRIORITIES AND TRADE-OFFS
Pro-Western liberals	Russian nineteenth-century Westernizes; modern liberal internationalism	Russia is a part of the West	Soft	Globalization; democratic versus authoritarian states	Economic
Great Power balancers	Multipolar world vision; civilizational approach	Global power; influential center in the multipolar world	Hard and soft	The attempts to establish a uni-polar world versus "real" multipolarity	Economic and security
Nationalists	Nineteenth-century Russian conservatism; twentieth-century Eurasianism; geopolitics; the concept of "divided nation"	Independent center of power; distinct civilization apart from the West	Hard	Hobbesian war of all against all; Anglo-American sea power versus Russia-led heartland	Security

with them ensures a parliamentary majority of more moderate political forces.

The findings regarding competing discourses on Russian identity, the preferred type of power it should project into the international arena, and different perceptions of the main global trends are summarized in Table 6.2.

The proposed classification reflects the evolution of Russian foreign policy debate as it has evolved since the early 1990s. However, the debate has started shifting the main focus.[33] Its dependency on the definitions of Russian identity is getting less evident. It has become more focused on the evolution of the international relations system. The discussion has become more nuanced in late 2000s. The implications of the relative decline of US power in the world are viewed with more discernment, and there is more open discussion of the pros and cons of China's rise. There is also more open acknowledgment of the importance of the West as a partner in Russia's efforts to modernize its economy. In sum, there are several signs of more realistic and more contentious views of the United States, its role in the world, and its implications for Russian interests.

Russian liberals used to be all pro-Western. Today, Westernizers can credibly promote a hardheaded national interest—at least they have developed robust argumentation to that effect. Westernizers can not only pursue modernization for the sake of becoming closer to the West but out of genuine motivation to promote the national interest. And Liberal Westernizers can define this interest in terms of power or in any other way typical of Realists or Nationalists. Many Westernizers often use typically Great Power balancers' (Realist) arguments: Russia needs to ally with NATO to balance off China. Other Westernizers point out the importance of good relations with China. Not unlike Realists or Nationalists they argue that Russo–Chinese diplomatic cooperation and trade are important assets for Russia.

This utilitarian approach can also explain the foreign policy document that was leaked to Russian *Newsweek* in May 2010.[34] The line is to take advantage of all opportunities whether through cooperation or competition, although the document emphasizes cooperation. It highlights pragmatism.

As the entire ideological discourse has narrowed and moved toward the right, it is often difficult to precisely pin down certain points of view. This may be because these categories still need to be refined, or also because it is now much easier to discredit more liberal sentiments and when they are voiced, they become "a-systemic" and so have little influence on foreign policy. The main difference between the liberals and the Great Power balancers is that, for the former, for Russia to attain its rightful role as a Great Power does not necessarily mean a decrease in the status of the West—the two can coexist in parity. For the balancers, it means that the West is overplaying its role and should cede some of it to Russia.

PERSPECTIVES ON THE UNITED STATES AND POLICY IMPLICATIONS

It may be argued that US policies after the end of the Cold War generated two processes on the international arena. First, the United States was engaged in a typical social process of interaction with other actors. Second, and more atypical, the US policies constituted an ecological process for other actors. In other words, they created and changed the whole environment for other states by structuring international relations in a way no other actor was capable.[35] This could alter the other states' policies significantly. Even if a country's international goals remained the same, structural changes on the world arena caused by the preeminence and assertiveness of the United States could require a different course of actions to achieve these goals. This might concern not only small and medium-sized states, but also the centers of global power. From this perspective, the beliefs about the United States held by major groups within the Russian foreign policy community may be a litmus test for their broader vision of the international arena and desirable foreign policy. This proposition looked less viable after the United States suffered major international setbacks during George Bush's presidency. During this period of time, particularly in 2003–2008, Russia made it clear that it did not recognize unconditional American leadership and insisted on its own status of Great Power. However, Russia, as a former superpower on par with the United States, still measured itself against a former Cold War rival. The differences in beliefs about the United States among major Russian groups are summarized in Table 6.3.

Table 6.3: *Beliefs about the United States*

MAJOR GROUPS	THE IMAGE OF THE UNITED STATES	THE US DESIRED RESPONSE
Pro-Western liberals	Proponent of liberal democratic values; strategic partner	Not to assume that this group is mainstream; not to discredit it by too close association; support indirectly
Great Power balancers	Power striving for dominance and unipolar world	Cooperate when possible and encourage more benign trends within the group
Nationalists	Ideological and strategic opponent	Understand that this group may strongly influence Great Power proponents or present a viable alternative

Russian perceptions of the United States and its role in the world provide a powerful lens for framing not only how Russia conceives its foreign and security policies—far more broadly than United States–Russia bilateral relations—but also for understanding deeply rooted notions of contemporary Russian identity and even its domestic political system.[36] For most of the second half of the twentieth century the United States and the Soviet Union were locked in a competitive struggle for global power and hegemony, and each country viewed its adversary as the principal "other" around which much of each country's identity and foreign policy revolved. The collapse of the Soviet Union was a searing event for citizens of Russia as well as the other newly sovereign states of the region, yet for most policy makers and elites in Moscow, old habits of measuring success or failure through a United States-centered prism have endured. Now nearly twenty years past the Soviet collapse, perceptions of the United States probably remain more significant for Russia than any other country in this study.

Since the collapse of the Soviet Union nearly twenty years ago, there has been a quite dynamic evolution in Moscow toward the role of US power in the world. For a brief period that definitively concluded with the defeat of Russian liberal reformist parties in the December 1993 parliamentary elections, the United States was regarded as a model for Russian development and key Russian government officials had high hopes for a "new world order" that would be comanaged by Washington and Moscow, and Russia even playing the role of a junior partner. In other words, the views of the United States held by pro-Western Liberals influenced the official Russian thinking strongly in 1992–1993. The results of the December 1993 parliamentary elections strengthened the assertive trends in the official policy. The defeat of the liberal reformers, caused principally by the economic crisis in the early 1990s, shifted Russian foreign policy to more traditional Realist concepts asserting national interests and expanding power and influence. Increasingly the US liberal democratic model was viewed as if not inappropriate for Russia, then at least should be introduced far more gradually taking greater account of Russian traditions and values.

Like other countries in this study, the dominant paradigm for Russian government officials and political elite is realism with probably a higher relative weight for the value of economic and military indices of power and lower relative weight for factors of soft power. In the traditional Russian calculus (Tsarist, Soviet, and post-Soviet), it is the power of coercion, typically through intimidation and/or buying off support—a very hard-edged realism—rather than the power of attraction that dominates. When Westerners emphasize values such as human rights or democracy, the default Russian reaction is deep skepticism. Promotion by the United States of democracy, liberal capitalism, rules-based system of global governance, and the like are interpreted as ideological fig leaves designed to conceal the naked American ambition to expand its own power and influence abroad.

From 1993 to 2003, Russian foreign policy was dominated by Great Power balancers who were joined by many liberals disappointed with reform and the West. From 1996, Evgeniy Primakov started playing the key role in Russian foreign policy and the views of pro-Western Liberals, as it was noted earlier, were gradually marginalized. Primakov is pragmatic and nonideological, but his most significant time in Russian politics came in the late 1990s when Russia's power was at its weakest, and US unipolar dominance, arguably, at its peak. Nevertheless, Russia tried to shape the perception that it was a Great Power.

The Great Power balancers' dominance in Russian foreign policy making was emphasized in March 1999 when then Prime Minister Primakov was in flight to Washington; on the flight he learned that the United States had begun war against Serbia, and he demanded that the plane not land in the United States but return to Moscow. The Russian paratroopers' march to Pristina airport later that year was yet another characteristic signal, a symbolic deed designed to project a desired image of a Great Power that could not be supported by more substantive actions. This led to a significant tension between self-perception and the perception of others, primarily the United States.[37]

Primakov wanted to see Russia as a Great Power and an influential center of a multipolar world. As the major trends in world development, he saw, on the one hand, the formation of such a world, and, on the other hand, United States-led Western attempts to dominate the world arena. Accordingly, he discerned a major challenge in efforts to form a unipolar world and considered the United States to be a country seeking to circumvent international law in order to form a unipolar structure and to establish its own economic and power dominion.

The proponents of Great Power status understand that the United States set the agenda and rules of the game in many interactions with Russia. It controlled Russia's options in many situations. However, they believe that the United States has had much less leverage in affecting Russia's preferences, desires, and thoughts.[38] It could not get Russia to want what the United States wanted in those areas where the two countries' preexisting fundamental beliefs about the world and corresponding national interests differed. According to Great Power status proponents, Russia does not need American protection, and does not feel that its views and interests are taken into consideration. American preponderance is seen by the Great Power proponents as a fact of life, but not as a source of legitimate authority. In their view, the United States has not successfully transformed its hard power into soft power in its relations with Russia. They would reject an argument that the underlying sources of American strength are entrepreneurial and societal freedoms that maximize competition and avoid catastrophic diversions into authoritarianism, right or left. Being true Realists, Russian Great Power balancers are not much interested in internal economic and political arrangements of other countries.

In 2000–2008, like many other nations in the world, Russia sought the means to balance, or more correctly, contain US unipolar hegemony. The United States was not viewed as malign but often as misguided and overbearing. This perspective on the United States endured pretty much through the first term of Vladimir Putin's presidency. For the purposes of this study, it is especially important to keep in mind the foreign policy conducted by Putin during his first term because it sheds light on the United States–Russian rapprochement in 2009–2011 and its potential path in the future. Mr. Putin is conventionally characterized as deeply opposed to US interests. For some, their analysis is based on his authoritarian centralization of power, that is, dictatorial rulers are inherently anti-American. For others, their analysis is more based on the growing rift in United States–Russian relations during Putin's second term. In our view, however, this characterization is flawed. It is conveniently forgotten that for a brief period of time in 2001–2002, Putin pursued his own version of a "reset" in United States–Russia relations, and his foreign policy orientation was at least as amenable to US interests as that under Dmitri Medvedev's presidency. Russia's circumstances started to change in the mid-2000s, but at least as important, Moscow's disappointment with the Bush administration's policies led to Putin's increasing willingness to oppose Washington on a number of issues. Russian public opinion grew more negative on the role of the United States, but this was fairly consistent with the rest of the world, including the NATO allies.

The period from 2003 to 2008 marked another shift in Russian foreign policy and Moscow's perception of US power capacity and intentions. Russia's confidence about its own reemergence strengthened as economic growth accelerated. The watershed moment came in 2006 when Moscow paid off its Paris Club debt early, and this sense of financial sovereignty equated with a renewed emphasis on political sovereignty. Differences beginning in 2003 over the Yukos affair and especially over the series of "color revolutions" in Georgia, Ukraine, and Kyrgyzstan gave more sustenance to the argument that the United States sought to weaken Russia and thwart Moscow's interests in a comprehensive manner. Russian foreign policy remained embedded in a realist and pragmatic framework for the most part; the most significant change was the perception that Russian power was growing, while the US "unipolar moment" was receding into history. Putin's position moved from that of a centrist power balancer with Western inclinations to more of one steeped in efforts to appeal to Russian nationalism and opposition to US policy, especially in post-Soviet space.

Throughout the whole history of post-Soviet Russia, the Nationalists saw the United States as the main ideological and geostrategic opponent.

Ethnic Nationalists are not as much concerned with the United States as neo-imperialists and proponents of Russian domination in Eurasia. Ethnic Nationalists are essentially isolationists and they "give away" the world to the United States. Neo-imperialists and "dominators" are , concerned primarily with American "meddling" in the Russian neighborhood.

This phase of dominance by absolute Great Power balancers in Russian foreign policy concluded in the second half of 2008 with the near concurrence of the Georgia war and the global financial crisis. While the Georgia war was a shock, the global economic crisis has had a far deeper impact on Russian leadership and elite perceptions on Russian interests in the ongoing changing balance of power in the world. In short, Russian elites are more unsure about the capacity and durability of American power, but also less confident that the shifting global balance of power in which China appears to be the principal beneficiary redounds to Moscow's favor. The almost knee-jerk inclination of the Russian leadership to identify the United States as the primary global threat to Russian interests on issues such as NATO expansion and missile defense has eroded. Obama administration policies have also helped to convince the Russian leadership that the United States does not seek to weaken Russia and that the role of US power in the world is counter to Russian interests.

There are certainly implications of this current trend for relations with other powers considered in this study. While Moscow may be more wary of being overleveraged in their relationship with China, Russia will probably hew to the current steady improvement in ties with China we have witnessed for the past twenty years. One would think that Moscow would seek to improve ties with Japan as a hedge with China, but in 2010–2011 we have witnessed the most antagonistic policy toward Tokyo in more than twenty years. This seeming anomaly does not lend itself to easy explanation. Likewise, we would expect increasing efforts to strengthen ties with India, but it has not been easy for these two traditional strategic partners to fill their positive relationship with much content. Finally, Russian ties with Iran have worsened considerably as Moscow has leaned more strongly to accommodating Western efforts to contain and isolate Tehran over its nuclear weapon program.

CONCLUSION

The collapse of the Soviet Union and the emergence of a newly independent Russian Federation facilitated quite far-ranging debates and diverse schools of foreign policy thinking in the early 1990s. The spectrum of debate with significance for Russian foreign policy has narrowed considerably as all those who aspire to be a "player" politically must frame their positions in ways that support a more significant role for the Russian state and in ideological terms that resonate with traditional themes of Russian nationalism.

Still the main magnetic pole in Russian debates over identity and foreign policy orientation is the status of the Western democratic market development model as well as the role of the United States and the West more broadly in international relations. Our three categories of pro-Western Liberals, Great Power balancers, and Nationalists can be approximately correlated to pro-Western, neutral toward the West, and anti-Western. The danger of Russian policy moving in an overtly anti-Western position peaked with the Georgia war and its aftermath in the summer of 2008. The main axis of debate revolves around the first two categories of liberals and Great Power balancers. The most significant external (or internal for that matter) factor with the potential to push the needle in one direction or the other is the world economy and how it affects the oil price. The lower price environment favors liberals who call for deeper structural reform of the Russian economic and political system to increase efficiency while the higher price environment discourages reform and fuels greater assertiveness.

At a rhetorical level, the worldviews of President Medvedev and his predecessor and successor, Vladimir Putin, have appeared at times in recent years to differentiate more clearly—with Medvedev in the liberal camp and Putin in the Great Power balancer camp with more nods to Russian Nationalists. However, we must be wary about exaggerating the differences.[39] It is true that Vladimir Putin has never been associated as a real proponent of democracy in Russia, but he did enter office more than ten years ago with his own economic modernization agenda and arguably pursued an overtly pro-Western foreign policy early in his first term.

Like the United States–Russia relationship, Russian elite perceptions of US power and role in the world has experienced great volatility in the past twenty years. How durable is the current Russian perception that not only is the United States less threatening but pursuing policies far more accommodating to Russian interests? There is no definitive answer to this question, but from reviewing the last ten years or so since Vladimir Putin first became Russian president, our conclusion is that US policies will be a far more important factor in affecting the views of the United States held by the Russian leader and the country's elite than who is the Russian president. The Russian perspective on the power and role of the United States in the world did not change in 2009–2012 because Dmitri Medvedev temporarily replaced Vladimir Putin as president of Russia. The Russian perspective changed because of the impact of the global economic crisis and changes in Obama administration policies of greatest interest to Moscow.

Historically, in more than a decade as Russia's de facto, if not always de jure, leader, Vladimir Putin has tapped into the intellectual discourses of all three leading schools of thought in the development and articulation of Russian foreign policy. The preponderence of evidence suggests he is a *Great Power balancer* in the mold of Evgeny Primakov. But depending on the internal and external circumstances he has faced, this essentially Realist orientation has been cast in a more liberal and pro-Western direction as it was in 2001–2002 or in a more Nationalist manner as it was from 2003 to 2008. We view Putin as essentially a pragmatic politician without strong ideological predilections.

Vladimir Putin returned to the presidency in 2012 to find a changed Russia and a changed world. Back in the early 2000s, he displayed natural political instincts in positioning himself as a leader promising to bring stability, predictability, and greater prosperity to the Russian people. Indeed, they responded. But now the domestic policy challenges are different. Russians are far wealthier today, with a per capita GDP based on purchasing power parity of close to $17,000 (it was just about $4,000 in 1999). Demands for better social services, better governance, and less corruption are growing. There is a natural tendency, as modernization theory argues, that as a nation's per capita GDP grows beyond a level of $10,000, citizens demand greater government openness and accountability. Increasingly, at least at the educated elite level, Russians want more democratic governance. This has been anything but Putin's priority in the past.

Putin also faces a potentially disastrous fiscal situation. National expenditures are going to have to be reined in. As former Finance Minister Alexei Kudrin said in an April 2009 speech in Washington, those felicitous circumstances that powered the Russian recovery before the financial crisis are not likely to recur in the near future, if ever. The Russian economy will have to rely on new engines of growth, which will require the Kremlin to return to a structural economic reform agenda and make extra efforts to improve Russia's investment climate.

Finally, the world Russia faces has changed dramatically since Putin first entered office on the last day of 1999. The United States has been humbled from its "unipolar moment," and the rise of China and other rapidly growing large emerging market economies makes for a rapidly shifting power away from the traditional West that has dominated international politics since the onset of the Columbian era more than 500 years ago. For Russia, rather than going back to Soviet and Tsarist days to define its identity, and setting its foreign policy goals and security threats in terms of the West, the orientation must genuinely be redirected 360 degrees to address the emerging challenges and opportunities.

Notes

We thank Vladimir Baranovskiy, Alexey Bogaturov, Alexandr Borisov, Fyodor Lukyanov, Dmitriy Polikanov, and Mikhail Troitskiy for helpful comments on the chapter draft. We also thank Olga Blyumin for her excellent research assistance.

1 · See Anders Aslund and Andrew C. Kuchins, "Russia's Historical Roots," in *The Russia Balance Sheet* (Washington, DC: Peterson Institute for International Economics, 2009). See also the insightful discussion of the interaction between Western and Russian IR theory in Andrei Tsygankov and Pavel Tsygankov, "A Sociology of Dependence in International Relations Theory: A Case of Russian Liberal IR," *International Political Sociology*, 1 (2007), 307–24.

2 · For an excellent history of the development of the field of Sovietology in the United States, see David C. Engerman, *Know Your Enemy: The Rise and Fall of America's Soviet Experts* (New York: Oxford University Press, 2009).

3 · Russian foreign policy debate is rooted in the discussion of IR theory but has its own purposes, structure, and dynamic. For the overviews of the Russian discipline of international relations theory, see Tatyana Shakleina, ed., *Vneshnyaya politika i bezopasnost' sovremennoi Rossiyi, 1991–2002*, vol. 4 (Moscow: ROSSPEN, 2002); Alexey Bogaturov, Nikolay Kosolapov and Mark Khrustalev, *Ocherki teoriyi i politicheskogo analiza mezhdunarodnykh otnosheni* (Moscow: Nauchno-obrazovatel'nyi forum po mezhdunarodnym otnosheniyam, 2002); M. Lebedeva, "International Relations Studies in USSR/Russia: Is There a Russian National School of

IR Studies?" *Global Society* 18, 3 (2004), 263–78; Andrey Tsygankov and Pavel Tsygankov, eds., *Rossiiskaya nauka mezhdunarodnykh otnoshenii: novye napravleniya* (Moscow: PER CE, 2005); Andrey Kokoshin and Alexey Bogaturov, eds., *Mirovaya politika: teoriya, metodologiya, prikladnoi analiz* (Moscow: KomKniga, 2005); Andrei Tsygankov and Pavel Tsygankov, "Russian Theory of International Relations," in Robert Denemark, ed., *International Studies Encyclopedia*, Vol. 10 (Hoboken, NJ: Wiley-Blackwell, 2010), 6375–87.

4 · Vladimir Putin, speech and the following discussion at the Munich conference on Security Policy, February 10, 2007, www.kremlin.ru. For more on the significance of this speech and how it fits with the evolution of Vladimir Putin's worldview and Russia's place in it, see Clifford Gaddy and Andrew C. Kuchins, "Putin's Plan," *Washington Quarterly* (Spring 2008), 117–29.

5 · See Henry Nau, *At Home Abroad: Identity and Power in American Foreign Policy* (Ithaca, NY: Cornell University Press, 2002).

6 · See Bill McSweeney, *Security, Identity and Interests: A Sociology of International Relations* (Cambridge: Cambridge University Press, 1999), 77–78.

7 · Our grouping is both similar and different from Anne Clunan's taxonomy; see Anne Clunan, *The Social Construction of Russia's Resurgence: Aspirations, Identity and Security Interests* (Baltimore: Johns Hopkins University Press, 2009). Clunan's analysis covers the period from 1991 to 2004 (to the end of Putin's first term). She identifies the following seven categories on a spectrum of national self-images which then inform foreign policy preferences: Western (liberal internationalist), Western (democratic developmentalist), statist (statist developmentalist), statist (Eurasian statism), national restorationist, neocommunist, and Slavophile. These categorizations collapse roughly into our three schools, Clunan argues that the statist and Western self-images and their subgroups are the most politically relevant to the formulation of Russian foreign policy.

8 · The discourse of national identity informs Russian theory of international relations, which in turn shapes foreign policy perspectives. Andrei Tsygankov and Pavel Tsygankov, when analyzing Russian theory of international relations, argued that "Russia has developed three traditions or schools of thinking about Self and Other—Westernist, Statist, and Civilizationist." See Tsygankov and Tsygankov, "Russian Theory of International Relations," 6376.

9 · See Marlene Laurelle, *Inside and Around the Kremlin's Black Box: The New Nationalist Think Tanks in Russia*, Stockholm Paper, Central Asia-Caucasus Institute, Paul H. Nitze School of Advanced International Studies, Washington, DC, 2009.

10 · Aleksei Arbatov, "Don't Throw Stones in a Glass House," *Russia in Global Affairs*, 3 (July–September 2008), http://eng.globalaffairs.ru/numbers/24/1227.html. See also Aleksei Arbatov, "Osobyi imperskii put Rossii," in Natalya Bubnova, ed., *20 let bez Berlinskoi steny* (Moscow: ROSSPEN, 2011), 31–63.

11 · Dmitri Trenin, *The End of Eurasia: Russia on the Border between Geopolitics and Globalization* (Washington, DC: Carnegie Endowment for International Peace, 2001).

12 · Dmitri Trenin, *Odinochnoe plavanie* (Moscow: Elenina, 2009).

13 · Dmitri Trenin, *Post-Imperium: A Eurasian Story* (Washington, DC: Carnegie Endowment for International Peace, 2011).

14 · Vladislav Inozemtsev, "The Post-Crisis World: Searching for a New Framework," *Russia in Global Affairs*, 3 (July–September 2009), http://eng.globalaffairs.ru/numbers/28/1304.html.

15 · Vladislav Inozemtsev, "Modernizatsya.ru: na svalku istoriyu!" *Vedomosti*, April 19, 2010, www.vedomosti.ru/newspaper/article/2010/04/19/231671.

16 · Vyacheslav Nikonov, "Back to the Concert. Global This Time," *Russia in Global Affairs* (November 2002), http://eng. globalaffairs.ru/numbers/1/447.html.

17 · See Clunan, *The Social Construction of Russia's Resurgence.*

18 · For critical analysis of this school of thought, see Lilia Shevtsova, *Lonely Power* (Washington, DC: Carnegie Endowment for International Peace, 2010).

19 · See the discussion of the concept of "civilization" in contemporary Russian discourse about national identity in Igor Zevelev, "Russia's Future: Nation or Civilization?" *Russia in Global Affairs*, 4 (October–December 2009).

20 · https://csis.org/files/attachments/110712_lavrov_transcript.pdf.

21 · See Andrew C. Kuchins, "Russia, the 360-Degree Regional Power," *Current History* (October 2011), 266–71.

22 · In September 2008, in his annual meeting with the Valdai Discussion Club, Putin was asked how he would describe himself and Dmitri Medvedev politically; he thoughtfully paused before responding that Medvedev was *liberal* and he himself was *conservative.*

23 · The following discussion of Russian nationalists' views is partly based on material in Igor Zevelev, *Russia and Its New Diasporas* (Washington, DC: United States Institute of Peace Press, 2001).

24 · *Trud,* January 1, 1995.

25 · Ibid.

26 · *Nezavisimaya Gazeta,* January 12 and 15, 1994.

27 · *Izvestiya,* January 2, 1992; *Mezhdunarodnaya Zhizn,* March–April 1992.

28 · Nikolai Berdyaev, *Russkaya Ideya. Osnovnye problemy russkoi mysli XIX veka i nachala XX veka* (Russian idea. Main problems of Russian thought in nineteenth and early twentieth century) (Moscow: Svarog i K, 1997), 322.

29 · Ibid., 232.

30 · Aleksandr Solzhenitsyn, *The Russian Question at the End of the Twentieth Century* (New York: Farrar, Straus & Giroux, 1995), p. 93.

31 · Kseniya Myalo and Nataliya Narochnitskaya, "Vosstanovlenie Rossii i evraziiskiy soblazn," *Nash sovremennik,* 11–12 (1994), 218–19.

32 · Nataliya Narochnitskaya, "Rossiya i russkie v mirovoy istorii," *Mezhdunarodnaya zhizn'*, 3 (1996), 76.

33 · The following discussion of the newest trends in Russian foreign policy debate is partly informed by valuable comments of Mikhail Troitskiy.

34 · www.government.ru/smi/press/1849/.

35 · When analyzing the sources of international norms, Paul Kowert and Jeffrey Legro suggested that there were three processes that generated, maintained, and changed them: ecological, social, and internal. See Paul Kowert and Jeffrey Legro, "Norms, Identity, and Their Limits: A Theoretical Reprise," in Peter J. Katzenstein, ed., *The Culture of National Security* (New York: Columbia University Press, 1996), 470.

36 · Much of the information in the following paragraphs is derived from Andrew C. Kuchins, "Russian Assessments of U.S. Power and Policy: Over-hyped Expectations, Bitter Disappointments, and Realism," in *Perceptions of US Primacy: Drivers and Implications* (Washington, DC: Center for Strategic and International Studies, 2011).

37 · See Igor Zevelev, "Russian and American National Identity, Foreign Policy, and Bilateral Relations," *International Politics,* 39, 4 (2002), 447–65.

38 · See a theoretical discussion of faces of power in David Baldwin, "Power and International Relations," in Walter Carlsnaes, Thomas Risse, and Beth Simmons, eds., *Handbook of International Relations* (London: Sage, 2002), 179.

39 · Andrew C. Kuchins, "The Speeding Troika," *Russia Behind the Headlines*, September 23, 2010, http://rbth.ru/articles/2010/09/21/the_speeding_troika04953.html.

7

Conclusion

Realists, Nationalists, and Globalists and the Nature of Contemporary Rising Powers

Nikola Mirilovic and Deepa M. Ollapally

Some of the most important questions for the contemporary international relations system have to do with the nature of the rise of key powers in Greater Asia, and with the future of the relations of those countries with the United States. Is the rise of China likely to be peaceful? How will emerging India orient its foreign policy making?

This chapter analyzes the key cross-national trends in domestic foreign policy debates in rising and aspiring powers in Asia and Eurasia. We also explore the likely implications of those trends for international relations in the region and for United States foreign policy. The chapter shows three key patterns: (1) the cross-national similarity of the spectrum of relevant foreign policy schools, (2) the tendency of the center of gravity within that spectrum to be located on its realist and/or nationalist side, and (3) the cross-national trend away from idealism toward realism and/or nationalism in general and, in some cases, toward their relatively pragmatic variants in particular.[1] We describe the key arguments of each school of thought, address the nature of their influence and how they relate to one another, and identify, based on the country chapters in this edited volume, their key proponents in the countries studied.

What do these trends mean for relations between key players in the region? How will they translate into their relationships with the United

States bilaterally and multilaterally? What do the shifting worldviews in Asian and Eurasian countries mean for US global leadership? These are some of the critical questions that will need to be answered as we consider the historic changes that are taking place internationally, driven by the power shifts in Greater Asia, and the parallel domestic debates that will influence policy choices in these countries.

The nature of the spectrum of foreign policy debates and the tracking of shifts in the center of gravity within that spectrum are important regardless of whether they have an independent causal effect on foreign policy choices or if they reflect underlying shifts in the strategic environment and in material interests. In the former case, their importance is obvious. In the latter case, we should track them as indicators of changes in those underlying phenomena. We are not attempting to explain the source of these shifts, which are affected by various factors; rather, our aim is to identify the center of gravity and what it means for regional politics and relations with the United States.

KEY PATTERNS

The Ideological Spectrum

Foreign policy debates in the countries studied tend to consist of four key schools of thought. Listed roughly in order of their cross-national prominence, they are Realists, Nationalists, Globalists, and Idealists. We proceed by addressing the key arguments of each school of thought, and by describing their key proponents and the nature of their influence on the debates.

Realists: The proponents of the Realist school of thought tend to emphasize the following set of ideas. First, they stress the importance of self-strengthening and self-reliance in the international arena. They hold that those strategies, labeled as internal balancing by the international relations literature, are often the optimal means of meeting perceived threats from other rising or established powers. According to realists, dealing with such threats is a pressing issue because the international system is anarchic; a country cannot rely on international institutions for protection. Second, realists are relatively open to forming alliances with other states: the external balancing strategy. Third, realists place an emphasis on great and rising powers, and prioritize relations with those states. Fourth, realists stress the importance of hard power: military and/or economic. By contrast, they argue that soft power and ideology matter less (or not at all), and they tend to view international institutions as ineffective.[2]

Realism is distinct from the other schools of thought discussed in this chapter due to the degree to which this perspective is embraced by members of the political and the military establishment. This school of thought influences debates and policy making in a straightforward manner: it is especially likely to be embraced by powerful people.

The country chapters in this edited volume identify numerous such individuals and institutions. In Russia, prominent Realists include the prime minister Vladimir Putin and the former prime minister Evgeniy Primakov. In China, the leadership of the People's Liberation Army and the majority of the senior leadership of the country belong to either the Realist or the Major Powers (which shares many realist principles) schools of thought. Proponents of Realism in India include members of the leadership of the Indian navy. According to Farhi and Lotfian, prominent Realists (offensive and defensive, respectively) in Iran include the president Mahmoud Ahmedinejad and the former president Akbar Rasfanjani. Proponents of the Balancers school of thought in Japan include many leading politicians, such as former defense minister Ishiba Sheguru of the Liberal Democratic Party (LDP), and former foreign minister Maehara Seiji of the Democratic Party of Japan (DPJ).

Nationalists: Nationalists, like the Realists, emphasize self-reliance and self-strengthening. However, nationalists may embrace these goals not only as a means to the end of meeting foreign threats, but also as a goal in and of itself. They may view the rise of their nation as a matter of pride and as a moral obligation. Other, isolationist nationalists are not interested in their country's rise internationally or in international relations in general. In their pursuit of self-reliance, what they desire from the rest of the world is to be left alone. Both of these approaches tend to share an emphasis on protecting their country's sovereignty and tend to perceive the rest of the world as at least potentially hostile to their country. Second, Nationalists are skeptical of international alliances in general, and of accepting a junior role in those alliances in particular. They emphasize the downside of alliances: the loss of autonomy. Moreover, some Nationalists perceive a junior partner role as an affront to national pride. Third, some nationalists emphasize domestic over international concerns. They prefer a foreign policy of limited scope and tend to perceive international initiatives as distractions from internal issues and problems that they perceive as more pressing.

Currently, proponents of the Nationalist school of thought do not tend to occupy dominant positions in the government. However, the influence of this perspective should not be underestimated for three key reasons. First, the Nationalist perspective is ubiquitous cross-nationally: there is an important Nationalist school of thought in each country studied. Second, there is evidence that Nationalism has significant popular appeal. For example, in many of the countries studied, Nationalist perspectives account for a significant section of the blogosphere. Third, Nationalist ideas sometimes transcend and structure the debates themselves. For example, in most of the countries we study there is a consensus on the importance of sovereignty or on the belief that the rise of one's country is just and desirable.

Proponents of the Nationalist school of thought tend to include opposition politicians as well as prominent public intellectuals and significant sections of the blogosphere. In Russia, Nationalist perspectives (of different types) are advocated by Vladimir Zhirinovsky, the leader of the Liberal Democratic Party of Russia (LDPR), and in some of the works of the author Aleksandr Solzhenitsyn. In Japan, the Autonomist school of thought (which builds on Nationalist ideas) has proponents from both the political right and the political left: LDP's Tokyo governor Ishihara Shintaro and Social Democratic Party chief Fukushima Mizuho, respectively. Chinese Nationalists have a support base in research institutes focused on Communist ideology under the Central Committee of the Communist Party, as well as in a number of institutes in the Chinese Academy of Social Sciences (CASS). In Iran, nationalist ideas help structure the terms of the debate that all schools of thought accept, such as the need to preserve national sovereignty and oppose imperialism (similar developments can also be observed in the other countries covered in this volume). In India the Standard Nationalist school of thought is associated with the ruling Congress Party.

Furthermore, the China, Russia, and India chapters all point out that the blogosphere in those countries includes a heavy dose of nationalist voices.

Globalists: Proponents of the Globalist school of thought tend to favor international political and/or economic integration.[3] They emphasize economic means and institutional goals. They believe that international institutions can resolve security and political issues in the region. In the economic realm, they tend to argue for free trade and fewer restrictions on international capital flows. Second, Globalists tend to favor democratic institutions. Some argue for emphasizing intergovernmental ties with other democracies. They are also likely to hold relatively positive views of the West and of the United States. Third, Globalists are relatively skeptical about military power as a tool of statecraft. Instead, they emphasize political, economic, and/or ideological mechanisms.

A Globalist school of thought is among the most influential perspectives in India and in Japan, and a Globalist school of thought is also present in China and in Russia. However, Globalists are not clearly dominant in any country. Representatives of this school of thought include constructivist scholars in China and opposition leaders in Russia such as Gary Kasparov. In India this view is often supported by the current prime minister Manmohan Singh and by the leaders of prominent businesses such as Infosys Limited.

Idealists: The Idealist (or Exceptionalist) category is the most diverse one cross-nationally. For example, in India, the Idealist schools of thought (the Leftists and the Neo-Nationalists) tend to emphasize leftist ideas, such as the need to reduce inequality within India and/or cross-nationally. In China, the Global South School seeks to build ties between developing countries. In Iran, Islamic Idealists are committed to Pan-Islamism.[4] These diverse perspectives tend to be characterized by two key shared attributes. First, they are committed to an international ideology or religion and they argue that that set of beliefs should be prioritized over concerns about power politics. Second, they tend to be skeptical about the current Western-dominated international system.

None of the countries covered, with the possible exception of Iran, has a dominant Idealist school of thought. Prominent proponents of these perspectives include left of center sections of the Congress Party in India, left of center newspapers in India (e.g., *The Hindu*), and, regarding the Pan-Islamic perspective in Iran, the Organization for Islamic Propaganda and the Ministry of Culture and Islamic Guidance.

The ideological spectrum is more distinct in some countries and less so in others; some have key intellectual anchor points, others do not. Olla-pally and Rajagopalan use intersecting circles to describe the broad areas of ideological overlap on foreign policy in India. The core of these schools of thought is a centrist version of Nationalism. Kuchins and Zevelev depict Russia in stark contrast, with extreme ideological swings from 1991 onward. While there is no single intellectual anchor for Russian foreign policy thought, Great Power Balancers are a dominant group throughout the post-Soviet period. Farhi and Lotfian acknowledge the essential bipo-larity in Iranian foreign policy debates, whether it is classified in terms of pragmatists versus ideologues, or revolutionary versus national interest. However, a shared idea of Iranian sovereignty is a single pivot around which Iranian thinking revolves. Shambaugh and Ren describe multiple schools of thought in China, and present them as not mutually exclusive, and mostly complementary. The key intellectual pillar for all Chinese thinking is the notion of anti-hegemony, coloring the way China looks at the world and every other power. Among this group of countries, contrary to expectations, Japan has the most-differentiated and well-developed for-eign policy debates in the twenty-first century as presented by Michishita and Samuels.

THE CENTER OF GRAVITY AND HOW THE SCHOOLS OF THOUGHT RELATE TO ONE ANOTHER

The schools of thought in the countries studied in this edited volume can be grouped into two broad camps based on those ideas that their propo-nents share. In the first camp are the Nationalists and the Realists. Propo-nents of these perspectives usually share the following views: they emphasize self-reliance in international relations, they stress the impor-tance of sovereignty, and they tend to view hard-power as a key tool of international statecraft.

A note on realism is in order. Some theorists might argue that realism is as much about power as it is about prudence, and prudence dictates a focus on power equations rather than just national hard-power. Put another way, realism requires recognizing weakness as much as strength. To capture the nuances of realist thought, we need to keep in mind differences between what has in recent years been termed offensive versus defensive realism.[5] The former takes a view of the world that most heavily emphasizes interstate competition and corresponding hard-power responses; the latter emphasizes the importance of security dilemmas and is willing to exercise self-restraint or be restrained by others. Offensive realists tend to believe that security dilemmas are not really dilemmas but conflicts that require more robust responses. The offensive–defensive aspect of realism might help us to see some important shades of differences among realists across countries.

The second camp consists of globalists and Idealists. These two groups tend to share a commitment to international ideologies or institutions and to nonmilitary (political, economic, and/or ideological) means of international statecraft.

The contemporary balance of power between foreign policy schools of thought tends to favor the Realist/Nationalist camp. Overall, the most common arrangement has Realists as the dominant school of thought with Nationalists in a supporting role and with an influence on areas of consensus that transcend the debates. According to the country case studies in this volume, the dominant perspective in each country studied is either Realist (China, Russia, Iran) or Nationalist (India), while in Japan, Realists and Globalists are both very influential. Moreover, at least one Nationalist and Realist school of thought is prominent in each country studied. A Globalist approach is prominent in most cases, but is not clearly dominant in any country. Idealist perspectives are the least ubiquitous.

Furthermore, the trends in most of the countries studied have tended to favor the Realists and/or the Nationalists.[6] In Russia, Realists have reasserted themselves following a brief period of Globalist dominance in the early 1990s. China has recently adopted a relatively assertive foreign policy following a period of emphasis on the peaceful and accommodative nature of its rise. In Iran, two of three key contemporary schools of thought identified by Farhi and Lotfian are Realist or heavily influenced by Realism.

Idealists were arguably more influential in the period more immediately following the Islamic Revolution and their influence has declined. The case of India is more open to debate: Realists emerged in India in the 1990s, but nationalist views arguably lost ground to globalist ones in the same period. Given these trends, it is important to specify in more detail the key similarities and differences between the schools of thought.

While the two camps differ in their view of the relative importance and/or desirability of international institutional integration, this disagreement is much less pronounced in the realm of economics. International economic integration tends to attract broad and increasing support both cross-nationally and across schools of thought (even though challenges to this approach do remain). The commitment of Globalists to international economic integration is obvious. Meanwhile, many Nationalists and Realists in the region have also embraced economic integration as a means of pursuing economic efficiency, growth, and power. Economic growth is a key ingredient of a country's rise, which in turn is a goal cherished by both Nationalists and Realists. Economic globalization is therefore likely to proceed even if Globalists are not the dominant school in key countries. That is the case because globalist ideas about the desirability of international economic integration are now shared by many proponents of the other schools of thought.[7]

In addition to important areas of agreement within the two camps, there are also important differences in terms of foreign policy scope and means between the two schools of thought within each camp. Those differences have relevant theoretical and policy implications. Realists tend to be more internationally oriented than Nationalists who are more sensitive to domestic political concerns. Nationalists may also be more concerned with questions of national pride and prestige, with Realists being more focused on maximizing or balancing power. An important policy implication of this divergence may be that Realists are more likely than Nationalists to embrace alliances, especially relations with the United States.[8]

Another important distinction between Nationalists and Realists is that the influence of the former has more of a bottom-up, populist, grassroots nature, while the influence of the latter is associated with the establishment and with the views of key policy makers. Elites play an important role in foreign policy making, and prominent Realists tend to be highly influential. However, they also have to be mindful of nationalist pressures from below.

In the Globalist/Idealist camp, Globalists are likely to embrace the contemporary international order, while some Idealist groups in the countries studied support globalism but have strongly anti-Western and revisionist views about the substance of globalization. Furthermore, because Idealists are a highly diverse group, their views are often incompatible cross-nationally.

It is important to underline, following Henry Nau's introductory chapter in this volume, that while there are important similarities cross-nationally within the key schools of thought, there are also important distinctions that can be made in further subdividing them. For example, the Nationalist category can be productively further subdivided. Extreme or Hyper-Nationalists might seek territorial expansion and military superiority and embrace diaspora-annexing strategies, while more moderate and/or isolationalist Nationalists may emphasize the pursuit of autonomy and the protection of sovereignty.

KEY IMPLICATIONS FOR THE REGION

Realists and Nationalists: Peer Competitors?

The current prevalence of Realists and Nationalists in all five countries to varying degrees could lead to a competitive environment in Greater Asia whereby each is vying for regional influence and even supremacy. In speculating about the longer-term policy choices, it may be important to understand the importance of historical claims, made particularly frequently by Nationalists—something the preceding chapters have laid out for each state. Not surprisingly, the main Nationalist schools of thought in Russia, China, India, and Iran, all locate their external role in fairly grand civilizational or "exceptionalist" narratives. While their foreign policy is limited in scope, it is ideological if not civilizational (anti-Western) in terms of goals. These historical evocations may not be entirely lost on the Realists either—Great Power Balancers in Russia, Major Power Realists in China, and Great Power Realists in India, for example, have an image of their countries that may not be derived solely from the modern period. While these visions have some common sociohistorical basis, domestic groups have different ideas of what their countries' policies ought to be, with some outlooks more amenable to regional cooperation than others. With China as the pivot, China's rise and the changing world order, and the prognosis for America's role are two key variables that drive the preferences of Realists and Nationalists across the region. Proximate to China and each other, these states and their geopolitical relationships take on special significance.

In Russia, the old habit of the Great Power Balancers and Nationalists to view foreign policy through a United States-centric prism seeking to contain American influence, now may be giving way to greater attention on China. For most of the decade until 2008, these two schools saw the United States as the greatest threat, seeing China's growth as redounding to Russia's benefit. The advent of the Shanghai Cooperation Organization illustrates this trend. It is then not surprising that Russian president Vladimir Putin, described by Kuchins and Zevelev as a Great Power Balancer, was the one to take the lead in 2006 to launch trilateral summitry between Russia, China, and India as a form of strategic consensus to promote global multipolarity. However, the Russia chapter explains that the Great Power Balancers and the Nationalists are now less confident of China's salutary impact on Russia, and are increasingly engaging in more open and discerning discussion of the pros and cons of China's rise.

If Russian Realists and Nationalists initially perceived China in a fairly benign manner, the same does not hold for India and Japan. As described by Ollapally and Rajagopalan, there is a fair degree of consensus among the Indian schools of thought on China's rise—a deep wariness. Still, at the present time, only the offensive realist Hyper-Nationalists want India to adopt a militarily confrontational posture toward China. They are far outnumbered by Standard Nationalists, some Neo-Nationalists, and Great Power Realists, all advocating diplomacy and negotiation as the best foreign policy means to deal with China. Great Power Realists do argue for strengthening India's defense capabilities, especially its naval arm, with a clear eye on China. They, along with the Hyper-Nationalists, are in the forefront of calling on the Indian political class to develop a grand strategy that pays more serious attention to coping with a rising China. But unlike the Hyper-Nationalists, others want to do this without provoking China.

To a much greater degree than Russia and India, China's rise has fundamentally affected Japan's foreign policy. Michishita and Samuels note how China and the United States are now nearly coequals in Japan's security calculus. The epochal 2009 election in Japan that brought the DPJ to power promised a shift away from subordination to Washington, and a tilt toward Asia. But owing to serious missteps by the DPJ and a new activism by China in 2010, including the high octane trawler showdown off the Senkaku/Diaoyu Islands, the DPJ platform never got off the ground. The traditional pro-US Balancers (or Realists) and Integrationists, who favor greater consolidation among Japan, United States, and China (and embrace some Globalist ideas), have regained power in Tokyo. The DPJ interlude, however, signaled the sentiment that chafes at Japan's junior partner status with the United States and a tendency toward greater solidarity with China/Asia, captured by some of the proponents of the Bandwagoners and Autonomists (Hyper-Nationalist) schools of thought.[9]

It would seem that given the foregoing discussion and the rise of Realists and Nationalists in the region, Russia, Japan, and India, all have some incentive for balancing against China's rise. However, this is not the scenario that has (yet) emerged. As Kuchins and Zevelev show, despite the expectation that Russia would try and improve relations with Japan as an insurance against China, Moscow showed the greatest hostility toward Japan in 2010–2011 in two decades. Indeed, the trend seems to be that India, Japan, and Russia are forging their own independent diplomatic and military strategies to deal with a growing China.

Why these three powerful neighbors of China have not moved more deliberately to counter China's influence is a good question. We can identify three reasons. First, the influence of Nationalists in Russia and Japan cuts both ways: their long-running dispute over the Kuril islands spilled over into hot public contestation when Dmitry Medvedev became the first Russian leader to visit the islands in late 2010. It continued to boil as Russia reinforced its defenses on the island in early 2011, stoking strong nationalist opinion in both countries. Second, many in Russia, Japan, and India believe that US power will erode in Asia. In the post-financial crisis environment, there is even less confidence in the durability and capacity of American power. Thus the need for each country to manage relations with China, if not accommo-date it. Globalists and defensive Realists lead this thinking, but some of the Nationalists who are inward-looking, especially in India, also share this view. Third, China appears both as a threat and an opportunity. Except for the extreme Nationalists in Japan, Russia, and India, the economic magnet of China is proving hard to resist. Japan has been taking the lead for East Asian economic integration, which allows it to exercise its own influence in the face of increasing Chinese advantages and even check China's role.

The independent approach of Japan, Russia, and India toward China may underline the importance of Nationalist thinking. At the same time, there is little indication of peer competition emerging among these states in the face of inevitable Chinese prominence in Asia. There is no foreign policy opinion in Japan, India, or Russia that views any of the others as a serious threat. For example, in India, Realists along with Nationalists of all stripes continue to value a strong relationship with Russia. Globalists and Realists in India are at the forefront of building more strategically signifi-cant ties with Japan, although the Realists and Nationalists would like to see Japan act with more autonomy from the United States in Asia.

The Pull of Liberal Globalizers

Key schools of thought tend to agree on international economic integra-tion while disagreeing on the desirability of international institutional integration. It is notable that even in countries where the Globalists are relatively weak there is significant integration into international markets (even though this is driven by energy exports in Russia and in Iran). The following is each country's trade/GDP (aggregated figures for 2007–2009) in descending order: China 59 percent; Iran 58 percent; Russia 51 percent; India 48 percent, and Japan 32 percent.[10] Moreover, China and India have both recently embraced the pursuit of economic liberalization through free trade deals, notably with ASEAN in 2010. China is the biggest trad-ing partner for Japan and India, overtaking the United States in 2006 and 2008, respectively. China is Russia's second most important trading partner, but trailing the European Union. For Iran, too, the EU is its key trading partner, but China and India are also important commercially.

According to the Asian Development Bank's *Asian Development Outlook 2011*, Asia has been in the forefront in pulling the world out of the post-2008 global economic crisis.[11] Domestically, it is not surprising that Globalists are on an upward trajectory given tangible economic results, but their numbers remain small in comparison to Nationalists and Realists since their starting base was smaller in most of the countries studied. *Outlook 2011* points out that China alone accounts for roughly 40 percent of all South–South trade. Given the market power of China, even some of the Realists and Nationalists in the region are acceding to the approach of the Japanese Bandwagoners with China (or Economic Hedgers), hedging with the United States against Chinese regional economic dominance. So far, the concerns regarding the potential for economic predation by an economically overweening China have been voiced loudly only by extreme Nationalists. This is unlikely to change unless Nationalist impulses in China challenge common rules, such as territorial sea boundaries, and create conflict, as in the South and East China Seas.

It is therefore more likely that international economic integration will continue to deepen more than the corresponding institutional integration. Even the Globalists across the region tend to prefer selective multilateralism and loose, informal institutions, rather than the European and United States model. This is especially true for the most rapidly growing economies of China and India. Russia is still outside the membership of the World Trade Organization (WTO); part of the delay has been Russia's Great Power Balancers blowing hot and cold on how actively to pursue admission. Japan, which has taken the lead for greater institutionalism, is somewhat of an exception in the region on this score. According to Farhi and Lotfian, the dominant groups of Regional and Global Power Balancers in Iran favor economic expansion through greater trade and investment. Once Russia gains membership in WTO, Iran will be the only major economy excluded. But, as we pointed out in the introduction, by then the United States may be retreating from a globalist stance.

IMPLICATIONS FOR THE UNITED STATES

Debates within rising powers about the United States are characterized by a contradiction. On one hand, in each case relations with the United States play an important part in structuring the debate. On the other hand, in many countries the emphasis is on the United States relative or absolute decline. We proceed by describing these patterns.

The importance of the United States to the debates is illustrated by the following examples from the country chapters in this volume. In Japan, choices about relations with the United States form one of the axes of division proposed by Michishita and Samuels. In other words, these choices structure the entire debate. In the case of Russia, Kuchins and Zevelev describe the United States as the key independent variable. In Iran, according to Farhi and Lotfian, the "America question" plays a key role in the foreign policy debate. Shambaugh and Ren point out the importance of the concept of hegemony, and of its application to the United States, in Chinese foreign policy thinking. Ollapally and Rajagopalan argue that relations with the United States are a key policy issue for India.

Even though the United States plays a profoundly influential role in the region and in its debates, the question of the US decline is also heatedly debated. Offensive realists in Iran argue that the decline is significant and that Teheran should consequently act more assertively; defensive realists dispute that premise. In China, analysts have repeatedly proclaimed the imminence of the decline of the United States, and have repeatedly been proven wrong. Shambaugh and Ren cite a Chinese scholar who points out that Chinese experts have consistently underestimated the United States. In Japan, the bandwagoning perspective views the US decline as a significant factor. Its proponents argue for a consequent reorientation of Tokyo toward Beijing. In Russia there is uncertainty about the durability of US power. In India, only some Great Power Realists are confident of America's resilience.

Evaluating the question of the US decline has important implications for policy making as well as for theory building.[12] The perceptions that the decline is steep unsurprisingly have negative implications for Washington. They tend to lead rising powers to either act more assertively or to look for alternative partners. Meanwhile, as Henry Nau notes in the Introduction, expectations of United States relative decline are often proclaimed by scholars and analysts. However, it is easy to misinterpret or to overestimate the relevance of this concept. Relative decline implies that the United States. is still the most powerful country, but by a smaller margin than before. This concept therefore tends to concede that the United States is still the most powerful state—but this often gets lost in the emphasis on the decline. How important is the US relative decline if choices about relations with Washington structure debates in key rising powers? Given the record of proclamations of the US decline that have been proven incorrect or overstated, there might be a tendency to overestimate the extent of the decline. If such perceptions and misperceptions indeed play an important role, it is important for the United States to emphasize its vitality and to reassert its commitment to the region.

The rise of realism and nationalism in the region has implications for the United States that are mixed rather than entirely negative. On the one hand, the rise of realism may hinder US efforts to promote international cooperation. Realists tend to endorse self-interested behavior and pursue common interests only to the extent that they advance national interests. On the other hand, Realists in the countries studied in this edited volume tend to place an emphasis on their country's relations with Washington. They are likely to focus the attention of their country in this direction because they want to sit at the table of great powers with the United States. Additionally, as China's power has grown more quickly than many anticipated, defensive Realists thinking seems to have propelled Japan, India, and Russia to solidify relations with the United States. This policy shift, especially notable in India and Russia, has so far exempted China's neighbors from having to engage in hard balancing behavior, evocative of Japan's realist and integrationist thinking. Not to be overlooked, it has also has given the United States a free pass in terms of its own presence in Asia—unlike earlier periods, there is presently no serious opinion to balance American power in the region.

The trends emphasized in this chapter have largely negative implications for US efforts to promote global burden-sharing. Self-interested rational actors (e.g., Realists) prefer to free ride and have someone else provide global public goods (e.g., open and safe sea-lanes). Nationalists in the countries studied (as well as some Realists) tend to be skeptical about international public good provision. Many perceive this as a Western trap designed to weaken their country.[13] The two new rising powers of China and India have tended to be reluctant to embrace greater responsibility, often citing their developing country status. The dissenting Great Power

Realists in India and the Globalists in these two countries do not currently seem to have the capacity to significantly change national policy in this regard. Earlier in the chapter, we described Realists and Nationalists currently holding the center of gravity in foreign policy debates in the countries we study. To glean implications for the United States, we need to see if the centers of gravity in these countries are moving closer or farther apart when compared with the United States. If the rise of Nationalists in aspiring powers coincides with a drift toward nationalist retrenchment in the United States, that could lead to seriously negative reinforcing behavior in terms of declining multilateral engagement and, at worst case, a turn toward mercantilism. For a country like India where the center of gravity is now shifting from a historically entrenched nationalist orientation toward the Globalist end of the spectrum, US nationalism would pose serious challenges. In Japan, if Nationalists in Washington come to power with Bandwagoners governing in Tokyo, the United States–Japan alliance would become shakier.

Likewise, if fiscally conservative thinking takes hold in Washington (or Europe for that matter) and demands for greater contribution to global security by other states become dominant, this could strengthen the Nationalists within several of the key aspiring powers. Uncertainty about United States intentions in Asia in the backdrop of growing Chinese power and/or assertiveness could lead to a recalibration of thinking in Japan, India, and Russia. Extreme Nationalists and Realists in these countries may then join forces on the question of military buildup by their countries. Under such a circumstance, Globalists who are not dominant in any of these countries at the moment would likely get even more marginalized.

With Realists riding the center of gravity in Asia, including notable offensive Realists in Russia and China, the United States has to walk a fine line in Asia to avoid unintended effects whoever gains power in Washington. United States policy vis-à-vis China will be the touchstone. If the United States takes a tough line, it is likely to bolster Nationalists and offensive Realists in China. But if Washington is seen as overly accommodating to any Chinese assertiveness or even growing Chinese power, it could make Realists and extreme Nationalists in India, Japan, and Russia rethink their strategy of moving closer to the United States as a hedge against China.

THEORETICAL IMPLICATIONS AND DIRECTIONS
FOR FURTHER POLICY RESEARCH

In this section we address the implications of the key patterns identified above for larger theoretical international relations debates. We also specify key questions for further policy-oriented research that flow from the project. Those questions relate to (1) the general applicability of analytical categories, (2) the implications of the rise of realism and nationalism, (3) the relationship between interdependence and stability, (4) the lingering issue of the theoretical link between ideas/worldviews and structure, and (5) the broader utility of our framework for other rising and aspiring powers.

First, the cross-national similarity of the ideological spectrum validates a premise of the project: that it is possible to productively compare foreign policy debates cross-nationally. Moreover, traditional categories of analyzing foreign policy making, such as realism or liberalism, adequately capture the current debates in the region. This finding answers a fundamental question raised by the project: it is possible to usefully apply analytical categories developed in Western contexts more generally. This is not to claim that these categories should be applied uncritically and that their meaning in each national context is exactly the same. However, by proceeding carefully we can effectively apply these analytical categories in a comparative research design. This is an important point to make because the general practice in international relations is to simply apply international relations theory developed in the West uncritically to non-Western contexts, assuming rather than assessing its validity. Terms such as Globalists and Realists are used in the literature without specifying what they constitute; this volume has tried to be explicit in what they refer to in the different countries.

Second, as we point out above, the further shift toward realism and/or nationalism might increase the likelihood of conflict and decrease the likelihood of cooperation in the region, but the likely consequences are more mixed than the conventional wisdom would predict. The study of those developments has important implications for the international relations literature in general, and for the study of the role of nationalism in international relations in particular. Nationalism can lead to aggressive behavior internationally.[14] According to the elite-led ethnic conflict literature, elites may manipulate nationalism as a means of staying in power domestically.[15] An international conflict, according to this argument, can provide legitimacy to the government and distract the populace from economic problems at home. Furthermore, several of the aspiring powers have diaspora populations in the region the presence of which could potentially spark nationalist conflicts. For example, Kuchins and Zevelev point out that some Nationalists in Russia call for the reunification of Russian communities abroad with Russia and/or for reunification of Russia with parts of Ukraine and Kazakhstan. This could lead to conflict with countries where those ethnic Russians reside. The strengthening of national identities might also work against constructivist solutions to international conflict, for example by making the construction of broader, regional identities more difficult. Examples from the country chapters illustrate some of these patterns: for example, in China, constructivist international relations scholars tend to belong to the less powerful Globalist school.

The rise of realism could also increase the likelihood of conflict. Realists emphasize self-interest, which may also, according to constructivists, hinder the construction of collective identities. The skepticism of Realists toward international institutions may hinder institutional solutions to security challengers.

The rise of realism and/or nationalism could, however, also increase stability. These effects are usually regarded as counterintuitive and are understudied in the literature. Realists might be quick to embrace balancing and meet a potential threat before it develops and results in a systemic challenge and a great power war. For example, Great Power Realists in India tend to favor cooperation with the United States in meeting regional threats. This could be an important source of stability in the region. Realists might also oppose conflict driven by ideological extremism. Moreover, international agreements arrived at by Realist actors might be particularly durable given that they are especially likely to reflect each participant's interests. Nationalism of the more defensive kind might decrease the likelihood of certain wars, via its emphasis on sovereignty and noninterference in other countries' internal affairs.

Third, the divergence we see between the drive for international economic integration and the reluctance toward institutional integration has important theoretical and policy implications. Is economic or political integration the key means to international peace? Is it possible to integrate economically without integrating politically? Is it the case that, as some Realists argue, international economic integration is more likely to generate conflict (e.g., due to concerns over economic dependence or trade imbalances) than peace?[16] These questions are particularly relevant to Greater Asia where economic relations have gotten way ahead of political relations, without any certainty in the latter.

Fourth, while the country chapters in this volume have not fully answered the first-order question of what are the sources of the worldviews we identify, we are not suggesting that this is not important for future work. In the Introduction, Nau gives an extended discussion about why we need to pay attention to domestic debates, rather than simply extrapolate policy preferences from international structural conditions facing the country. Each chapter does touch upon the sources for the different worldviews that groups hold: for example, several of the authors of the country chapters claim that historical experience of colonialism or national humiliation loom large for Nationalists in China, India, and Russia, and for all schools of thought in Iran. In contrast, the views of Globalists in China and India, Liberals in Russia, and Integrators in Japan are fueled by a postglobalization era understanding of the benefits of greater economic cooperation. The latter want to take advantage of the contemporary liberal economic system and even shape how it evolves.

Fifth, a preliminary literature review indicates that the framework developed in this volume can be productively applied to other key countries that are often identified as rising or aspiring powers: Brazil, South Africa, and Turkey. Even if we focus only on "rising powers," defining these states is not straightforward. Experts disagree over which countries should be regarded as such in the contemporary world. They also disagree over the nature of the key causes of a country's rise and/or international influence. Finally, the trend that those cases will take in the future can often only be projected with uncertainty. Rising powers are states that have the potential to attain great power status, but that have not fully reached that potential yet. Rising powers tend to be characterized by two key attributes: a large population and a relatively underdeveloped but fast-growing economy.

While large population size is neither a sole nor a sufficient determinant of great power status, it is probably a necessary prerequisite for that status.[17] The second key determinant of great power status is the level of economic development. Economic development trends are usually measured by changes in the Gross Domestic Product (GDP) per capita over a period of time (i.e., the yearly GDP per capita growth rate). Rising powers tend to be populous countries having a GDP per capita that is relatively low but exhibiting high GDP per capita growth rates. This description fits particularly well the two key contemporary rising powers, China and India.

While most analysts would likely agree that population and economic development matter in explaining great or rising power status, there are other potentially relevant variables the importance of which is more contested. Those variables include domestic political institutions in general and regime type in particular, soft power, and geographic location. Political scientists debate whether or not democracy facilitates economic growth, whether democracies are better at fighting wars than authoritarian states, and whether and/or why they avoid fighting wars against other democracies. Meanwhile, the concept of soft power, according to Joseph Nye, refers to being able to influence other states so that their preferences become more similar to one's own.[18] Finally, geographic location can affect a country's relevance on the world stage. For example, being located in a region rich in natural resources has increased the international profile of Iran. Furthermore, countries located in geographic proximity to one another are more likely to interact with one another in both productive (e.g., trade) and destructive (e.g., war) ways.

The countries covered in detail in this book are located in relative geographic proximity to one another. For example, China has land borders with Russia and India, while its maritime claims partially overlap with those of Japan. Consequently, these countries are interlinked with one another, and are likely to consider one another's capabilities and/or intentions when making international strategic decisions. While this volume has confined itself to the fast-growing Greater Asian region, the countries included here do not exhaust the list of rising powers in the contemporary world that we should study. In the next section, we suggest that the framework developed in this book can be productively applied to three other countries—Brazil, South Africa, and Turkey—while leaving it to future analysts for further work.

ADDITIONAL CASES: A PRELIMINARY OVERVIEW

Brazil is the fifth most populous country in the world. Its current GDP per capita adjusted for purchasing power parity is only 103rd in the world,[19] but its recent GDP per capita growth has tended to be strong (e.g., 7 percent in 2010).[20] Brazil's rise is often noted by experts and analysts who include it, along with Russia, India, China, and South Africa among the key rising powers that make up the acronym BRICS.

A cursory survey of the recent social science literature on the topic of the sources of Brazilian foreign policy making indicates that the analytical framework developed in this book could also be useful in understanding Brazil's foreign policy. That is the case for three reasons. First, several scholars claim that there is a lively foreign policy debate within Brazil. According to Paulo Sotero (2010), Brazil's domestic debate about its international role is intense.[21] Jeffrey W. Cason and Timothy J. Power (2009) argue that interest in international relations has expanded rapidly among Brazilian students and scholars. They also claim that global affairs play an increasingly important role in Brazil's domestic politics.[22]

Second, an increasing number of actors are taking an interest in and attempting to influence Brazil's foreign policy. Cason and Power argue that the increasing pluralization of actors involved in foreign policy making is one of two major trends affecting Brazil's foreign policy making since the 1990s. The process of pluralization involves a growing role for societal outreach initiatives by the government in foreign policy making. Tullo Vigevani and Gabriel Cepaluni (2009) also identify a trend whereby additional actors, including labor unions and businesspeople, are becoming more influential in shaping foreign policy making.[23] Simone Diniz and Claudio Oliveira Ribeiro (2008) argue that the literature plays insufficient attention to the role the Brazilian Congress plays in Brazilian foreign policy making.[24]

Third, some of those actors adopt arguments and perspectives similar to those advanced by the representatives of the schools of thought in the other countries covered by this book. For example, Vigevani and Cepaluni (2009) argue that government of former president Luiz Inácio Lula da Silva was seeking to build an international identity among developing countries as one part of a larger strategy of pursuing autonomy through diversification.[25] This approach could be similar to those of the Global South schools of thought in China and in India. Sean W. Burges (2009) argues that Brazilian foreign policy making is shaped in part by ideational variables that set the boundaries of conceivable action. He cites democracy, liberal economics, and a "clear vision of globalization" among such key ideas.[26] This perspective is similar to the views held by Globalists across several of the countries covered by this edited volume.

The worldviews approach can also shed light on foreign policy making in South Africa. The sources of Pretoria's foreign policy making are subject to a debate within South Africa, as some of the citations included below indicate. Furthermore, South Africa is attracting increasing attention on the international stage, partly due to Pretoria's prominent regional role in its region. This development is illustrated by South Africa's inclusion in the BRICS group of key countries on the rise.

Domestic sources of foreign policy making may be particularly important in South Africa for two reasons. First, partly as a legacy of the apartheid regime, internal divides persist within South Africa's society. Those divides, among their other effects, also affect foreign policy (see e.g., Bischoff).[27] Second, South Africa democratized following the end of the apartheid system. This regime-type change has led to scholarly debates over the extent to which democracy shapes Pretoria's foreign policy making. For example, the *Democratizing Foreign Policy?* edited volume includes a number of chapters on the relationship between democratic consolidation and Pretoria's foreign policy making (Nel and van der Westhuizen).[28]

A preliminary literature review indicates that, similarly to the countries covered in detail in this edited volume, multiple worldviews that shape foreign policy making can be identified in South Africa. For example, according to Paul Williams (2000), the conceptual rationale guiding the foreign policy decisions of the African National Congress (ANC) government is "an eclectic synthesis of neo-realist and neo-liberal principles." This approach, Williams argues, combines an emphasis on the importance of the global economy with the view that states remain the most important actors in the international system.[29] This state of affairs might be comparable to that in some of the countries covered in detail in this edited volume (e.g., Japan), where both Realists and Globalists play important roles.

In addition to multiple schools of thought being represented, we can also identify a number of actors and institutions who shape South Africa's foreign policy making. For example, Bishoff provides a list of actors who influenced Pretoria's foreign policy making during the presidencies of Nelson Mandela and of Thabo Mbeki. According to Bishoff, those actors include, the Department of Foreign Affairs, the president, the Department of Trade and Industry, members of parliament, members of civil society, and the ANC party leadership.

A worldviews approach to foreign policy analysis can also be applied to the case of Turkey. Istanbul's claim to rising power status is based in part on the following facts and developments. Turkey's current population is estimated at almost seventy-nine million, making Turkey the seventeenth largest country in the world. Furthermore, the Turkish economy has recently attained high GDP per capita growth rates. Finally, the geographic location of Turkey, connecting the Middle East with Europe, provides Istanbul with strategic advantages.

One example for how the worldviews approach can be applied to Turkish foreign policy making can be found in the work of Josh Walker. In "Understanding Turkey's Foreign Policy through Strategic Depth," Walker analyzes the links between Turkish foreign policy making and the ideas of Ahmet Davutoğlu. Davutoğlu is the current foreign minister of Turkey and a former International Relations professor. In his 2001 book *Strategic Depth,* Davutoğlu emphasized two variables: Turkey's geostrategic location and its historical ties in its neighboring areas. Examples of such ties include Turkey's legacy as an heir to the Ottoman Empire and its potential to become a "Muslim superpower."[30] Geostrategic location is a variable that is often emphasized by Realists. Meanwhile, shared historical experiences and the importance of religion are often emphasized by Idealists. As is the case in many of the country case studies included in this edited volume, we observe the debate between a Realist and an Idealist perspective—sometimes in the work of a single policy maker and/or analyst.

The findings of this volume strongly support the notion that tracking contending ideas and political cleavages within aspiring powers has important payoffs in understanding a country's strategy and actions. States do have to be cognizant of the international structure and adopt ideas that make them survive and succeed. In the long run, winning strategies are often those that Kenneth Waltz laid out reflecting a state's international capability—in essence, balancing and bandwagoning.[31] However, domestic politics matter as well and looking inside of the "black box" of a sovereign state provides insights that help us understand international relations. We neglect domestic political cleavages, and the foreign policy ideas and interests being forged in the most dynamic, yet uncertain, Asian and Eurasian region at our own peril.

Notes

1 · For consistency's sake we capitalize the names of schools of thought and of their proponents throughout this chapter, even if they are by convention not usually capitalized (e.g., Nationalists).

2 · Some of the definitive works on realism in the international relations literature include Hans J. Morgenthau, *Politics among Nations: The Struggle for Power and Peace* (New York: Alfred A. Knopf, 1978); Stephen Walt, *The Origins of Alliances* (Ithaca, NY: Cornell University Press, 1997); Kenneth Waltz, *Theory of International Politics* (New York: McGraw-Hill, 1979); John J. Mearsheimer, *The Tragedy of Great Power Politics* (New York: Norton, 2001); Robert Gilpin, *War and Change in World Politics* (New York: Cambridge University Press, 1981); and Charles Glaser, "Realists as Optimists: Cooperation as Self-Help," *International Security*, 19, 3 (1994), 50–90.

3 · On liberal institutionalism in the larger international relations literature, see, for example, Robert O. Keohane and Joseph S. Nye, *Power and Interdependence: World Politics in Transition* (Boston: Little, Brown, 1977), or Robert O. Keohane and Lisa L. Martin, "The Promise of Institutionalist Theory," *International Security*, 20, 1 (Summer 1995), 39–51.

4 · For a prominent argument on the role of religion and culture in international relations, see Samuel Huntington, *Clash of Civilizations* (New York: Simon & Schuster, 2003).

5 · For a good overview of offensive and defensive Realism, see Shiping Tang, *A Theory of Security Strategies for Our Time: Defensive Realism* (New York: Palgrave Macmillan, 2010), 148–52. Two noted exponents of defensive realism are Glaser and Kydd: Glaser, "Realists as Optimists," and Charles Glaser, *Rational Theory of International Politics* (Princeton, NJ: Princeton University Press, 2010); and Andrew Kydd, "Sheep in Sheep's Clothing: Why Security Seekers Do Not Fight Each Other," *Security Studies*, 7, 1 (1997), 114–55.

6 · See also Nikola Mirilovic, "Back to the Future? A Revival of Realpolitik in Asia and Eurasia," Policy Brief (Washington, DC: Sigur Center for Asian Studies, George Washington University, 2010).

7 · Whether one of the countries studied is likely to (attempt to) lead globalization in the future remains an open question.

8 · For example, this debate might play out in the case of India.

9 · On how the concept of bandwagoning fits into international relations debates, see for example, Randall Schweller, "Bandwagoning for Profit—Bringing the Revisionist State Back In," *International Security*, 19, 1 (Summer 1994), 72–107.

10 · World Bank Development Indicators, http://data.worldbank.org/indicator.

11 · Asian Development Bank, *Asian Development Outlook 2011: South-South Economic Links*, www.adb.org/documents/books/ado/2011/default.asp.

12 · On the question of US decline and its consequences, see Fareed Zakaria, *The Post-American World* (New York: Norton, 2008).

13 · For example, Shambaugh and Ren describe the prevalence of this point of view in China.

14 · On the relationship between nationalism and international conflict, see Stephen van Evera, "Hypotheses on Nationalism and War," *International Security*, 18, 4 (Spring 1994), 5–39.

15 · On elite manipulation of nationalism, see V. P. Gagnon Jr., *The Myth of Ethnic War: Serbia and Croatia in the 1990s* (Ithaca, NY: Cornell University Press, 2004).

16 · For an overview of the debate on the consequences of international interdependence, see Susan McMillan, "Interdependence and Conflict," *Mershon International Studies Review*, 41 (May 1997), 33–58.

17 · Mearsheimer, *The Tragedy of Great Power Politics*.

18 · Joseph S. Nye Jr. coined the term "soft power." For a full treatment of this concept, see *Soft Power: The Means to Success in World Politics* (New York: PublicAffairs, 2004).

19 · The figures cited in this section of the chapter are from the *CIA World Factbook* (www.cia.gov/library/publications/the-world-factbook) unless indicated otherwise.

20 · World Bank Development Indicators, http://data.worldbank.org/indicator.

21 · Paulo Sotero, "Brazil's Rising Ambition in a Shifting Global Balance of Power," *Politics*, 30, (December 2010), 71–81.

22 · Jeffrey W. Cason and Timothy J. Power, "Presidentialization, Pluralization, and the Rollback of Itamaraty: Explaining Change in Brazilian Foreign Policy Making in the Cardoso-Lula Era," *International Political Science Review*, 30 (March 2009), 117.

23 · Tullo Vigevani and Gabriel Cepaluni, *Brazilian Foreign Policy in Changing Times* (Lanham, MD: Lexington Books, 2009).

24 · Simone Diniz and Claudio Oliveira Ribeiro, "The Role of Brazilian Congress in Foreign Policy: An Empirical Contribution to the Debate," *Brazilian Political Science Review* (Online), 2, 2 (2008).

25 · Tullo Vigevani and Gabriel Cepaluni, *Brazilian Foreign Policy in Changing Times* (Lanham, MD: Lexington Books, 2009).

26 · Sean W. Burges, *Brazilian Foreign Policy after the Cold War* (Gainesville: University Press of Florida, 2009).

27 · Paul-Henri Bischoff, "External and Domestic Sources of Foreign Policy Ambiguity: South African Foreign Policy and the Projection of Pluralist Middle Power," *Politikon*, 30, 2 (2003), 183–201.

28 · Philip Nel and Janis van der Westhuizen, *Democratizing Foreign Policy? Lessons from South Africa* (Lanham, MD: Lexington Books, 2004).

29 · Paul Williams, "South African Foreign Policy: Getting Critical?" *Politikon*, 27, 1 (2000), 73–91.

30 · Joshua W. Walker, *"Understanding Turkey's Foreign Policy through Strategic Depth,"* Transatlantic Academy, www.transatlanticacademy.org/sites/default/files/publications/Josh_Walker%20UnderstandingStrategi%20Depth(2).doc.

31 · Waltz, *Theory of International Politics*.

Index